VOICES OF EXPERIENCE

Practical Ideas to
Start Up the Year

Grades K-3

VOICES OF EXPERIENCE

Practical Ideas to
Start Up the Year

Grades K-3

COLLEEN POLITANO • JOY PAQUIN
CAREN CAMERON • KATHLEEN GREGORY

PORTAGE & MAIN PRESS

Portage and Main Press acknowledges the financial support of the
Government of Canada through the Book Publishing Industry
Development Program (BPIDP) for our publishing activities.

Printed and bound in Canada by Friesens

06 07 08 5 4 3

Since the first printing of this book in 2003, we have added new
pictures and descriptions to further clarify the activities.

National Library of Canada Cataloguing in Publication

Practical ideas to start the year : grades K-3 / Colleen
Politano ... [et al.].

Includes bibliographical references.
ISBN 1-55379-028-6

1. Activity programs in education. 2. Creative activities and seat
work. I. Politano, Colleen, 1946-

LB1139.35.A37P73 2004   372.13   C2004-900628-2

PORTAGE & MAIN PRESS

100-318 McDermot Ave.
Winnipeg, MB Canada R3A 0A2
Email: books@portageandmainpress.com
Tel: 204-987-3500
Toll-free fax: 1-866-734-8477
Toll free: 1-800-667-9673

Printed on recycled paper

FOR JOY PAQUIN

In the summer of 2003, the four of us (Joy, Colleen, Caren, and Kathleen) worked together and planned the ideas for all the books in the Voices of Experience series. Shortly before the first two books went to press, Joy died suddenly. The ideas in this series reflect Joy's spirit.

Joy Paquin was a teacher's teacher. She was committed to making classrooms the best places for children and to sharing ideas with others. She was known for her enthusiasm, tireless dedication, and the fun she brought to teaching. Joy did more than teach children to read and write; she taught her students and her friends  how to live a full and joyous life. Her professional legacy – one of love, caring, humor, knowledge, and wisdom – will live on for thousands of children, parents, educators, and colleagues.

We dedicate this series to Joy, our dear friend, with love.

Colleen, Caren, and Kathleen

ACKNOWLEDGMENTS

Our thanks to:

Fran Beckow, Joy's teaching partner, who shared in the creation of an environment where the ideas in this book could flourish.

Joy and Fran's students for being such a delight to work with.

Bernie Johnston, Joy's mom, for being an inspiration to us all. We believe that no mother ever chose a more appropriate name for her child. Joy lived her name, and it was our joy to share in her life.

Contents

Introduction

Who is this series for?

Voices of Experience is a series of six books – three for grades K-3, three for grades 4-8. Each book is full of practical ideas designed for new teachers, teachers new to a grade level, and teachers who want new ideas to reenergize their practice.

What's in the books?

We have compiled our best ideas and organized them into two sets of three books:

■ Book 1: for the start of the year when teachers are just getting to know their students

■ Book 2: for during the year when teachers need to get themselves and their students "fired up"

■ Book 3: for the end of the year when teachers need to wrap things up

Each book is organized into four sections around the acronym ROAR.

R = ideas for building relationships

O = ideas for classroom organization

A = ideas for classroom assessment that support student learning

R = ideas that are reliable and ready to use tomorrow

"Create a new model of teacher-teacher support so that every teacher knows every other teacher's best ideas."

— Eric Jensen,
Brain-Based Learning

For each idea we provide a brief discussion and easy-to-follow steps. Many also include student examples and unique adaptations. In addition, we have included current information about the brain and how students learn.

We have also included a variety of ways to use this series of books to support professional development activities in different settings; for example, educators' book clubs; team and department meetings and staff meetings; in-service and pre-service workshops; and seminars with student teachers (see appendix A).

Final Note:

The single, most important message we want to leave you with is to listen to your own voice and the voices of your students. Adapt our ideas to fit for you, your students, and your school community.

Introduction to Relationships

Establish trust and build relationships before anything else.
Then, place relationships above the rest.

■

Show students you care about them as people,
and let them see you as a person.

■

When relationships are established, students
can take risks and accept new challenges.

■

Emotion is a huge part of the classroom;
it often sets the stage for learning.

■

Relationships: First in the book. First in our classrooms.

■

In this chapter on relationships, we offer practical
ideas for you and your students for the start of the
school year. Activities include ways to:

- develop a classroom agreement

- invite families to the classroom

- build relationships with the students' families

- help children learn one another's names

- find out the talents and interests of the students

Classroom Agreement:
developing expectations with students

DISCUSSION

Classrooms run smoothly when students know what is expected of them. Take time to create a class agreement together. When students' ideas and words are used, students understand the expectations and feel committed to the agreement.

STEPS

1. Ask students: "What kind of classroom do we want?" Make a list of students' ideas (see figure 1). Leave the list posted for two or three days so that you and your students can talk about it, think about it, and add to it.

2. Discuss with students what they think it means to agree to something or to make a promise. When we ask students about their experiences with making a promise, we have had responses that range from "I promised my best friend I would…" to "At Brownies

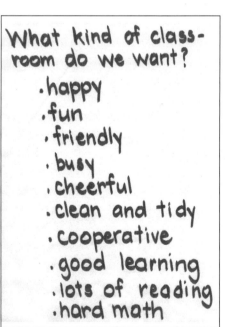

What kind of class-
room do we want?
· happy
· fun
· friendly
· busy
· cheerful
· clean and tidy
· cooperative
· good learning
· lots of reading
· hard math

Figure 1. This list was "brainstormed" and recorded. It was posted for two or three days so students could talk about it and add to it.

we promise to…" to "When we say the Pledge of Allegiance in our classroom, we promise to…"

3. Read the posted list of ideas to students, and work with them to sort the ideas into three to five key categories. Typically, we end up with key words such as *safe*, *thoughtful*, *caring*, *friendly*, and *helpful* for each category.

4. Ask students: "If we want our classroom to be like this, what will we need to agree to or promise to do?" Take a key word from the list, and ask students: "If we want our classroom to be safe, what do we have to agree to do?" Record students' suggestions.

Figure 2. All members (including adults) are asked to read and sign the "class promise" to signify all agree to it.

5. Make a chart to display the key words and the promises that students suggested be included in the class agreement (see figure 2).

6. Read the agreement as part of the classroom routine. At the beginning of the year, we read the agreement aloud daily to remind students of what they have promised.

7. Help students become more familiar with the agreement: Ask them to work in groups to illustrate a key word (for example, *safety*) to show what it could "look like, sound like, feel like." We ask students to use three-fold sheets to show their ideas (see figure 3).

Figure 3. Doing "looks like, sounds like, feels like," helps students develop a visual, auditory, and kinesthetic connection to each point in the promise.

Conversation Starters:
connecting with families

DISCUSSION

Provide families opportunities to give information about their children and to ask questions about the classroom. We offer two ways to start conversations with families at the beginning of the school year.

IDEA #1: FAMILY LETTER

STEPS

1. Write a letter to introduce yourself and other adults in the classroom to the families of your students (see figure 4). To be respectful of all family situations, we address this letter, "Dear Families."

2. Decide what information you want to ask family members to share about their children. We make a response sheet for families to complete and return (see figure 5).

Dear Families,

I am delighted to be your child's teacher this year. Now that I've had the opportunity to meet the students who will make up this class, I know we are going to have a great year!

We have the good fortune to have an enthusiastic and creative student teacher, Michelle King, working with us for the first four months of school. We will also be receiving excellent support from our teaching assistant, Fern Simpson, who will be in our classroom three mornings a week. We welcome family members. If you can volunteer to spend some time in our class, please let me know.

No one knows your children quite the way you do. Would you please take a few minutes to fill in the attached form? The information you share will help get this year off to a great start.

Regards,
Colleen

Figure 4. We address our letter to "Dear Families" to respect the different family compositions our children come from.

3. Set aside some time to read the responses, and find ways to use or refer to the information. For example, when a child is having a tough Monday, start a conversation with: "Your mom told me you play soccer on weekends. Did you play this weekend? How did it go?" At a parent-teacher conference, begin the conversation with something like: "You mentioned on your response sheet to the Family Letter that you really want your son to improve his printing. I've brought these two samples so you can see how much he has improved."

IDEA #2: READ AND RESPOND

STEPS

1. Display a quotation or information poster about topics that might interest students' families; for example, how children learn to spell or nutritional snacks that help the brain learn.

2. Invite families to write their thoughts and questions on cards that you have placed by the poster (see figure 6).

3. Read the cards. If and when it is appropriate, respond to families' concerns through your class newsletter or individual conversations.

Child's name: _____

The most important people in _____ 's life are _____

My child's favorite activities are _____

You can always get _____ 's attention by _____

You might want to be careful about _____

If _____ is upset, it is most helpful to_____

One thing that might surprise you about our child is _____

Our best advice to help our child as a learner is _____

Our hopes and dreams for _____ are

Please add any other comments you have.

Black line master on p. 56

Figure 5. This form gives valuable information at the beginning of the year and can also be a catalyst for celebration at the end of the year.

Families

Your thoughts and questions are important. Please take the time to read the information on display and fill out a card to let us know what you are thinking. Thank you.

_____

_____

_____

_____

Black line master on p. 57

Figure 6. When our families fill out cards like this, we gain insight into what they value in the classroom life.

"We are basically a social species."

— Robert Sylwester, *Student Brains, Student Issues*

Getting Together:
building relationships with families

DISCUSSION

Build relationships with students' families at the beginning of the school year by inviting them for a "get-together." There is no one best way to organize these occasions and we've learned to keep them quick, casual, positive, and to involve the learners.

IDEA #1: PRESENTING OUR CLASS AND OUR DAY

STEPS

1. Tell students that their families are going to be invited to visit the classroom. Explain to students that they will take turns talking about what a day in the classroom is like.

2. Write a typical day's agenda on a chart. Have students work with a partner to decide what part of the school day they would like to talk about. Have partners "sign up" for their parts by writing their names on the agenda.

3. Set a date, and invite families to attend. We ask parents to let us know who will be attending so we can make all necessary arrangements (see figure 7).

4. Give time for partners to rehearse their part and to practice introducing family members.

Dear Families,

The children would like you to meet their classmates. They would also like the opportunity to tell you about some of the things we do at school. You are invited to our classroom at 6:45 pm on Tuesday, September 16th. If you are unable to attend, you are welcome to send a grandparent, other relative, or family friend with your child.

This is our agenda for the evening:

6:45: Children introduce their family members to the whole group
7:00: Children take turns taking guests through our daily agenda
7:20: Children do activities in our classroom supervised by our student teacher, Miss King. Adults go to the library for a short information session with me
7:40: Adults return to classroom to look through their child's folder
7:55: That's all, folks!

We look forward to seeing you on Tuesday evening. Please fill out the form below and return it with your child so we have an idea of how many people we'll have with us.

Thanks for sending such well-cared-for children!

Colleen

- - - - - - - - - - ✂- - - - - - - - - - - - - - - -

On Tuesday, September 16th, _____ people from the _____family will be attending.

Figure 7. Having the students do a presentation encourages families to attend a get-together.

5. Have students introduce their family members as they arrive. Have student partners, in turn, present each part of the agenda.

6. End the event with cookies and juice.

IDEA #2: FAMILY PICNIC

STEPS

1. Set a time and a place for the picnic. We find that most of our family members can attend on their way home from work.

Figure 8. Using child-designed stationery sends the message that our classrooms are about children.

2. Make class stationery: Have each student draw a picture of him/herself along the perimeter of a sheet of copy paper.

3. Have each student use the "letterhead" to send a letter inviting family members to attend the picnic (see figure 8). Make several master copies of the "letterhead" to use for letters and notices throughout the year.

ADAPTATION

We know a kindergarten teacher who holds a Teddy Bear Picnic each year. She asks her students to bring a teddy bear, six cookies, and a family member to the picnic. She supplies cups and juice. Children play together while the guests meet one another and mingle. For the last ten minutes, the children are supervised by the principal, and the teacher meets briefly with family members to inform them of routines and plans for the year. The entire picnic takes thirty minutes.

Name Games:
getting to know each other

DISCUSSION

It is important for students to learn the names of all of their classmates in order to develop relationships. We find children often do not know the names of many of their classmates even after being together for a few months. To help our students get to know one another we introduce name games.

IDEA #1: TRAVELLING NAMES

STEPS

1. Tell students they are going to play a game that will help them learn and remember everyone's name.

2. Make a name card for each student in the class. Place the name cards in a bag or in some kind of interesting container.

3. Have the children sit on the floor in a large circle.

4. Explain to them that when the music starts to play, they will pass around the bag of names.

5. Start the music, and have students pass around the bag of names. After five to ten seconds, stop the music. Have the student holding the bag take a name card out, read it aloud, and give it to the person whose name is written on the card. Ask them to shake hands and say, "Hi, [each other's name]!"

6. Repeat step 5 until all the names have been drawn.

ADAPTATION

With younger children, have a child draw a name out of the bag, hold up the name card, and show it to the class rather than try to read it. The child whose name is on the card can then stand up and read his/her name aloud. Have everyone in the class say: "Hi, [student's name]!"

IDEA #2: THE TELEPHONE GAME

STEPS

1. Have the children sit on the floor in a circle. Give one student a toy telephone or a recycled phone.

2. Teach the following pattern to the children:

   All say: "Hey, [a student's name]."

   That student answers: "I think I hear my name."

   All say: "Hey, [same student's name]."

   That student answers: "I think I hear it again."

   All say: "You're wanted on the telephone."

   Student answers: "If it isn't [different student's name], then I'm not home."

   All say: "With a rick-tick, tickedy, ticko-yeah"

   "With a rick-tick, tickedy, ticko-yeah"

   Repeat, with the new student's name inserted.

ADAPTATION

To turn these name games into singing games check Mary Helen Richards' CD or book, *Experience Games Through Music*. The tune to "There's a Penny in My Hand" fits well for Idea #1. Here is a contact address:

Richards Institute of Education and Research
PO Box 2122, Sarnia, ON N7T 7L1
Toll free phone: 800.859.6804
Fax: 519.864.1686

> *"Learners need to interact to integrate learning."*
>
> — Eric Jensen,
> *Learning With the Body in Mind*

Who Am I?:
using personal artifacts

DISCUSSION

Helping students find out about one another is an important step in building relationships. One way to start exciting and interesting conversations is to ask students to bring in things that they really care about and that represent who they are.

STEPS

1. Bring personal artifacts to the classroom in a box or a bag, and show and talk about them. Pictures of family members, special books, and unique objects from home are examples of things that show who we are. Take approximately two to three minutes to model the process so students have an idea of how much time each person has to "show and tell."

2. Have students sign up for a turn. We have four to six students present each day, which allows everyone to have a turn within a school week.

3. Invite classmates to make brief, specific comments or connections when each presenter is finished (for example, "I like your car. I have one like it").

4. Set aside space in the room so students can put their items on display for the day.

Figures 9a & 9b. The items that students bring vary; the pride they take in sharing is similar.

ADAPTATION

When we have children who are struggling to put together
a collection of personal artifacts from home, we give them support
and time in class to draw, paint, or write about themselves.

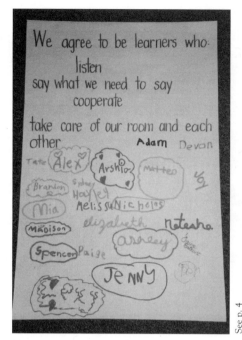

See p. 4

Figure 10. Each student signs the "classroom agreement."

See p. 42

Figure 11. Student shares his "fact frieze" with a friend.

See p. 29

Figure 12. The "daily observer" uses a class list to include all class members.

INTRODUCTION TO ORGANIZATION

Organize in ways that maximize learning.

■

Take time at the beginning to set up routines and procedures with students; it saves time in the long run.

■

Organize in ways that allow all students to make independent use of materials, spaces, and routines in the classroom.

■

Organization is more than having a neat and tidy classroom. Organization is about creating a positive, safe, and orderly environment.

■

The best way to organize is the way that works best for you and your students.

■

In this chapter on organization, we offer practical ideas for you and your students for the start of the school year. Activities include ways to:

- arrange the classroom to support learning

- use an agenda to help teachers and students have a sense of the day as a whole

- create job routines to involve the students in the day-to-day running of the classroom

- use signal songs to make transitions go smoothly

- organize school supplies with students

A Room for Everyone:
setting up the classroom

*"Environments
do matter."*

— Eric Jensen,
Learning Smarter

DISCUSSION

Students need to know where things belong in their classroom, where they can find what they need, and where different workspaces are located. We set up our classrooms so that students can be independent, resources are easily accessible to everyone, and time can be spent learning and working together in organized and appropriate workspaces.

STEPS

1. Make a map of the classroom. On it, indicate electrical outlets, windows, doors, and shelving. Make a list of work and play areas needed. We designate seven areas that we use all year.

2. Create a workspace for yourself. We like to make sure this area has a panoramic view of the classroom. Some teachers choose to have a desk in this space; others use a small table or shelves.

3. Establish a library space. For us, the library needs to be easily accessible to everyone – it is the center of our classroom life.

4. Set up student seating space by arranging tables or by putting desks together to make groups (see figure 13). We set up this area so that all students can see the teacher easily when instructions are being given.

5. Choose a group meeting area. Look for a space where the agenda can be on permanent display and where a whiteboard or chalkboard is available. We like to include a big book easel in this space.

Figure 13. The classroom is organized to invite students to interact with materials and each other.

Figure 14. Storage areas are established so that students have easy access to materials and supplies.

6. Decide on the types and number of centers or activity areas that will be required. Set aside areas for painting, math, writing, construction, creative arts, music, puppets, toys and games, science and nature, and dramatic play. We start the year by giving only a few choices and adding more as we establish expectations and routines.

7. Establish a storage and materials area (see figure 14) so that children have independent access to resources such as paints, paper, magazines, craft supplies, and any other materials needed on a regular basis.

8. Designate a space for lost-and-found items. One colleague calls this her "everything table" and has containers labelled "library books," "no-name papers," and a variety of other labels for items that do not have a home.

The Agenda:
posting the daily plan

DISCUSSION

Posting a daily agenda can help everyone have a productive day. Students see what to expect during the day, and they can look forward to their favorite events. Teachers can use an agenda as a way to organize the day and to stay "on track."

STEPS

1. Choose an area of the classroom that can be a permanent display place for the agenda. We make this in the area set aside for group meetings.

2. Decide how to display the agenda. Some people use a chalkboard, some use a whiteboard, while others prefer chart paper (see figure 15).

Figure 15. The kindergarten agenda gives students the "big picture" of their day.

3. Place a shelf, basket, or other container next to the agenda area for materials such as markers, pointers, highlighter pens, and tape so everything is ready to go.

4. Talk through the agenda with the class at the beginning of each day. Point out any changes in the regular routine. This discussion helps children who have a difficult time with transitions; it gives them a sense of the way the day will develop. After students are familiar with the routine, have them read the agenda themselves.

5. Add arrows or notes to the agenda to show any adjustments made during the day.

6. Take a few minutes at the end of the school day to read over the agenda, and ask students to reflect on the highlights. For example, ask: "What was your favorite part of the day? What was the hardest part? What part would you like more time for?"

"Not knowing what will happen during the course of the day can create anxiety for many students. Posting a morning agenda can make such students involved, curious and eager."

— Martha Kaufeldt,
Begin With the Brain

ADAPTATIONS

■ We find it helpful to put the main agenda words on laminated cards that have magnetic tape on the back. This saves writing the words each day.

■ For our younger students and students with special needs, we add picture cards that represent each main activity (such as a computer icon for computer time and a book to represent reading time). (See figure 16.) Boardmaker™ is an excellent resource for these symbols.

Figure 16. Picture cards that represent activities work well with younger students and those with special needs.

Job Routines:
sharing classroom responsibility

DISCUSSION

To keep the classroom clean and organized, involve students in setting up job routines. We find that when everyone is responsible for doing a specific job every day, students are filled with feelings of pride and a sense that the classroom belongs to everyone.

STEPS

1. Ask the students what jobs need to be done in the classroom to keep it clean and organized. Make a list of their suggestions on whiteboard or the chalkboard, and add ideas that you want on the list (see figure 17).

2. From the list of suggestions, make a chart listing the specific jobs. Make a name card for each student; include a photo of each student above his/her name. Use these cards to indicate the job that each student is responsible for. We include our own picture card with the students' cards (see figure 18).

Jobs We Need To Do

clean sinks
computers
stack chairs
put buckets away
tidy books
clean boards
vacation read or volunteer
put out name tags
bins
shelves
tidy toys
tidy science table
floor fix up
put out notices

Figure 17. List of suggestions

3. Take time to practice and demonstrate each job. Discuss how many people might need to be assigned to each job and what the responsibilities are.

4. Decide how often the jobs will be rotated. With some classes we use a one-day schedule; with other classes the students keep their jobs for a week.

5. Set aside a time to talk with students about what is going well with job routines and what changes can be made.

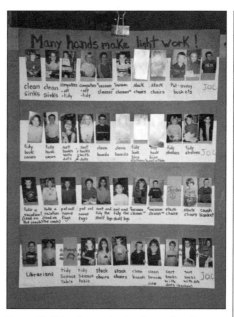

Figure 18. Using photographs of students makes this an attractive and easily read display.

ADAPTATION

We include a "day off" and/or teacher's personal assistant on the job list. We also like to create a "snappy title" for each job. For example, "floor fixer" and "greeter" provide novelty titles that students enjoy.

Signal Songs:
making transitions go smoothly

DISCUSSION

Use music to help students make a smooth transition from activity to activity. We use signal songs to let students know when it is time to finish an activity, clean up, and come together as a group. Below, we offer three of our favorite activities.

IDEA #1: SIGNAL SONG

STEPS

1. At the beginning of the week, play three lively songs for the students. We use rock and roll tunes because the energy creates momentum.

2. Make a quick graph with the three song titles, and have students vote on their favourite song. The most popular song becomes the "signal song" for the week.

3. Tell the students that whenever they hear the song of the week, it is a signal to stop what they are doing, start their clean-up, and meet at a designated spot by the time the song has finished playing.

(To the tune "Shortenin' Bread")

Everybody have a seat, have a seat, have a seat

Everybody have a seat, a seat on a chair.

Not on the ceiling, not in the air,

Everybody come and have a seat on a chair.

(Variation)

Everybody have a seat, have a seat, have a seat

Everybody have a seat, a seat on the floor.

Not on the ceiling, not on the door,

Everybody come and have a seat on the floor.

Black line master on p. 58

Figure 19. Everybody Have a Seat

Idea #2: Three Time Song

Steps

1. Teach students the song, *Everybody Have a Seat* (see figure 19).

2. Sing the song together for the *first* time at a quick tempo.

3. Sing the song together a *second* time, and this time have everyone sing in a soft voice. By now some students will have cleaned up. Have them sit in the meeting area and sing while they wait for all of the students to be ready.

4. Sing the song together once again. This time, though, have students mouth the words so there is no sound. By the end of this third round of the song, all students are expected to be quietly sitting in the meeting area, ready to begin a new activity.

Idea #3: Countdown

Steps

1. Show students how a countdown chant can be used to let them know how long they have to clean up and come to a designated meeting area (see figure 20).

2. Ask all students to sit together in the designated meeting area by the end of the chant.

3. Begin the countdown with the first line: "We'll be starting in 5" [clap clap].

4. Continue the countdown: "We'll be starting in 4" [clap, clap].

5. Continue the countdown, adjusting the speed of the chant according to how much clean-up is necessary.

We'll be starting in 5 [clap, clap]

We'll be starting in 4 [clap, clap]

We'll be starting in 3 [clap, clap]

We'll be starting in 2 [clap, clap]

We'll be starting in 1 [clap, clap]

We're starting now.

Figure 20. Having a transition routine respects children's need to finish their thoughts before joining the group.

Supply Round-Up:
sorting school supplies

DISCUSSION

Sort and organize school supplies with students during the first week of school. We have learned that school supplies are very important to young children, and we need to reassure them that their supplies belong to them and will be available when needed.

STEPS

1. Explain that everyone is going to work together to sort and put away their school supplies. Students' supplies usually fall into one of three groups: fit in with the desk supplies; too big for the desk supplies; use-a-few-at-a-time supplies.

2. Have students come to an area on the floor with all of their school supplies. Reassure students that their supplies belong to them, will not get lost or mixed up with others' "stuff," and will be available to them whenever they need them.

3. Ask students to "round up" supplies that take up room and are too big for their desks (such as paints and glue). Have students place these supplies into two classroom containers labelled "glue" and "paint." To prevent loss or mix up, make sure that the name of each student is on his/her supplies.

4. Ask students to "round up" supplies that fit in their desks and are used every day (for example, felt pens, crayons, pencil crayons, pencil sharpener, ruler, scissors). Have students select two pencils, one eraser, four notebooks, and have them put all of these supplies in their desks.

Figures 21a & 21b.
Children know they have access
to their own school supplies.

5. Give each student a large envelope or clear plastic bag with
    his/her name printed on it. Ask the students to "round up"
    their extra supplies that come in multiples, such as extra
    pencils, notebooks, and erasers, and put these in the envelope
    or clear plastic bag (see figures 21a & 21b). Have students
    place their packed supplies in a box or on a shelf labeled
    "students' extra supplies."

ADAPTATION

If students work at tables rather than at desks, each student needs
a container with his/her name on it to store the supplies that he/she
uses daily.

See p. 44

Figure 22. Class is organized into groups — each has one helper role.

See p. 24

Figure 23. Students help keep the classroom library organized.

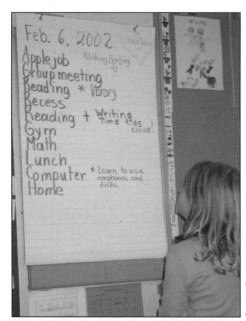

Feb. 6, 2002
Apple job
Group meeting
Reading * library
Recess
Reading + Writing Time kids choice!
Gym
Math
Lunch
Computer *Learn to use earphones and disks.
Home

See p. 18

Figure 24. A student checks the agenda during the day to find out what's next.

INTRODUCTION TO ASSESSMENT

Assessment is information about learning: what
is working, what is not, what happens next.

■

Our first goal for assessment practices is to support
student learning, not simply measure it.

■

Descriptive feedback is what contributes most
dramatically to learning.

■

The more students are involved in their own assessment,
the more they learn.

■

Students are more likely to achieve goals they set
for themselves than ones set for them.

■

In this chapter on assessment, we offer practical ideas
for you and your students for the start of the school year.
Activities include ways to:

■ help students recognize accomplishments of others

■ offer students descriptive feedback

■ start a system for organizing students' work samples

■ involve students in self-reflection

■ help families and students appreciate the
growth of learning over the year

Daily Observer:
involving students in observation

DISCUSSION

It is important to take notice of the positive things that are done in the classroom every day. We involve students in observation by giving them a turn to be the "daily observer." Student observers look for, record, and tell others what they see happening that makes our classroom work smoothly.

STEPS

1. Set aside an "observer's" desk and chair, and place a clipboard, pencil, and paper on it.

2. Tell students some of the thoughtful, kind, respectful, and hard-working things you see happening in the classroom. For example: "I notice you take turns, speak politely, help others, are supportive of one another, and do so many other great things."

3. Explain that when you are teaching or reading a story aloud, it is difficult to notice and make notes of all the positive things taking place in the classroom. Tell students you need their help: each day a different student will take on the job of being the "observer."

4. Demonstrate the process. Record on a sheet on the clipboard some of the specific behaviors you observe during a short period of time. Gather as a class, and show and read to the students what you have recorded.

5. Ask students to volunteer to be the "daily observer." Ask the observer (see figure 25) to record as many positive actions as he/she can. To start, give students approximately fifteen to thirty minutes of activities (such as story time or clean-up time), and then have them stop. Say: "Let's see what our observer has noticed about our class." Make the student observer's role clear by assuring students it is not their job to deal with any problems. We often need to repeat the message: "If you notice something that could be a problem, leave that for me to deal with. Your only job is to write down as many positive things as you observe."

6. Have the observer read his/her comments aloud to the class. We find that the first few times the notes might not be very specific or include every child. To help students be more specific, ask questions such as: "What exactly did Railyn do to be helpful?" With practice children become better at noticing and recording specifics (see figure 26).

Figure 25. Children enjoy the privilege of describing their classmates in positive ways.

Note: Children who cannot write, can draw their observations, have the teacher scribe the information, or put a smiley face beside students' names.

ADAPTATION

It is important that students *volunteer* to be daily observers – not all students feel confident enough to do the job. One way to involve more reluctant students is to give them the choice of working with a partner.

Our students suggest adaptations for example, when they realized the need to include everyone in their observations, they came up with the idea to record as many comments as possible and finish with a summary comment like: "Everyone helped clean up today." Another student asked for a class list so that when comments were recorded no one was left out.

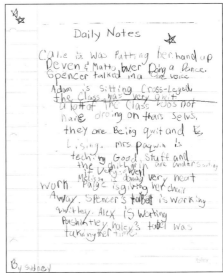

Figure 26. Student sample of "daily observer."

Feedback Frames:
making descriptive feedback a habit

"One of the best ways to boost learning is to dramatically increase the quality and quantity of feedback. For growing greater dendrites in the brain, increased feedback is king."

— Eric Jensen,
Brain Compatible Strategies

DISCUSSION

Feedback is information that learners receive about what they are doing well and what they still need to improve. We find that using simple frames or prompts helps us develop the habit of offering our students specific, immediate, and descriptive feedback.

STEPS

1. Tell students it is important for them to receive specific information on how they are doing in their learning. Say: "To help you do your best learning, I am going to tell you things I notice about your work and about your behaviour. When I am really specific it gives you information that you can use. For example, if I say 'nice job,' you know I like it. But if I say, 'I like the way you used so many colors and used black to make your words stand out,' you know exactly what might be worth doing again."

2. Post feedback frames in the classroom where they are easy for all to see (see figure 27a). Having the frames visible helps teachers and students develop the habit of giving descriptive feedback.

3. Practice using one of the frames to give students descriptive feedback. For example, say: "Sultan, I have two stars for you. You got your supplies out and started right to work, and you've got your name on your paper already. My wish is that you will add some colourful pictures to your letter." We start by offering only "stars," or specific compliments as descriptive feedback.

2 Stars and 1 Wish	Two to glow and One to grow...
☆ _____	
☆ _____	Glow _____
Wish _____	
2 Hurrahs and 1 Hint	Glow _____
Hurrah _____	
Hurrah _____	Grow _____
Hint _____	

Black line master on p. 59

Figure 27a (left) & 27b. Feedback frames help students develop the language of reflection.

4. Add wishes or suggestions for improvement when students are used to receiving feedback. We use different frames to add variety (see figure 27b).

ADAPTATIONS

■ Give students opportunities to use the frames and prompts for offering descriptive feedback to themselves and others. Have students stop what they are doing, and ask them to tell themselves or a partner two stars (things they have done well) and one wish (something they want to change or improve).

■ To offer written feedback to students, photocopy the black line masters on p.59.

Four-Pocket Folders:
collecting authentic evidence

DISCUSSION

When we invest time at the beginning of the year to set up a way to collect student work samples, that time pays off throughout the year. We use a four-pocket folder, which gives our students, parents, and ourselves a visual, concrete, and dramatic way to see growth and development over time. We find the folders are particularly useful at conference and report card time.

STEPS

1. Decide on the type of student samples to collect. We find collecting samples for all subjects is overwhelming so we focus on literacy and collect one reading, one writing, and one visual representation (drawing, painting, or mind map) sample.

2. Tell students they will help collect samples of their work four times during the year so that their families can see how much they have learned. We do the first collection early in the school year, and use it as baseline data. This allows growth and development to be tracked for the first reporting period.

3. Set up a four-pocket folder for each student: Attach two pocket folders with wide cellophane tape (see figure 28). We put a name label on each folder so the folders can be reused each year.

4. Save a first sample of student writing. Use the original or photocopy it, and place it in the folder. We add a brief comment about the writing to highlight what is important for parents to notice. Later in the year, when students have many writing pieces to choose from,

they look through their writing notebooks and files and select a sample.

Figures 28. The brain needs the whole picture. Four-pocket folders help parents, students, and teachers see progress over time.

5. Have each student select a piece of reading material that he or she is comfortable reading. We meet with each child during class time when all students are busy reading, writing, or working on other literacy activities and ask him/her to read the piece aloud. As the child reads we record brief comments.

6. Photocopy a page or two of each student's reading selection. Place this along with comments into the child's folder. To make the process work for children who are just beginning to understand the process of reading, have them select a book they can retell or one they have memorized.

7. Include an example of a visual representation from each student. Use of these samples are an important part of a literacy portfolio because young children are often more able to express their ideas through visual representations than through words.

8. Repeat the collection of student samples four times during the year. We collect in September to establish baseline data and then again in November, February, and June to fit with our reporting times. We also use four-pocket folders at conferences and report card time to show specific student examples.

9. Give students time in class to look at and talk about their samples in their folders and to celebrate their accomplishments.

ADAPTATION

We invite families to the classroom to look at four-pocket folders and talk with their son or daughter about the growth that has taken place over the year.

Reflection:
taking time to pause and think

DISCUSSION

Reflection is essential for learning. When students are taught how to recognize and appreciate their own learning, they can begin to take an active role in directing and monitoring their own progress. A starting place for us is to give all learners time to figure out their strengths and what they need to work on.

STEPS

1. Talk with students about the importance of taking time to pause and think. Say, for example: "Sometimes we get so busy working that we don't take time to think about our learning. In our class we're going to start a new habit of stopping at different times during the day so we can think about what we are doing well and what we need to work on to get better."

Thinking about Your Thinking

What do you like about what you did?

What would you change if you did it again?

Figure 29. Chart of reflection questions

2. Record reflection questions on a chart for students to think about and respond to. We start with: "What do you like about what you did?" "What might you change if you did it again?"

(See figure 29.) Add more questions as students become familiar with the process.

3. Ask students to meet together as a group after they complete an activity. Have each student sit next to a partner. Read aloud one question at a time to students, and ask them to take turns with their partner responding to each one.

4. Leave the chart posted in the classroom, and give students opportunities to use these questions with other activities and assignments. To make reflection a habit, ask students to think about activities outside the classroom; for example, how the morning went at home, recess and lunch, playtime with friends, and other real-life events.

ADAPTATION

At the end of the day, we schedule time to have the students sit together and think about how the day went. We invite students to share their thoughts with the group about how they feel about the day and what they learned. Some of the questions we ask are: "Does anyone want to tell about something that went really well today? Did anyone do something they might do differently another time?"

"As students begin to know their own personal strengths and challenges, they can make better choices and set realistic goals."

— Martha Kaufeldt,
Begin With the Brain

Self-Portrait Wall:
organizing a year-long record of growth and development

DISCUSSION

Families often record growth marks on a wall or doorjamb to show their children how much taller they grow each year. To help students see how much they are growing as learners throughout the school year we designate a space in the classroom for a "Self-Portrait Wall" – a place where students can see how they are growing as learners throughout the school year.

STEPS

1. Select a bulletin board or wall space large enough to hold a self-portrait of each student in the class.

2. Give each student a sheet of white paper. Letter size works well.

3. Demonstrate how to draw a self-portrait, taking time to talk about features, details, use of space, and use of materials. Have each student complete a self-portrait. Then give students a slip of paper, and ask them to print their name on it.

4. Have students choose a piece of coloured paper for a background and glue their completed self-portrait and name slip on this coloured paper. Staple the portraits onto display board (see figure 30).

5. Have students complete new portraits and name cards once a month throughout the school year. Staple each new portrait and name strip on top of the previous one.

6. At the end of the school year, have students add a cover (the same size as the background paper), decorate it, and take the self-portraits home.

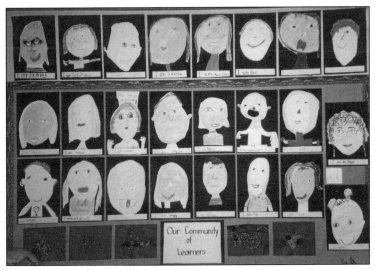

Figure 30. Self-portrait wall is an ongoing display that shows growth over time.

ADAPTATION

Ask children in kindergarten to draw a full-body self-portrait on legal-size paper. It is informative to see how their body image evolves over the year.

"Colorful, interesting environments boost learning. Learners need rituals and routines which give them positive feedback."

— Eric Jensen,
Learning With the Body in Mind

See p. 30

Figure 31. Teacher offers "descriptive feedback" using the frame "2 hurrahs and 1 hint."

See p. 32

Figure 32. Student gets her "four-pocket folder" ready to share.

Figure 33. The teacher takes notes while the student reads her "just right" book.

See p. 32

INTRODUCTION TO RELIABLES

Reliables are ideas that can be depended
on to keep students active and engaged.

■

Reliables are activities that work with a wide range of learners.

■

Reliables offer students choices to show what they know.

■

Reliables let students personalize their learning.

■

With reliables, students know what to anticipate,
and they can say: "Oh, we know how to do this!"

■

In this chapter on reliables, we offer practical ideas
for you and your students for the start of the school
year. Activities include ways to:

■ provide choice and variety

■ teach students unique ways to represent learning

■ help groups use roles effectively

■ get great results with quick and easy projects

■ use movement and music

Exploration Time:
providing choice and variety

DISCUSSION

Ensuring that there is enough time in the day for students to choose an activity to work on is one of the single most important ways we can help children build relationships, use conflict resolution, be creative, and apply their academic skills for real purposes. Exploration Time is a self-directed, risk-free time in the day when children make choices.

STEPS

1. Tell students that they are going to have time set aside in the day to choose what they want to work on and "explore." Ask them what materials, books, and topics might interest them. Record their ideas on a chart (see figure 34).

2. Schedule a regular time for exploration (from fifteen to forty minutes depending on grade level, time of year, and age of students).

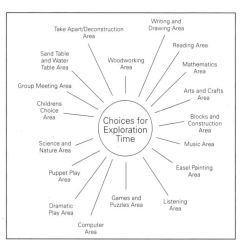

Figure 34. Having a wide variety of choices for exploration time gives all children opportunities to be successful.

3. Start with a limited number of activities for students to choose from. For example, writing, drawing, reading, math games, arts and crafts, and blocks and construction all work well at the beginning of the school year. As the year progresses, add such activities as sand, water, science and nature table; music, painting, puppets; listening, games and puzzles, computers; dramatic play; and woodwork.

4. To develop clear guidelines for exploration time, ask the students: "What do you think we can all do to make exploration time work well for everyone?" We have found that the more we involve our students in decision making, the more we create opportunities for learning.

5. Set aside time at the end of the exploration period for reflection. Ask questions such as: "What did you learn today at exploration time?" "What went well today?" "Did you have any problems?" "What did you do to solve them?" Our students, for example, decided on the number of participants who could work at the block and construction area when they had a problem with too many in the area at one time.

6. Teach students to give each other specific compliments related to exploration time. We hear comments such as: "I'd like to compliment Ben because when I asked him if I could join in the building, he said, 'Sure!'"

ADAPTATION

We invite students to set up and run exploration areas called "children's choice." For example, one student brought materials and taught a craft; another brought a board game for students to play. We also invite family members, student teachers, and other adults who visit the class to bring materials and activities for an "exploration special."

"Brain development may, in fact, be enhanced by play. In the early years of a child's development, the complex interaction of social, physical, and emotional factors contribute toward neural connectednes.

Connectivity is a crucial feature of brain development because the neural pathways formed during the early years carry signals that allow us to process information throughout our lives."

— W. Dixon and C. Shore, *Infant Behavior & Development*

Fact Frieze:
providing alternate ways to represent

DISCUSSION

For variety and to help more students be successful, provide them with alternate ways to represent information. A fact frieze is an effective way for students to use pictures and words to show what they know about a particular book or topic.

IDEA #1: CLASS FACT FRIEZE

STEPS

1. Draw a frieze sample to show the horizontal arrangement of the panels.

2. Read aloud a nonfiction book to the students. Ask them to tell the most important facts and information. Record their ideas on a chart.

3. Have students choose one of the facts from the list to illustrate. Have students sign up on the chart for the idea they select.

4. Give each student a sheet of legal-size paper (turn it sideways so it looks like the panel of a frieze), and provide time for students to illustrate their frieze panels. Have them copy the fact they illustrated on the bottom of the panel and sign their name.

5. Ask students to hand in their completed panels and, as a class, arrange the drawings in a connected horizontal, linear display.

Figure 35. Having students do a fact frieze about themselves several times a year can demonstrate their development.

Note: Due to lack of space, this work sample cannot be shown in its original horizontal configuration.

Idea #2: Individual Fact Frieze

Steps

1. Draw a sample of a frieze to show the horizontal arrangement of the panels.

2. Give each student a long, narrow strip of paper, and have him/her fold it into four panels.

3. Ask each student to think of four facts that he/she knows about a theme or topic the class is studying. Have students then draw an illustration of the theme or topic for each panel and add text if they wish (see figure 35).

4. Display these panels as a frieze that extends around the perimeter of the classroom.

Adaptation

A frieze provides a way for students to respond to a video, a demonstration, or a field trip. Each student can also make a fact frieze to illustrate what he/she does at school. The frieze can then be shown at conferences or included with report cards.

Forming Groups:
setting the stage for group work

"From a succession of experiences that build community, a sense of belonging, or groupness, can emerge, where no one feels isolated."

— Barbara Given,
Teaching to the Brain's Natural Learning Systems

DISCUSSION

Have students work in groups early in the school year, and introduce the idea of "helper roles." We find that when our students give and receive help from others, they feel supported, recognized for their own talents, and safe to try new things in the classroom.

STEPS

1. Let students know they will be doing some work in groups. For example, say: "We are going to learn how to work in groups and how we can use our talents to help each other."

2. Organize the class into groups of four students. To decide who will be in each group, carefully consider a balance of gender, skills in literacy and numeracy, as well as social skills.

3. Decide on a helper role for each student in the group. Match the role of each student to his/her strengths. To indicate the different helper roles, we use colours such as blue (writing helper), green (math helper), purple (speaking helper), yellow (social helper), red (reading helper), and orange (artistic helper). Hand out a different colour to each student in the group so there are four helper roles in each group.

4. Ask students to meet with their group, and give them time to get to know one another and feel comfortable as a group. For example, have them decide on a group name, make up a group cheer, or design a banner that they will present to the class.

5. Give time for students to practice their helper roles in a group activity. Begin with activities that students are familiar with so they can focus on developing group skills. For example, reread a favourite story to the class, and ask groups to show what they know about the story (see figure 36).

6. Plan for reflection time after group work. We ask students to respond to three questions:
   - How did you help your group today?
   - How did someone else in your group help you?
   - What would you like to change the next time you work in a group?

Figure 36. When students work in groups, they feel supported and are willing to try new things in the classroom.

Instant Murals:
responding to shared experiences

DISCUSSION

Instant murals provide an opportunity for students to give individual responses to a shared experience. We find that having student-created murals in our classrooms lets every child see his/her individual response and helps develop a sense of community.

STEPS

1. Tell students they are going to make a mural for family night. The theme of the mural is, "Things I do at school." Explain that half the class will be working on the mural; the rest of the students will be doing another activity until it is their turn.

2. Place two strips of paper on the floor. Each strip should be long enough for four to six children to work on at once (see figure 37). Have the students draw a large picture of themselves doing something they like to do in school. We find it best to have students use felts or crayons the first time they do instant murals. (Repeat step 2 for the second half of the class.)

Figures 37. Students draw themselves doing a favourite activity at school.

3. Give students an opportunity to go back to the mural to add details, captions, and background features. When the students have completed their murals (figure 38), we draw a picture of ourselves in the mural and ask other adults who work in the classroom to do the same.

4. Display the completed murals.

5. Ask students to reflect on what they enjoyed doing, what could make the activity better, and what other materials they could use next time. Repeat this exercise frequently throughout the year.

ADAPTATION

Some shared experiences we use for instant murals are field trips, videos, performances, and "wrapping up" a theme.

Figure 38. Students create an instant mural at the end of a theme.

> "Real learning, the kind of learning that establishes meaningful connections in the learner, is not complete until there is some output, some physical, personal expression of thought."
>
> — Carla Hannaford, *Smart Moves*

Stress Busters:
using movement and music

DISCUSSION

Schedule regular times during the day for physical breaks and other stress busters. Teaching students a variety of ways to lower their own stress levels is one of the most important things we can do in the classroom. Here, we offer two of our favourites.

IDEA #1: CROSSOVERS

STEPS

1. Explain to children what crossovers are and why they are important: "When we do activities that require us to cross over the center or midline of our body with our arms and legs, it's called a *crossover*. During the day, the two sides of our brain take turns being in charge so when we do crossovers it helps us use both sides of our brain."

2. Show the children some simple crossovers (see figure 39):
   - bring one hand to opposite side of back
   - place hands on opposite knees, hips, elbows, heels, toes
   - use one thumb and then the other to make horizontal figure 8s and cross in front of face
   - touch nose, and hold opposite ear and then switch

Figure 39. Crossovers help the two sides of the brain communicate and add some fun to the day.

Knees, Knees

Knees, knees
Slap knees twice

Shoulders, shoulders
Cross hands over chest, and tap shoulders twice

Knees, knees
Slap knees twice

Shoulders, shoulders
Cross hands over chest, and tap shoulders twice

Knees, one shoulder
Slap knees once, and cross one hand over and tap opposite shoulder

Knees, the other shoulder
Slap knees once, and cross the other hand over and tap opposite shoulder

Knees, crossover, knees
Tap knees once, cross hands over and touch knees, uncross hands and tap again

Snap!
Snap fingers in front of body

Brush, brush
Brush hands together in front of body

Elbow, elbow
Touch inside of elbow with opposite hand, repeat other side

Nod, nod
Bend head to chest twice

Back, back
Bring head back for two counts

Wax on, wax off
Circle palm of hand and arm in front of body with one hand, then the other

Wax together!
Circle both hands and arms in front of body

Black line master on p. 63

Figure 40. Actions for "knees knees" cross over activity

Black line master on p. 63

> "Enjoyable breaks promote the production of dopamine through social bonding and celebration. This improves storage and retrieval of information and helps put students in a positive state for learning."
>
> — Eric Jensen, *Learning With the Body in Mind*

3. Practice simple crossovers as a class and then teach the movements for "Knees, Knees" (see figure 40).

4. Add music after students have tried the actions a few times. Our favourite songs to use are: "Build Me Up Buttercup," by The Foundations; "We Are Family," by Sister Sledge; and "Rock Around the Clock," by Bill Haley and the Comets.

IDEA #2: CHAIR AEROBICS

STEPS

1. Explain to students that they can take a break without getting off their chairs. Have students move their chairs so they have room to stretch their feet out in front of them. They can now do a stress buster without getting out of their chairs.

2. Lead students in chair aerobics. Our favourite tune for this activity is "Footloose," by Kenny Loggins. Some of our favourite moves are in figure 41.

Chair Aerobics

- lift shoulders up – first together, then one at a time
- roll shoulders
- slap knee with arm, and stretch up
- stretch arms up, and cross them in front of the body
- pump arms and lift legs, and move them as if running on the spot
- hold onto the chair, and extend one leg, then the other
- hold onto the chair, and extend both legs at once
- twist in chair
- roll ankles

Black line master on p. 62

Figure 41. Actions for "chair aerobics"

Appendix A
professional development

USING THIS BOOK WITH ADULT LEARNERS

The ideas in this book can be used to support professional development activities in different settings; for example, educators book clubs; team and department meetings and staff meetings; and in-service and pre-service workshops.

Consider the following possibilities

BRAIN BITS

This idea works well as a way to introduce the book at a staff meeting (where only two or three books might be available).

1. Make a copy of Brain Bits black line master (page 62) for each participant.

2. Organize the participants into small groups (three or four per group), and have each member in the group do the following:

    (a) Choose a "brain bit."

    (b) Read aloud the quotation to the others in the group.

    (c) Discuss how he/she can relate the "brain bit" to his/her students and experiences in the classroom.

    (d) Invite group members to make comments or ask questions.

3. Have the groups continue until each person in the group has had a turn.

4. Bring all the groups together, show them copies of Voices of Experience, and invite a couple of volunteers to read the books and try some of the ideas with their students.

5. At the next staff meeting, ask the volunteers to discuss what ideas they tried and what they learned.

JIGSAW

Jigsaw is a quick way to introduce the book to the participants. This idea works well at staff meetings or pre-service teacher seminars (when there are a large number of participants).

1. Divide participants into groups of four. Assign a different section of the book (Relationships, Organization, Assessment, Reliables) to each person in the group.

2. Ask each person to read his/her assigned section and to be prepared to summarize and retell a favourite activity.

3. Each person, in the group of four, takes a turn to talk about his/her section.

4. Invite participants to select one idea that they will try out with their students. Ask each person to come to the next meeting with student samples and stories to share.

BOOK CLUB

This idea works when at least two people are interested in the book.

1. Invite colleagues to form a book club (two or more people make a club).

2. Agree on a time, place, and schedule for the first meeting.

3. At the meeting, discuss how to work with the book. A couple of suggestions: (a) each member reads a different section of the book and selects one activity to try with students, or (b) the group comes to an agreement on one section of the book to read and one idea to have everyone try out before the book club meets again.

4. At the end of the meeting, set a time to get together again. Agree to bring back student samples and stories about what worked, what did not work, and what adaptations were made.

5. Invite participants to record their next steps on a planning sheet (see page 64).

INDEPENDENT STUDY

This idea works well for teachers who choose to work on their own – especially those who are new to the profession and those who are working at a new grade level.

1. Read the book to get an overall sense of its contents (20 ideas for a 20-minute read).

2. Select one or two ideas to try out with students.

3. Use the record sheet to keep track of the idea you have tried, how well it worked, and what idea to try next (see Recording Sheet, page 65).

TAKE ACTION

This idea works well at meetings and workshops.

1. Invite adult learners to try out activities for themselves during staff meetings and workshops. Here are some possibilities:

■ "Who Am I?" (page 12)
Participants can bring, list, or sketch three to five items that reflect their interests. Organize small groups, and have participants share their interests with others in the group.

■ "Classroom Agreement" (page 4)
Have staff or other working groups list expectations and develop an agreement for working together. Agreements can be developed for all meetings.

■ "The Agenda" (page 18)
Post an agenda for all staff meetings and workshop sessions. At the beginning of the meeting or workshop, review the agenda as a group and give participants an opportunity to consider the plan for the session.

- "Signal Songs" (page 22)
  Use a signal song to call participants back from breaks during meetings and workshop sessions.

- "Reflection" (page 34)
  Provide participants with time to reflect during and immediately following meetings and workshop sessions. Reflection gives participants time to connect the content presented to their own practice.

- "Self-Portrait Wall" (page 36)
  Give each staff member an area (other than the classroom) to display different students' work throughout the school year. Alternatively, have staff use the area to post interesting articles or reading recommendations.

- "Stress Busters" (page 48)
  Adult learners need breaks just as often as young learners. Participants can process the information from meetings or workshops while doing crossovers or stretching their arms and their legs.

- "Fact Frieze" (page 42)
  Invite groups of participants to use a fact frieze to summarize a meeting or workshop. Provide them with strips of paper, and have them draw quick sketches and write captions to represent the main points of the session.

Appendix B
black line masters

Child's name: _____

The most important people in _____'s life are _____

_____

My child's favorite activities are _____

_____

You can always get _____'s attention by _____

_____

You might want to be careful about _____

If _____ is upset, it is most helpful to_____

_____

One thing that might surprise you about our child is _____

_____

Our best advice to help our child as a learner is _____

_____

Our hopes and dreams for _____are

_____

_____

_____

Please add any other comments you have.

Figure 5 (page 7).

Families

Your thoughts and questions are important. Please take the time to read the information on display and fill out a card to let us know what you are thinking. Thank you.

_____

_____

_____

_____

Figure 6 (page 7).

(To the tune "Shortenin' Bread")

Everybody have a seat,
have a seat, have a seat

Everybody have a seat,
a seat on a chair.

Not on the ceiling,
not in the air,

Everybody come and
have a seat on a chair.

(Variation)

Everybody have a seat,
have a seat, have a seat

Everybody have a seat,
a seat on the floor.

Not on the ceiling,
not on the door,

Everybody come and
have a seat on the floor.

Figure 16 (page 22).

2 Stars and 1 Wish

☆ ____________________

☆ ____________________

Wish ____________________

Figure 21a (page 33).

2 Hurrahs and 1 Hint

Hurrah ____________________

Hurrah ____________________

Hint ____________________

Figure 21a (page 33).

Two to glow and One to grow...

Glow ____________________

Glow ____________________

Grow ____________________

Figure 27ab (page 31).

Knees, Knees

Knees, knees
Slap knees twice

Shoulders, shoulders
Cross hands over chest, and tap shoulders twice

Knees, knees
Slap knees twice

Shoulders, shoulders
Cross hands over chest, and tap shoulders twice

Knees, one shoulder
Slap knees once, and cross one hand over and tap opposite shoulder

Knees, the other shoulder
Slap knees once, and cross the other hand over and tap opposite shoulder

Knees, crossover, knees
Tap knees once, cross hands over and touch knees, uncross hands and tap again

Snap!
Snap fingers in front of body

Brush, brush
Brush hands together in front of body

Elbow, elbow
Touch inside of elbow with opposite hand, repeat other side

Nod, nod
Bend head to chest twice

Back, back
Bring head back for two counts

Wax on, wax off
Circle palm of hand and arm in front of body with one hand, then the other

Wax together!
Circle both hands and arms in front of body

Figure 40 (page 49).

Chair Aerobics

- lift shoulders up – first together, then one at a time

- roll shoulders

- slap knee with arm, and stretch up

- stretch arms up, and cross them in front of the body

- pump arms and lift legs, and move them as if running on the spot

- hold onto the chair, and extend one leg, then the other

- hold onto the chair, and extend both legs at once

- twist in chair

- roll ankles

Figure 41 (page 50).

1. "Be sure that students understand the rules. It is always good to have the students help you make them. Post them, send them home, and follow them."

   –Marilee B. Sprenger, *Becoming a "Wiz" at Brain Based Learning*

---

2. "We are basically a social species."

   –Robert Sylwester, *Student Brains, School Issues*

---

3. "Learners need to interact to integrate learning."

   –Eric Jensen, *Learning With the Body in Mind*

---

4. "Environments do matter"

   –Eric Jensen, *Learning Smarter*

---

5. "The brain's capabilities are enhanced by positive social interactions."

   –Martha Kaufeldt, *Begin With the Brain*

---

6. "One of the best ways to boost learning is to dramatically increase the quality and quantity of feedback. For growing greater dendrites in the brain, increased feedback is king."

   –Eric Jensen, *Brain Compatible Strategies*

---

7. "By facilitating students' attentional focus on personal goals and immediate feedback, we can actually help their brains direct their attention by bringing these goals to a conscious level."

   –Martha Kaufeldt, *Begin With the Brain*

---

8. "Not knowing what will happen during the course of the day can create anxiety for many students. Posting a morning agenda can make such students involved, curious and eager."

   –Martha Kaufeldt, *Begin With the Brain*

Brain Bits (page 51).

9. "As students begin to know their own personal strengths and challenges, they can make better choices and set realistic goals."

   –Martha Kaufeldt, *Begin With the Brain*

10. "Colorful, interesting environments boost learning. Learners need rituals and routines which give them positive feedback."

    –Eric Jensen, *Learning With the Body in Mind*

11 "Brain development may, in fact, be enhanced by play. In the early years of a child's development, the complex interaction of social, physical, and emotional factors contribute toward neural connectedness. Connectivity is a crucial feature of brain development because the neural pathways formed during the early years carry signals that allow us to process information throughout our lives."

   –W. Dixon and C. Shore, *Infant Behavior & Development*

12. "From a succession of experiences that build community, a sense of belonging, or groupness, can emerge, where no one feels isolated."

    –Barbara Given, *Teaching to the Brain's Natural Learning Systems*

13. "Real learning, the kind of learning that establishes meaningful connections in the learner, is not complete until there is some output, some physical, personal expression of thought."

    –Carla Hannaford, *Smart Moves*

14. "Enjoyable breaks promote the production of dopamine through social bonding and celebration. This improves storage and retrieval of information and helps put students in a positive state for learning."

    –Eric Jensen, *Learning With the Body in Mind*

Brain Bits (page 51).

Planning Sheet

Name: _____

The section I'm focusing on is _____

_____

The idea I'm going to try is _____

_____

_____

Subject/topic/assignment I'm using it for is _____

_____

Time frame: by _____

(date of next meeting)

Comments:

What worked: _____

_____

_____

What didn't work: _____

_____

_____

Adaptations made: _____

_____

_____

Recording Sheet

Name: _____

Contents	Ideas Tried	Comments
RELATIONSHIPS Introduction to Relationships Classroom Agreement Conversation Starters Getting Together Name Games Who Am I?		
ORGANIZATION Introduction to Organization A Room for Everyone The Agenda Job Routines Signal Songs Supply Round-up		
ASSESSMENT Introduction to Assessment Daily Observer Feedback Frames Four-Pocket Folder Reflection Self-Portrait Wall		
RELIABLES Introduction to Reliables Exploration Time Fact Frieze Forming Groups Instant Murals Stress Buster		

Bibliography

Dixon, W. Shore C. Temperamental Predictors of Linguistic Style During Multiword Acquisition. *Infant Behavior and Development*, Jan-Mar, 20, 99-103, 1997.

Given, Barbara. *Teaching to the Brain's Natural Learning System.* Alexandria, VA: Association for Supervision and Curriculum Development, 2002.

Hannaford, Carla. *Smart Moves: Why Learning Is Not All in Your Head.* Arlington, VA: Great Ocean Publishers, 1995.

Jensen, Eric. *Learning With the Body in Mind: The Scientific Basis for Energizers, Movement, Play, Games, and Physical Education.* San Diego: The Brain Store, 2000.

——. *Different Brains, Different Learners: How to Reach the Hard to Reach.* San Diego: The Brain Store, 2000.

——. *Learning Smarter: The New Science of Teaching.* San Diego: The Brain Store, 2000.

——. *Brain Compatible Strategies.* Del Mar, CA: Turning Point Press, 1997.

——. *Brain-Based Learning.* Del Mar, CA: Turning Point Publishing, 1996.

Kaufeldt, Martha. *Begin With the Brain: Orchestrating the Learner-Centered Classroom.* Tucson, AZ: Zephyr Press, 1999.

Sprenger, Marilee B. *Becoming a "Wiz" at Brain-Based Teaching: How to Make Every Year Your Best Year.* Thousand Oaks, CA: Corwin Press, 2002.

Sylwester, Robert, ed. *Student Brains, School Issues: A Collection of Articles.* Arlington Heights, IL: Skylight, 1998.

Workshops

The authors are available to do workshops on the Voices of Experience series of books. If you enjoyed this book, you'll love their workshops!

Here's what participants are saying:

"Brilliant. Thank you for giving me such wonderful ideas to take back to my class."

"The ideas are easy, inexpensive, and require little preparation."

"Great energy. Wonderful ideas that can be used immediately!"

"Many of my ideas will show up in my class this week. Thanks, too, for the chuckles."

"Thanks, I had fun. I learned a lot, and my kids will benefit right away."

"Your ideas help me do the best for my students and still have a life for myself."

For more information, please contact Portage & Main Press at 1-800-667-9673.

You may have noticed that the products in Question 2 did not contain an imaginary number, even though the original expression contained imaginary numbers. Each pair of expressions in Question 2 are called *complex conjugates*.

Complex conjugates are pairs of numbers of the form $a + bi$ and $a - bi$. The product of a pair of complex conjugates is always a real number and equal to $a^2 + b^2$.

Remember that a polynomial is a mathematical expression involving the sum of powers in one or more variables multiplied by coefficients. The definition of a polynomial can now be extended to include imaginary numbers.

A polynomial in one variable is an expression of the form $a_0 + a_1x + a_2x^2 + \ldots + a_nx^n$, where the coefficients (a_0, a_1, a_2, . . .) are complex numbers (real or imaginary) and the exponents are nonnegative integers.

A polynomial can have a special name, according to the number of terms it contains. A polynomial with one term is called **a monomial**. A polynomial with two terms is called a **binomial**. A polynomial with three terms is called a **trinomial**.

3. Maria says that the expression $3x + xi - 5$ is a trinomial because it has three terms. Dante says that the expression is a binomial because it can be rewritten as the equivalent expression $(3 + i)x - 5$, which has two terms. Jermaine says that it is not a polynomial. Who is correct? Explain your reasoning.

4

4. Identify each expression as a monomial, binomial, trinomial, or other. Explain your reasoning.

   a. $3 + 5i$

   b. $-4xi + 2x - 5i + 1$

   c. $\frac{3}{2}x^2 - \frac{1}{4}x^2i$

   d. $1.5x + 3i + 0.5x^3i$

You can simplify some polynomial expressions involving *i* using methods similar to those you used to operate with numerical expressions involving *i*.

5. Simplify each polynomial expression, if possible. Show your work.

   a. $xi + xi =$

You just need to remember the rules for multiplying two binomials.

   b. $xi + xy =$

   c. $-2.5x + 3i - xi + 1.8i + 4x + 9 =$

   d. $(x + 3i)^2 =$

   e. $(2i - 4x)(i + x) =$

6. Analyze each method. Explain each student's reasoning. Then, identify which of the two methods seems more efficient and explain why.

a.

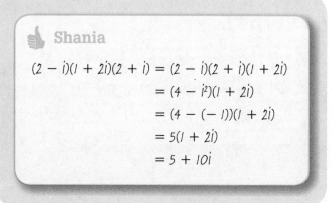

Shania

$(2 - i)(1 + 2i)(2 + i) = (2 - i)(2 + i)(1 + 2i)$
$= (4 - i^2)(1 + 2i)$
$= (4 - (-1))(1 + 2i)$
$= 5(1 + 2i)$
$= 5 + 10i$

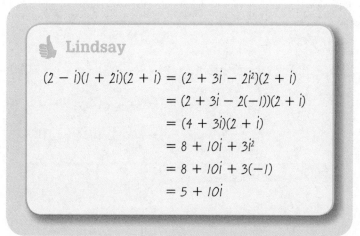

Lindsay

$(2 - i)(1 + 2i)(2 + i) = (2 + 3i - 2i^2)(2 + i)$
$= (2 + 3i - 2(-1))(2 + i)$
$= (4 + 3i)(2 + i)$
$= 8 + 10i + 3i^2$
$= 8 + 10i + 3(-1)$
$= 5 + 10i$

b.

👍 **Elijah**

$(x + i)(x + 3) + (x + 3i)(x + 3)$

$= (x^2 + 3x + xi + 3i) + (x^2 + 3x + 3xi + 9i)$

$= (x^2 + x^2) + (3x + 3x) + (xi + 3xi) + (3i + 9i)$

$= 2x^2 + 6x + 4xi + 12i$

👍 **Aiden**

$(x + i)(x + 3) + (x + 3i)(x + 3) = (x + 3)(x + i + x + 3i)$

$= (x + 3)(2x + 4i)$

$= 2x^2 + 4xi + 6x + 12i$

7. Simplify each expression.

    a. $(2 - i)(1 + 2i)(2 + i)$ **b.** $(x + i)(x + 3) + (x + 3i)(x + 3)$

Rewriting Quotients of Complex Numbers

Division of complex numbers requires the use of complex conjugates, thus changing the divisor into a real number. Recall, the complex conjugate of $a + bi$ is $a - bi$.

1. For each complex number, write its conjugate. Then calculate each product.

    a. $7 + i$ **b.** $-5 - 3i$

Remember that
$(a + bi)(a - bi) = a^2 + b^2$.

    c. $12 + 11i$ **d.** $-4i$

You can rewrite the division of a complex number by multiplying both the divisor and the dividend by the conjugate of the divisor, thus changing the divisor into a real number.

You can rewrite $\dfrac{3 - 2i}{4 + 3i}$ without a complex number in the denominator.

You are just multiplying by a form of 1.

$$\dfrac{3 - 2i}{4 + 3i} = \dfrac{3 - 2i}{4 + 3i} \cdot \dfrac{4 - 3i}{4 - 3i}$$

$$= \dfrac{12 - 9i - 8i + 6i^2}{4^2 + 3^2}$$

$$= \dfrac{12 - 17i - 6}{16 + 9}$$

$$= \dfrac{6 - 17i}{25}$$

$$\dfrac{3 - 2i}{4 + 3i} = \dfrac{6}{25} - \dfrac{17}{25}i$$

2. Rewrite each quotient without a complex number in the denominator.

a. $\dfrac{2 - i}{3 + 2i}$

b. $\dfrac{3 - 4i}{2 - 3i}$

c. $\dfrac{5 + 2i}{1 + i}$

d. $\dfrac{20 - 5i}{2 - 4i}$

Be prepared to share your solutions and methods.

You Can't Spell "Fundamental Theorem of Algebra" without F-U-N!

Quadratics and Complex Numbers

LEARNING GOALS

In this lesson, you will:

- Determine the number and type of zeros of a quadratic function.
- Solve quadratic equations with complex solutions.
- Use the Fundamental Theorem of Algebra.
- Choose an appropriate method to determine zeros of quadratic functions.

KEY TERMS

- imaginary roots
- discriminant
- Fundamental Theorem of Algebra
- double root

I'm sure you've heard these sayings: "That's it! I'm drawing a line in the sand!" or "You've crossed that line a long time ago!" So what is the human fascination with lines and boundaries and the implications if these boundaries are crossed?

You might remember that as a young child, you might have been told to stay within the lines of a drawing when coloring in your coloring book; though young toddlers seem to have a tough time with that motor skill. The implication of coloring *outside* of the lines was not a big deal—unless it just drove you crazy as a kid! However, crossing a line over international flying zones, at sea, or on the ground can have much greater impacts on global situations. For example, in 2009, three Americans were hiking in Iraqi Kurdistan when they inadvertently crossed the Iranian border. Upon doing so, Iranian border guards detained the hikers. A long ordeal of negotiating followed between the U.S. and Iranian governments led to the release of Sarah Shourd on September 2010, and the release of Shane Bauer and Joshua Fattal on September 21, 2011.

These of course are two extremes of crossing lines or boundaries. And of course, it is more than governments and conventions that establish lines and boundaries. People establish certain boundaries and etiquette in social settings. What are some social boundaries people have established? What are the implications when those boundaries are crossed?

PROBLEM 1 X-Axis Intersection Inspection

1. Analyze each graph. Identify the *x*-intercepts, if possible.

Group A

$g(x) = x^2 - 4$

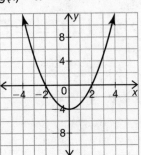

$h(x) = -x^2 - 6x$

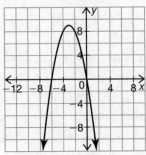

Group B

$m(x) = -x^2 - 6x - 9$

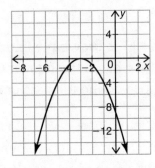

$n(x) = \frac{1}{2}x^2 - 4x + 8$

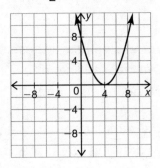

Group C

$p(x) = 2x^2 - 12x + 19$

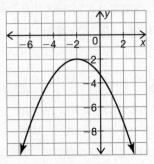

$q(x) = -\frac{1}{3}x^2 - \frac{4}{3}x - \frac{10}{3}$

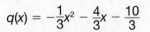

The *x*-intercepts of a quadratic function $f(x)$ are the solutions of the equation $f(x) = 0$.

2. If $f(x)$ is a quadratic function, explain how to determine the number of solutions of $f(x) = 0$ given the graph of $f(x)$.

3. Choose one of the two functions from each group in Question 1. Use the Quadratic Formula and what you know about imaginary numbers to solve an equation of the form $f(x) = 0$ for each function you choose.

Group A

$$g(x) = x^2 - 4 \qquad\qquad h(x) = -x^2 - 6x$$

Group B

$$m(x) = -x^2 - 6x - 9 \qquad\qquad n(x) = \frac{1}{2}x^2 - 4x + 8$$

Group C

$$p(x) = 2x^2 - 12x + 19 \qquad\qquad q(x) = -\frac{1}{3}x^2 - \frac{4}{3}x - \frac{10}{3}$$

Equations that have imaginary solutions have **imaginary roots**.

4. Consider the three equations you chose to solve in Question 3.

   a. Which of the three equations have imaginary roots?

   b. When you used the Quadratic Formula to solve the equations, at what point did you know the solution was going to include an imaginary number?

The radicand expression in the Quadratic Formula, $b^2 - 4ac$, is called the **discriminant** because it "discriminates" the number and type of roots of a quadratic equation.

5. Describe how you can tell whether a quadratic equation has real or imaginary roots from the:

   a. discriminant.

   b. graph.

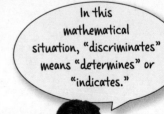

In this mathematical situation, "discriminates" means "determines" or "indicates."

6. Consider the three equations that you did not solve in Question 3. Use the discriminant to determine whether the roots are real or imaginary. Show your work. Then, look at each graph to verify.

Just as equations may have imaginary roots, functions may have imaginary zeros. Imaginary zeros are zeros of quadratic functions that do not cross the x-axis. Remember that zeros of a function $f(x)$ are the values of x for which $f(x) = 0$. Zeros, roots, and x-intercepts are all related.

Oh! So, graphs have x-intercepts, equations have roots, and functions have zeros!

7. Use any method to determine whether each function has real or imaginary zeros. You do not need to calculate the zeros.

   a. $f(x) = -3x^2 + 2x - 1$

   b. $f(x) = -\frac{1}{2}x^2 + x - \frac{1}{2}$

   c. $f(x) = 2x^2 - 5x - 6$

Remember, a quadratic equation is a special type of polynomial equation. The degree of a polynomial equation is the greatest exponent in the polynomial equation.

8. What is the degree of a quadratic equation? a linear equation? a constant equation?

The *Fundamental Theorem of Algebra was* first proposed in the early 1600s, but would not be proven until almost two centuries later. The **Fundamental Theorem of Algebra** states that any polynomial equation of degree n must have exactly n complex roots or solutions; also, every polynomial function of degree n must have exactly n complex zeros. However, any root or zero may be a multiple root or zero.

Now that we have covered both real and imaginary roots and zeros, we can refer to them as complex roots and complex zeros.

9. Look at the graphs of the functions in Group B of Question 1. Even though the functions intersect the x-axis once, according to the Fundamental Theorem of Algebra, how many complex zeros do these functions have?

If the graph of a quadratic function $f(x)$ has 1 x-intercept, the equation $f(x) = 0$ still has 2 real roots. In this case, the 2 real roots are considered a **double root.**

10. Analyze the discriminants of the quadratic functions in Question 1. What must be true about the discriminant of a quadratic equation that has a double root?

11. Explain why it is not possible for a quadratic equation to have 2 equal imaginary solutions, or a double imaginary root.

12. Circle the function(s) shown that could describe the given graph. Explain your reasoning.

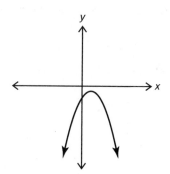

$h(x) = -2x^2 + 3x - 2$

$k(x) = -0.5x^2 + 1.5x + 1$

$t(x) = -\dfrac{1}{2}x^2 + 3x - \dfrac{9}{2}$

$w(x) = 2x^2 - 4x - 10$

PROBLEM **2** **What Does the Form Tell Me?**

1. Consider each quadratic function written in vertex form. Determine whether the zeros of each function are real or imaginary without calculating the zeros. Explain how you know.

a. $f(x) = -2(x - 3)^2 - 4$

I'll give you a hint. Use the key characteristics of a function in vertex form to sketch a graph.

b. $f(x) = 2(x - 3)^2 - 4$

c. $f(x) = -2(x - 3)^2$

2. Complete the table to show how you can use the vertex form of a quadratic function to determine whether it has real or imaginary solutions. The first row has been completed for you.

Location of Vertex	Concavity	Sketch	Number of x-Intercepts	Number and Type of Roots	Number and Type of Zeros
Above the x-axis	Up		0	2 imaginary roots	2 imaginary zeros
	Down				
Below the x-axis	Up				
	Down				
On the x-axis	Up				
	Down				

3. Consider the quadratic function $f(x) = \frac{1}{2}(x - 3)(x + 2)$. Describe the type of zeros for this function. How do you know?

4. Tony and Ava each attempt to factor $f(x) = x^2 - 2x + 2$. Analyze their work.

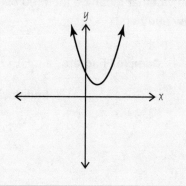

Tony

I sketched the graph $f(x) = x^2 - 2x + 2$ and noticed there are no real zeros. So, $f(x) = x^2 - 2x + 2$ cannot be factored.

Eva

$x^2 - 2x + 2 = 0$

$x = \dfrac{-(-2) \pm \sqrt{(-2)^2 - 4(1)(2)}}{2(1)}$

$x = \dfrac{2 \pm \sqrt{-4}}{2}$

$x = \dfrac{2 \pm 2i}{2}$

$x = 1 \pm i$

The function in factored form is
$f(x) = [x - (1 + i)][x - (1 - i)]$.

a. If you consider the set of real numbers, who's correct? If you consider the set of imaginary numbers, who's correct? Explain your reasoning.

4

b. Use the distributive property to rewrite Eva's function to verify that the function in factored form is the same as the original function in standard form.

Remember, the set of complex numbers is the super set of numbers . . . it includes both real and imaginary numbers.

c. Identify the zeros of the quadratic function $f(x)$.

Some functions can be factored over the set of real numbers, while other functions can be factored over the set of imaginary numbers. However, all functions can be factored over the set of complex numbers.

5. Analyze each expression.

$x^2 + 4$	$x^2 - 4$	$x^2 + 2x + 5$	$x^2 + 4x - 5$
$-x^2 + x + 12$		$x^2 + 4x - 1$	$-x^2 + 6x - 25$

a. Sort each expression based on whether it can be factored over the set of real numbers or the set of imaginary numbers.

Complex Factors	
Real Factors	**Imaginary Factors**

b. Factor each expression over the set of complex numbers.

6. Suppose that you know that one zero of a quadratic function $b(x)$ is $2 + 3i$.

   a. What is the other zero of the function $b(x)$? Explain how you know.

   b. Write the quadratic function $b(x)$ in standard form, using an a-value of 1. Show all your work.

Talk the Talk

The table shown summarizes multiple methods to determine the complex zeros of a quadratic function based specific given information.

<table>
<tr><td rowspan="3">Given Information</td><td rowspan="3">Type of Zeros</td><td colspan="3" align="center">Number of Complex Zeros of a Quadratic Function</td></tr>
<tr><td colspan="2" align="center">Two Real Zeros</td><td align="center">Two Imaginary Zeros</td></tr>
<tr><td align="center">Two Distinct Zeros</td><td align="center">Two Repeated Zeros</td><td align="center">Two Distinct Zeros</td></tr>
<tr><td>Graph</td><td align="center">two x-intercepts</td><td align="center">one x-intercept</td><td align="center">zero x-intercepts</td></tr>
<tr><td>Equation in Standard Form: $f(x) = ax^2 + bx + c$</td><td align="center">$b^2 - 4ac > 0$</td><td align="center">$b^2 - 4ac = 0$</td><td align="center">$b^2 - 4ac < 0$</td></tr>
<tr><td>Equation in Vertex Form: $f(x) = a(x - h)^2 + k$</td><td align="center">$k > 0$ and $a < 0$
or
$k < 0$ and $a > 0$</td><td align="center">$k = 0$</td><td align="center">$k > 0$ and $a > 0$
or
$k < 0$ and $a < 0$</td></tr>
<tr><td>Equation in Factored Form: $f(x) = a(x - r_1)(x - r_2)$</td><td align="center">$r_1 \neq r_2$, r_1 and r_2 are real numbers</td><td align="center">$r_1 = r_2$, r_1 and r_2 are real numbers</td><td align="center">$r_1 \neq r_2$, r_1 and r_2 are imaginary numbers</td></tr>
</table>

Determine the number of zeros and the type of zeros for each quadratic function. Justify your reasoning.

1. $k(x) = -2(x + 3)^2$

2. $v(x) = 0.5x^2 - 3x + 10$

3. $c(x) = -\frac{1}{3}x(x - 9)$

4. $p(x) = 5(x - 1)^2 + 6$

Be prepared to share your solutions and methods.

Chapter 4 Summary

KEY TERMS

- standard form of a quadratic function (4.1)
- factored form of a quadratic function (4.1)
- vertex form of a quadratic function (4.1)
- concavity of a parabola (4.1)
- reference points (4.2)
- transformation (4.2)
- rigid motion (4.2)
- argument of a function (4.2)
- translation (4.2)
- vertical dilation (4.3)
- vertical stretching (4.3)

- vertical compression (4.3)
- reflection (4.3)
- line of reflection (4.3)
- horizontal dilation (4.4)
- horizontal stretching (4.4)
- horizontal compression (4.4)
- the imaginary number i (4.6)
- principal square root of a negative number (4.6)
- set of imaginary numbers (4.6)
- pure imaginary number (4.6)
- set of complex numbers (4.6)
- real part of a complex number (4.6)

- imaginary part of a complex number (4.6)
- complex conjugates (4.6)
- monomial (4.6)
- binomial (4.6)
- trinomial (4.6)
- imaginary roots (4.7)
- discriminant (4.7)
- Fundamental Theorem of Algebra (4.7)
- double root (4.7)

4.1 Using Characteristics of a Quadratic Function to Describe Its Graph

4

The graphs of quadratic functions can be described using key characteristics:

- x-intercept(s)

- y-intercept

- vertex

- axis of symmetry

- concave up or down

The y-intercept (c) and whether the parabola is concave up ($a > 0$) or down ($a < 0$) can be determined when the quadratic is in standard form, $f(x) = ax^2 + bx + c$.

The x-intercepts (r_1, 0), (r_2, 0), and whether the parabola is concave up ($a > 0$) or down ($a < 0$) can be determined when the quadratic is in factored form, $f(x) = a(x - r_1)(x - r_2)$.

The vertex (h, k), whether the parabola is concave up ($a > 0$) or down ($a < 0$), and the axis of symmetry ($x = h$) can be determined when the quadratic is in vertex form, $f(x) = a(x - h)^2 + k$.

The example shows that using the key characteristics of a graph can also determine the function represented by the graph.

Example

Analyze the graph. Then, circle the function(s) which could model the graph. Describe the reasoning you used to either eliminate or choose each function.

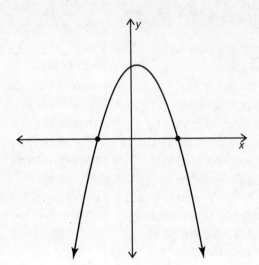

$f_1(x) = 2(x - 3)(x + 4)$

The function f_1 can be eliminated because the a-value is positive.

$f_2(x) = \frac{1}{2}(x + 3)(x - 4)$

The function f_2 can be eliminated because the a-value is positive.

$\boxed{f_3(x) = -\frac{1}{2}(x + 3)(x - 4)}$

The function f_3 is a possible function because it has a negative a-value and one positive and one negative x-intercept.

$f_4(x) = -\frac{1}{2}(x - 3)(x - 4)$

The function f_4 can be eliminated because it has two positive x-intercepts.

4.1 Determining the Best Form in Which to Write a Quadratic Function

Given the roots or x-intercepts and an additional point, a quadratic function can be written in factored form: $f(x) = a(x - r_1)(x - r_2)$.

Given a minimum or maximum point or vertex and an additional point, a quadratic function can be written in vertex form: $f(x) = a(x - h)^2 + k$.

Given a y-intercept and two additional points, a quadratic function can be written in standard form: $f(x) = ax^2 + bx + c$.

Example

vertex (2, −5) and point (3, 1): vertex form

points (2, 0), (6, 5), and (9, 0): factored form

y-intercept (0, −2) and points (−4, 3), (5, 2): standard form

4.1 Writing a Quadratic Function in Standard Form

When a quadratic function is in vertex or factored form, the function can be rewritten in standard form by multiplying the factors and combining like terms.

Example

$f(x) = (x - 2)(x + 8)$ $\qquad\qquad$ $f(x) = -2(x - 3)^2 + 6$

$$f(x) = (x - 2)(x + 8)$$
$$= x^2 + 8x - 2x - 16$$
$$= x^2 + 6x - 16$$

$$f(x) = -2(x - 3)^2 + 6$$
$$= -2(x^2 - 6x + 9) + 6$$
$$= -2x^2 + 12x - 18 + 6$$
$$= -2x^2 + 12x - 12$$

4.1 Writing a Quadratic Function to Represent a Situation

Determine the important information from the problem situation, including a possible vertex or *x*-intercepts. Substitute the information into either the vertex or factored form of a quadratic function and solve for *a*. Write the complete function.

Example

Hector launches a rocket from a platform 5 feet above the ground. The rocket reaches a maximum height of 50 feet at a distance of 75 feet. Write a function to represent the rocket's height in terms of its distance.

$$h(d) = a(d - 50)^2 + 75$$

$$5 = a(0 - 50)^2 + 75$$

$$5 = 2500a + 75$$

$$-70 = 2500a$$

$$\frac{-7}{250} = a$$

$$h(d) = -\frac{7}{250}(d - 50)^2 + 75$$

4.2 Identifying the Reference Points of a Quadratic Function

Reference points are a set of key points that help identify a basic function.

Reference Points of Basic Quadratic Function	
P	(0, 0)
Q	(1, 1)
R	(2, 4)

If the vertex of a quadratic function and two points to the right of that vertex are known, the axis of symmetry can be used to draw the other half of the parabola. These key points are reference points for the quadratic function family.

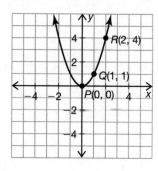

Understanding the Effect of the *C*-Value and the *D*-Value in the Transformational Function Form $g(x) = Af(B(x - C)) + D$

A translation shifts an entire graph the same distance and direction. When $f(x)$ is transformed to $g(x) = Af(B(x - C)) + D$, the *C*-value shifts the graph horizontally and the *D*-value shifts the graph vertically. When $C < 0$, the graph shifts left *C* units, and when $C > 0$, the graph shifts to the right *C* units. When $D < 0$, the graph shifts down *D* units, and when $D > 0$, the graph shifts up *D* units.

Example

$f(x) = x^2$

$m(x) = (x + 3) + 1$

$C = -3$ and $D = 1$

The original function $f(x)$ will translate to the left 3 units and translate up 1 unit.

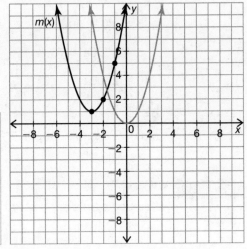

Reference Points on $f(x)$	→	Apply the Transformations	Corresponding Points on $m(x)$
(0, 0)	→	(0 − 3, 0 + 1)	(−3, 1)
(1, 1)	→	(1 − 3, 1 + 1)	(−2, 2)
(2, 4)	→	(2 − 3, 4 + 1)	(−1, 5)

Writing the Function of a Transformed Graph

Identify the location of the new vertex. Use the *x*- and *y*-coordinates of the new vertex as the *C*- and *D*-values. Write the transformed function in terms of the original function in the form $g(x) = f(x - C) + D$.

Example

Given $y = f(x)$

$g(x) = f(x - 2) - 4$

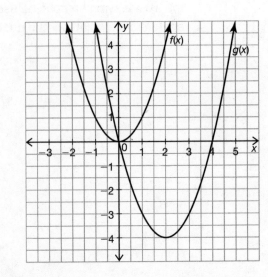

Understanding the Effect of the A-Value in the Transformational Function Form $g(x) = Af(B(x - C)) + D$

A translation shifts an entire graph the same distance and direction. When $f(x)$ is transformed to $g(x) = Af(B(x - C)) + D$, the A-value stretches or compresses the graph vertically. The C-value shifts the graph horizontally and the D-value shifts the graph vertically.

When $|A| \geq 1$, the graph stretches away from the x-axis, and when $0 < |A| < 1$, the graph compresses towards the x-axis. When $A < 0$, the graph is reflected across the x-axis or across the horizontal line $y = D$. Any point on the transformed graph can be represented in coordinate notation as

$$(x, y) \rightarrow \left(\frac{1}{B}x + C, Ay + D\right).$$

Example

$f(x) = x^2$

$b(x) = -4(f(x + 1) - 3$

The C-value is -1 and the D- value is -3 so the vertex will be translated 1 unit to the left and 3 units down to $(-1, -3)$.

The A-value is -4, so the graph will have a vertical stretch by a factor of 4 and will be reflected across the line $y = -3$.

$(x, y) = (x - 1, -4y - 3)$

Writing a Quadratic Function to Represent a Graph

Given $y = f(x)$, the coordinate notation represented in the transformational function $y = Af(x - C) + D$ is (x, y) becomes $(x + C, Ay + D)$. Using this coordinate notation and reference points, you can work backwards from the graph to write the function in vertex form.

Example

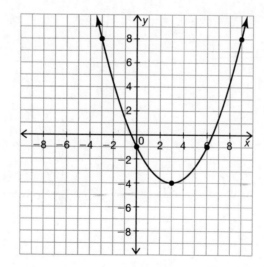

$f(x) = \frac{1}{3}(x - 3)^2 - 4$

Considering the transformational function $g(x) = Af(B(x - C)) + D$, B determines the horizontal dilation.

- Horizontal stretching is the stretching of a graph away from the y-axis and happens when $0 < |B| < 1$.

- Horizontal compression is the squeezing of a graph towards the y-axis and happens when $|B| > 1$.

The factor of horizontal stretch or compression is the reciprocal of the B-value. When $B < 0$, the dilation will also include a reflection across the y-axis, but because a parabola is symmetric, it will look identical to the function when $B > 0$.

Example

$p(x) = f(2x)$

Reference Points on $f(x)$	$\rightarrow$	Apply the Transformations	Corresponding Points on $p(x)$
$(0, 0)$	$\rightarrow$	$\left(\frac{1}{2} \cdot 0, 0\right)$	$(0, 0)$
$(1, 1)$	$\rightarrow$	$\left(\frac{1}{2} \cdot 1, 1\right)$	$(0.5, 1)$
$(2, 4)$	$\rightarrow$	$\left(\frac{1}{2} \cdot 2, 4\right)$	$(1, 4)$
$(3, 9)$	$\rightarrow$	$\left(\frac{1}{2} \cdot 3, 9\right)$	$(1.5, 9)$

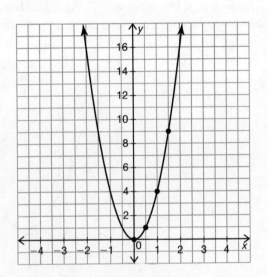

4.4 Identifying Multiple Transformations Given Quadratic Functions

Analyzing the transformations of $y = f(x)$, it is possible to graph a function from information given by the form of the equation.

Function Form	Equation Information	Description of Transformation of Graph
$y = Af(B(x - C)) + D$	$D > 0$	vertical shift up D units
	$D < 0$	vertical shift down D units
	$C > 0$	horizontal shift right C units
	$C < 0$	horizontal shift left C units
	$|A| > 1$	vertical stretch by a factor of A units
	$0 < |A| < 1$	vertical compression by a factor of A units
	$A < 0$	reflection across the line $y = k$
	$|B| > 1$	horizontal compression by a factor of $\frac{1}{|B|}$
	$0 < |B| < 1$	horizontal stretch by a factor of $\frac{1}{|B|}$
	$B < 0$	reflection across the y-axis

Example

$h(x) = -3(x + 7)^2 - 8$

The A value is -3 so the graph will have a vertical stretch by a factor of 3 and be reflected over the x-axis. The C-value is -7 and the D-value is -8, so the vertex will be shifted 7 units to the left and 8 units down to $(-7, -8)$. The A-value is -3 so the graph will have a vertical stretch by a factor of 3 and be reflected across the line $y = D$, or $y = -8$

Example

Given the graph of $y = f(x)$, the graph of $g(x) = -f\left(\frac{1}{2}(x - 4)\right) - 5$ is sketched.

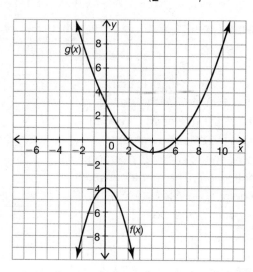

4.4   Writing Quadratic Functions in Terms of a Given a Graph

Determine by how much and in what direction the reference points of the graph have moved and if there has been a reflection, horizontal dilation, or vertical dilation. Use coordinate notation $\left(\frac{1}{B}x + C, Ay + D\right)$ to help identify A, B, C, and D values. Write the transformed function in terms of the original function in the form $g(x) = Af(B(x - C)) + D$.

Example

The function of $g(x)$ in terms of $f(x)$ is
$g(x) = f(-x) - 5$, or $g(x) = f(x - 12) - 5$.

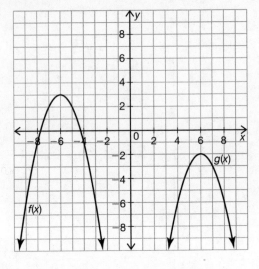

4.5   Deriving a Quadratic Equation Given Certain Information and Reference Points

To write a unique quadratic function, use the reference points of the basic quadratic function and consider the vertical distance between each point. If given the x-intercepts and another point on the parabola, a function can be written in factored form or if given the vertex and another point on the parabola, a function can be written in vertex form; but in both cases the a-value must also be determined. To do this, first determine the axis of symmetry as directly in the middle of the two x-intercepts or at the location of the vertex. Plot the axis of symmetry and points on a coordinate plane and assign each point a letter based on its horizontal distance from the line of symmetry. The vertical distance between A' and B' will be the vertical distance between A and B of the basic function times a.

Example

x-intercepts and 1 point: $(-3, 0)$, $(5, 0)$, $(4, 14)$

$\dfrac{r_1 + r_2}{2} = \dfrac{-3 + 5}{2} = \dfrac{2}{2} = 1$ so the axis of

symmetry is $x = 1$. Point $(5, 0)$ is point D' because it is 4 units from the axis of symmetry. Point $(4, 14)$ is point C' because it is 3 units from the axis of symmetry. The range between the C and D point on the basic function is 7. The range between point D' and point C' is $7 \times (-2) = -14$, therefore the a-value must be -2.

$f(x) = -2(x + 3)(x - 5)$

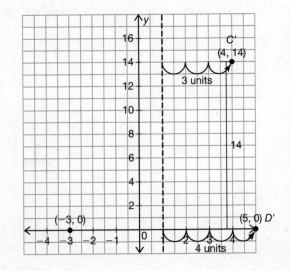

4.5 Deriving a Quadratic Equation Given Three Points Using a Graphing Calculator

 You can use a graphing calculator to determine a quadratic regression equation given three points on the parabola.

Step 1: Diagnostics must be turned on so that all needed data is displayed. Press **2nd CATALOG** to display the catalog. Scroll to **DiagnosticOn** and press **ENTER**. Then press **ENTER** again. The calculator should display the word **Done**.

Step 2: Press **STAT** and then press **ENTER** to select **1:Edit**. In the **L1** column, enter the x-values by typing each value followed by **ENTER**. Use the right arrow key to move to the **L2** column. Enter the y-values.

Step 3: Press **STAT** and use the right arrow key to show the **CALC** menu. Choose **5:QuadReg**. Press Enter. The values for a, b, and c will be displayed.

Step 4: To have the calculator graph the exact equation for you, press **Y=**, **VARS**, **5:Statistics**, scroll right to **EQ**, press **1:RegEQ**, **GRAPH**.

Example

$(-8, 1), (-1, 13.25), (6, -48)$

$f(x) = -0.75x^2 - 5x + 9$

To use a system of equations, first create a quadratic equation in the form $y = ax^2 + bx + c$ for each of the points given. Then, use elimination and substitution to solve for a, b, and c.

Example

$(-1, -11), (2, -5), (4, -41)$

Equation 1: $-11 = a(-1)^2 + b(-1) + c$

$-11 = a - b + c$

Equation 2: $-5 = a(2)^2 + b(2) + c$

$-5 = 4a + 2b + c$

Equation 3: $-41 = a(4)^2 + b(4) + c$

$-41 = 16a + 4b + c$

Subtract Equation 1 from Equation 2 and solve in terms of a:

$$\begin{aligned} -5 &= 4a + 2b + c \\ -(-11 &= a - b + c) \\ \hline 6 &= 3a + 3b \\ 2 - b &= a \end{aligned}$$

Subtract Equation 2 from Equation 3:

$$\begin{aligned} -41 &= 16a + 4b + c \\ -(-5 &= 4a + 2b + c) \\ \hline -36 &= 12a + 2b \\ -18 &= 6a + b \end{aligned}$$

Substitute the value for a into this equation:

$-18 = 6(2 - b) + b$

$-18 = 12 - 5b$

$-30 = -5b$

$b = 6$

Substitute the value of b into the equation for the value of a:

$a = 2 - 6$

$a = -4$

Substitute the values of a and b into Equation 1:

$-11 = -4 - 6 + c$

$-11 = -10 + c$

$-1 = c$

Substitute the values for a, b, and c into a quadratic equation in standard form:

$f(x) = -4x^2 + 6x - 1$

Calculating Powers of i

The imaginary number i is a number such that $i^2 = -1$. Because no real number exists such that its square is equal to a negative number, the number i is not a part of the real number system. The values of i^n repeat after every four powers of i, where $i = \sqrt{-1}$, $i^2 = -1$, $i^3 = -\sqrt{-1}$, and $i^4 = 1$.

Example

$i^{25} = (i^4)^6 (i^1)$

$\quad = (1)^6 (\sqrt{-1})$

$\quad = \sqrt{-1}$

Rewriting Expressions with Negative Roots Using i

Expressions with negative roots can be rewritten. For any positive real number n, the principal square root of a negative number, $-n$, is defined by $\sqrt{-n} = i\sqrt{n}$.

Example

$\sqrt{-63} + \sqrt{-24} = i\sqrt{63} + i\sqrt{24}$

$\qquad\qquad\qquad = i\sqrt{(9)(7)} + i\sqrt{(6)(4)}$

$\qquad\qquad\qquad = 3\sqrt{7}i + 2\sqrt{6}i$

Adding, Subtracting, and Multiplying on the Set of Complex Numbers

The set of complex numbers is the set of all numbers written in the form $a + bi$, where a and b are real numbers. The term a is called the real part of a complex number, and the term bi is called the imaginary part of a complex number. When operating with complex numbers involving i, combine like terms by treating i as a variable (even though it's a constant). Complex conjugates are pairs of numbers of the form $a + bi$ and $a - bi$. The product of a pair of complex conjugates is always a real number in the form $a^2 + b^2$.

Example

$4x + (x + 3i)(x - 3i) - 5x + 7$

$4x + (x + 3i)(x - 3i) - 5x + 7 = 4x + x^2 - 9i^2 - 5x + 7$

$\qquad\qquad\qquad\qquad\qquad\qquad = x^2 + (4x - 5x) + (7 \quad 9(-1))$

$\qquad\qquad\qquad\qquad\qquad\qquad = x^2 - x + 16$

4.6 Identifying Complex Polynomials

A polynomial is a mathematical expression involving the sum of powers in one or more variables multiplied by coefficients. The definition of a polynomial can be extended to include imaginary numbers. Some polynomials have special names, according to the number of terms they have. A polynomial with one term is called a monomial. A polynomial with two terms is called a binomial. A polynomial with three terms is called a trinomial. Combine like terms to name the polynomial.

Example

$5x - 3xi + x^2 - 3i + 9$

The expression is a trinomial because it can be rewritten as $x^2 + (5 - 3i)x + (9 - 3i)$, which shows one x^2 term, one x term, and one constant term.

4.6 Adding, Subtracting, and Multiplying Complex Polynomials

Some polynomial expressions involving i can be simplified using methods similar to those used to operate with numerical expressions involving i. Whenever possible, multiply the complex conjugates first to get a real number.

Example

$(3x + 7i)(2x + 5i)$

$$(3x + 7i)(2x + 5i) = 6x^2 + 15xi + 14xi + 35i^2$$
$$= 6x^2 + 29xi + 35(-1)$$
$$= 6x^2 + 29xi - 35$$

4.6 Rewriting the Quotient of Complex Numbers

When rewriting the quotient of complex numbers, multiply both the divisor and the dividend by the complex conjugate of the divisor, thus changing the divisor into a real number. The product of a pair of complex conjugates is always a real number in the form $a^2 + b^2$.

Example

$$\frac{3 - i}{5 + 2i} = \frac{3 - i}{5 + 2i} \cdot \frac{5 - 2i}{5 - 2i}$$
$$= \frac{15 - 6i - 5i + 2i^2}{5^2 + 2^2}$$
$$= \frac{15 - 11i - 2}{25 + 4}$$
$$= \frac{13 - 11i}{29}$$
$$= \frac{13}{29} - \frac{11}{29}i$$

Using the Quadratic Formula to Determine the Zeros of a Function

If the graph of $f(x)$ intersects the x-axis 2 times, then the quadratic equation $f(x) = 0$ has 2 solutions, or roots. If the graph of $f(x)$ intersects the x-axis 1 time, then the quadratic equation $f(x) = 0$ has 1 solution and double roots. If the graph of $f(x)$ does not intersect the x-axis, then the quadratic equation $f(x) = 0$ has no solution, or imaginary roots. Use the Quadratic Formula and what you know about imaginary numbers to solve an equation of the form $f(x) = 0$ to calculate the roots, or zeros of the function.

Remember the Quadratic Formula is: $x = \dfrac{-b \pm \sqrt{b^2 - 4ac}}{2a}$.

Example

$g(x) = x^2 - 7x + 12$

$x^2 - 7x + 12 = 0$

$a = 1, b = -7, c = 12$

$x = \dfrac{-b \pm \sqrt{b^2 - 4ac}}{2a}$

$x = \dfrac{-(-7) \pm \sqrt{(-7)^2 - 4(1)(12)}}{2(1)}$

$x = \dfrac{7 \pm \sqrt{1}}{2}$

$x = 4, x = 3$

4

Determining Whether a Quadratic Function in Standard Form Has Real or Imaginary Zeros

The radicand in the Quadratic Formula, $b^2 - 4ac$, is called the discriminant because it "discriminates" the number and type of roots of a quadratic equation. If the discriminant is greater than or equal to zero, the quadratic equation has two real roots. If the discriminant is negative, the quadratic equation has two imaginary roots. If the discriminant is equal to zero, the quadratic equation appears to have only 1 root, but still has 2 real roots called a double root. The Fundamental Theorem of Algebra states that for any polynomial equation of degree n must have exactly n complex roots or solutions; also, every polynomial function of degree n must have exactly n complex zeros. Zeros of a function $f(x)$ are the values of x for which $f(x) = 0$ and are related to the roots of an equation.

Example

$f(x) = x^2 - 3x + 14$

$b^2 - 4ac = (-3)^2 - 4(1)(14)$

$\qquad = 9 - 56$

$\qquad = -47$

The discriminant is negative, so the function has two imaginary zeros.

Determining Whether a Quadratic Function in Vertex Form Has Real or Imaginary Zeros

If the graph of $f(x)$ intersects the x-axis 2 times, then the quadratic equation $f(x) = 0$ has 2 solutions, or roots. If the graph of $f(x)$ intersects the x-axis 1 time, then the quadratic equation $f(x) = 0$ has 1 solutions and double roots. If the graph of $f(x)$ does not intersect the x-axis, then the quadratic equation $f(x) = 0$ has no solution, or imaginary roots. So, by using C and D of vertex form to locate the vertex above or below the x-axis and using A to determine if the parabola is concave up or down, you can tell if the graph intersects the x-axis or not.

Example

$f(x) = -5(x - 2)^2 + 7$

Because the vertex $(2, 7)$ is above the x-axis and the parabola is concave down ($a < 0$), it intersects the x-axis. So, the zeros are real.

 ## Determining Whether a Quadratic Function in Factored Form Has Real or Imaginary Zeros

Some functions can be factored over the set of real numbers, while other functions can be factored over the set of imaginary numbers. However, all functions can be factored over the set of complex numbers. If necessary, use the Quadratic Formula to determine the roots and write the function in factored form.

Example

$p(x) = x^2 + 6x + 18$

$p(x) = [x - (-3 + 3i)][x - (-3 - 3i)]$

$x = -3 + 3i, x = -3 - 3i$

The function $p(x)$ has two imaginary zeros.

Polynomial Functions

5

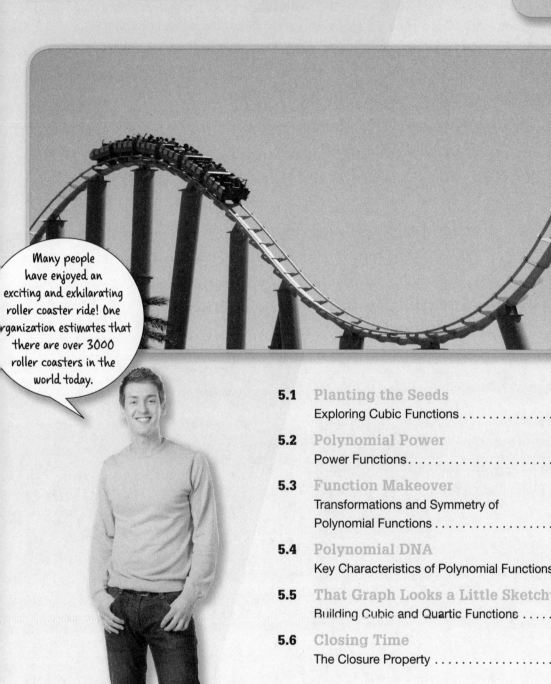

Many people have enjoyed an exciting and exhilarating roller coaster ride! One organization estimates that there are over 3000 roller coasters in the world today.

313

Planting the Seeds
Exploring Cubic Functions

In this lesson, you will:

- Represent cubic functions using words, tables, equations, and graphs.
- Interpret the key characteristics of the graphs of cubic functions.
- Analyze cubic functions in terms of their mathematical context and problem context.
- Connect the characteristics and behaviors of cubic functions to its factors.
- Compare cubic functions with linear and quadratic functions.
- Build cubic functions from linear and quadratic functions.

- relative maximum
- relative minimum
- cubic function
- multiplicity

If you have ever been to a 3D movie, you know that it can be quite an interesting experience. Special film technology and wearing funny-looking glasses allow movie-goers to see a third dimension on the screen—*depth*. Three dimensional filmmaking dates as far back as the 1920s. As long as there have been movies, it seems that people have looked for ways to transform the visual experience into three dimensions.

However, your brain doesn't really need special technology or silly glasses to experience depth. Think about television, paintings, and photography—artists have been making two-dimensional works of art appear as three-dimensional for a long time. Several techniques help the brain perceive depth. An object that is closer is drawn larger than a similarly sized object off in the distance. Similarly, an object in the foreground may be clear and crisp while objects in the background may appear blurry. These techniques subconsciously allow your brain to process depth in two dimensions.

Can you think of other techniques artists use to give the illusion of depth?

Business Is Growing

The Plant-A-Seed Planter Company produces planter boxes. To make the boxes, a square is cut from each corner of a rectangular copper sheet. The sides are bent to form a rectangular prism without a top. Cutting different sized squares from the corners results in different sized planter boxes. Plant-A-Seed takes sales orders from customers who request a sized planter box.

Each rectangular copper sheet is 12 inches by 18 inches. In the diagram, the solid lines indicate where the square corners are cut and the dotted lines represent where the sides are bent for each planter box.

> It may help to create a model of the planter by cutting squares out of the corners of a sheet of paper and folding.

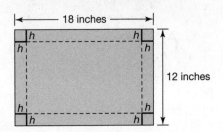

1. Organize the information about each sized planter box made from a 12 inch by 18 inch copper sheet.

   a. Complete the table. Include an expression for each planter box's height, width, length, and volume for a square corner side of length h.

Square Corner Side Length (inches)	Height (inches)	Width (inches)	Length (inches)	Volume (cubic inches)
0				
1				
2				
3				
4				
5				
6				
7				
h				

> Recall the volume formula $V = lwh$.

b. What patterns do you notice in the table?

2. Analyze the relationship between the height, length, and width of each planter box.

    a. What is the largest sized square corner that can be cut to make a planter box? Explain your reasoning.

    b. What is the relationship between the size of the corner square and the length and width of each planter box?

    c. Write a function $V(h)$ to represent the volume of the planter box in terms of the corner side of length h.

3. Louis, Ahmed, and Heidi each used a graphing calculator to analyze the volume function, $V(h)$, and sketched their viewing window. They disagree about the shape of the graph.

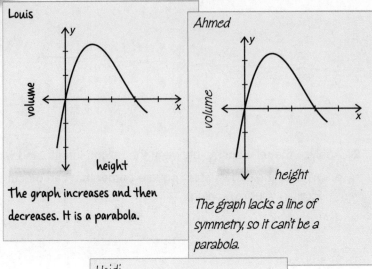

Louis

The graph increases and then decreases. It is a parabola.

Ahmed

The graph lacks a line of symmetry, so it can't be a parabola.

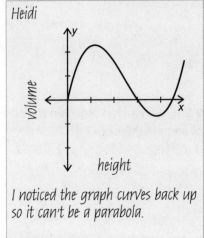

Heidi

I noticed the graph curves back up so it can't be a parabola.

Evaluate each student's sketch and rationale to determine who is correct.
For the student(s) who is/are not correct, explain why the rationale is not correct.

4. Represent the function on a graphing calculator using the window
$[-10, 15] \times [-400, 400]$.

a. Describe the key characteristics of the graph?

In this problem you are determining the maximum value graphically, but consider other representations. How will your solution strategy change when using the table or equation?

b. What is the maximum volume of a planter box?
State the dimensions of this planter box.
Explain your reasoning.

c. Identify the domain of the function $V(h)$.
Is the domain the same or different in terms of the context of this problem?
Explain your reasoning.

d. Identify the range of the function $V(h)$.
Is the range the same or different in terms of the context of this problem?
Explain your reasoning.

e. What do the *x*-intercepts represent in this problem situation? Do these values make sense in terms of this problem situation? Explain your reasoning.

The key characteristics of a function may be different within a given domain. The function $V(h) = h(12 - 2h)(18 - 2h)$ has x-intercepts at $x = 0$, $x = 6$, and $x = 9$.

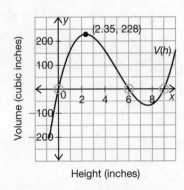

As the input values for height increase, the output values for volume approach infinity. Therefore, the function doesn't have a maximum; however, the point (2.35, 228) is a *relative maximum* within the domain interval of (0, 6). A **relative maximum** is the highest point in a particular section of a graph. Similarly, as the values for height decrease, the output values approach negative infinity. Therefore, a *relative minimum* occurs at (7.65, −68.16). A **relative minimum** is the lowest point in a particular section of a graph.

The function $v(h)$ represents all of the possible volumes for a given height h. A horizontal line is a powerful tool for working backwards to determine the possible values for height when the volume is known.

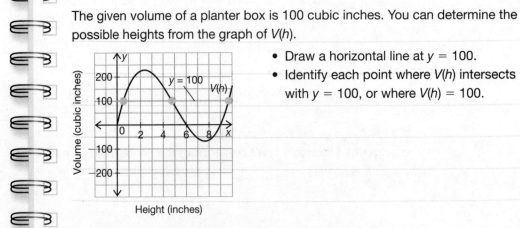

The given volume of a planter box is 100 cubic inches. You can determine the possible heights from the graph of $V(h)$.

- Draw a horizontal line at $y = 100$.
- Identify each point where $V(h)$ intersects with $y = 100$, or where $V(h) = 100$.

The first point of intersection is represented using function notation as $V(0.54) = 100$.

5. A customer ordered a particular planter box with a volume of 100 cubic inches, but did not specify the height of the planter box.

   a. Use a graphing calculator to determine when $V(h) = 100$. Then write the intersection points in function notation. What do the intersection points mean in terms of this problem situation?

   b. How many different sized planter boxes can Plant-A-Seed make to fill this order? Explain your reasoning.

6. A neighborhood beautifying committee would like to purchase a variety of planter boxes with volumes of 175 cubic inches to add to business window sill store fronts. Determine the planter box dimensions that the Plant-A-Seed Company can create for the committee. Show all work and explain your reasoning.

5

7. Plant-A-Seed's intern claims that he can no longer complete the order because he spilled a cup of coffee on the sales ticket. Help Jack complete the order by determining the missing dimensions from the information that is still visible. Explain how you determined possible unknown dimensions of each planter box.

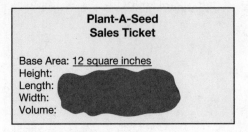

**Plant-A-Seed
Sales Ticket**

Base Area: <u>12 square inches</u>
Height:
Length:
Width:
Volume:

8. A customer sent the following email:

To Whom It May Concern,
I would like to purchase several planter boxes, all with a height of 5 inches. Can you make one that holds 100 cubic inches of dirt? Please contact me at your earliest convenience.

Thank you,
Muriel Jenkins

Write a response to this customer, showing all calculations.

How is the volume function built in this problem?

PROBLEM 2   A Dirty Business

The Plant-A-Seed Company also makes cylindrical shaped planters for city sidewalks and store fronts. The cylindrical shaped planters come in a variety of sizes, but all have a height to radius ratio of 2:1.

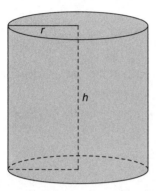

Recall from Geometry that this constant ratio makes the planters in this problem similar.

1. Why do you think Plant-A-Seed might want to manufacture different sizes of a product, but maintain a constant ratio, such as height to radius ratio of 2:1?

2. Consider different sized cylindrical planters.

    a. Complete the table.

Recall the following formulas:
Volume of a cylinder:
$V = $ (base area)(height)
Area of a circle:
$A = \pi r^2$

Radius	Height (inches)	Base Area (square inches)	Volume (cubic inches)
0			
1			
2			
3			
4			
			2000
x			

    b. Describe how you determined the volume when you are given the radius.

c. Describe your method to determine the base area and the height when you are given the volume.

d. Analyze your table of values. For every unit increase in the radius, describe the rate of change in the height, area, and volume of each planter.

3. The base area function $A(x) = 3.14x^2$ and the height function $h(x) = 2x$ are multiplied to build the volume function $V(x) = (3.14x^2)(2x)$. Let's analyze this problem situation graphically.

a. Sketch and label the functions $h(x)$, $A(x)$, and $V(x)$ on the same coordinate plane.

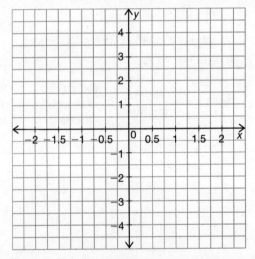

b. In what ways is the graph of $V(x)$ similar to the graph of $h(x)$? In what ways is it different?

c. In what ways is the graph of $V(x)$ similar to the graph of $A(x)$? In what ways is it different?

d. Does $V(x)$ have a relative maximum or relative minimum? Explain your reasoning in terms of the function and in terms of this problem situation.

e. Gene and Douglas disagree about the key characteristics of the graph of the cylindrical shaped planter compared to the graph of the rectangular planter box.

Gene	Douglas
The volume function from the rectangular planter boxes had three x-intercepts, so the graph of the cylindrical shaped planter also must have three. If I extend my viewing window on my graphing calculator I can determine where this graph crosses the x-axis again.	Both the linear and quadratic functions that built the volume function for the cylindrical shaped planter only cross the x-axis at (0, 0). A function can't have an x-intercept different from its factors, so (0, 0) is the only one.

Who is correct? Explain your reasoning.

The volume functions for the rectangular planter box and the cylindrical shaped planter are examples of *cubic functions*. A **cubic function** is a function that can be written in the standard form $f(x) = ax^3 + bx^2 + cx + d$ where $a \neq 0$. In other words, a cubic function is a polynomial function of degree 3.

The volume of the rectangular planter box was represented as $V(h) = h(12 - 2h)(18 - 2h)$. You can multiply the three factors to express the function in standard cubic form.

$$V(h) = h(12 - 2h)(18 - 2h)$$
$$= h(216 - 60h + 4h^2)$$
$$= 216h - 60h^2 + 4h^3$$
$$V(h) = 4h^3 - 60h^2 + 216h$$

The volume of the cylindrical shaped planter was represented as $V(x) = (3.14x^2)(2x)$. You can multiply the two factors to express the function in standard cubic form.

$$V(x) = 6.28x^3$$

The Fundamental Theorem of Algebra tells you that a cubic function must have 3 zeros. Roots may be any number in the set of complex numbers, and can even appear multiple times. **Multiplicity** is how many times a particular number is a zero for a given polynomial function. For example in the polynomial function that represents the volume of the cylindrical shaped planter, $V(x) = (3.14x^2)(2x)$, the zero, $x = 0$, has multiplicity 3.

4. The Fundamental Theorem states that a cubic function must have 3 zeros. Explain why the volume function in this problem crosses the x-axis only one time, yet still satisfies the Fundamental Theorem of Algebra.

5. When analyzing a table, the values in a linear function have a common first difference while quadratic functions have a common second difference. What pattern is present in cubic functions? Do you think this pattern always holds true? Explain your reasoning.

An important mathematical habit is to explore ideas informally. Examine different cubic functions on your calculator. Look for patterns, make predictions, and come up with questions instead of answers.

6. The graphs of linear functions are always lines while quadratic functions are always parabolas. How would you describe the shape of a cubic function? Do you think all cubic functions will have the same general shape? Explain your reasoning.

PROBLEM 3   Cubic Equivalence

Let's consider the volume formula from Problem 1, *Business is Growing*.

1. Three forms of the volume function $V(h)$ are shown.

$V(h) = h(18 - 2h)(12 - 2h)$	$V(h) = h(4h^2 - 60h + 216)$	$V(h) = 4h^3 - 60h^2 + 216h$
The product of three linear functions that represent height, length, and width.	The product of a linear function that represent the height and a quadratic function representing the area of the base.	A cubic function in standard form.

   a. Algebraically verify the functions are equivalent. Show all work and explain your reasoning.

   b. Graphically verify the functions are equivalent. Sketch all three functions and explain your reasoning.

   c. Does the order in which you multiply factors matter? Explain your reasoning.

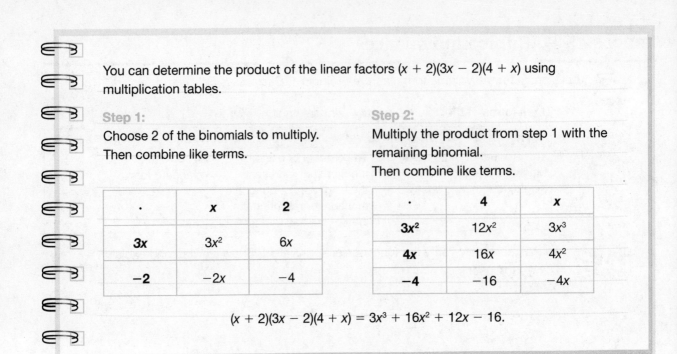

You can determine the product of the linear factors $(x + 2)(3x - 2)(4 + x)$ using multiplication tables.

Step 1:

Choose 2 of the binomials to multiply. Then combine like terms.

Step 2:

Multiply the product from step 1 with the remaining binomial. Then combine like terms.

·	x	2
3x	$3x^2$	$6x$
−2	$-2x$	-4

·	4	x
$3x^2$	$12x^2$	$3x^3$
4x	$16x$	$4x^2$
−4	-16	$-4x$

$$(x + 2)(3x - 2)(4 + x) = 3x^3 + 16x^2 + 12x - 16.$$

2. Analyze the worked example for the multiplication of three binomials.

   a. Use a graphing calculator to verify graphically that the expression in factored form is equivalent to the product written in standard form.

   b. Will multiplying three linear factors always result in a cubic expression? Explain your reasoning.

3. Determine each product. Show all your work and then use a graphing calculator to verify your product is correct.

   a. $(x + 2)(-3x + 2)(1 + 2x)$

   b. $(10 + 2x)(5x + 7)(3x)$

4. Determine the product of the linear and quadratic factors. Then verify graphically that the expressions are equivalent.

   a. $(x - 6)(2x^2 - 3x + 1)$

   b. $(x)(x + 2)^2$

5. Max determined the product of three linear factors.

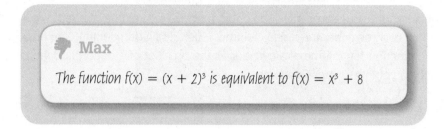

Max

The function $f(x) = (x + 2)^3$ is equivalent to $f(x) = x^3 + 8$

a. Explain why Max is incorrect.

b. How many *x*-intercepts does the function $f(x) = (x + 2)^3$ have? How many zeros? Explain your reasoning.

Talk the Talk

In this lesson, you represented the cubic function for volume of a rectangular prism as the product of three linear functions, volume = (length)(width)(height). You also represented the cubic function for volume of a cylinder as the product of a quadratic function and a linear function, volume = (base area)(height).

1. How are cubic functions similar to linear functions? How are they different?

Consider all representations: graph, table, equation, and context.

2. How are cubic functions similar to quadratic functions? How are they different?

Be prepared to share your solutions and methods.

Polynomial Power
Power Functions

LEARNING GOALS

In this lesson, you will:

- Determine the general behavior of the graph of even and odd degree power functions.
- Derive a general statement and explanation to describe the graph of a power function as the value of the power increases.
- Use graphs and algebraic functions to determine symmetry of even and odd functions.
- Determine whether a function is even or odd based on an algebraic function or graph.
- Understand the structure of the basic cubic function.
- Graph the basic cubic function using reference points and symmetry.

KEY TERMS

- power function
- end behavior
- symmetric about a line
- symmetric about a point
- even function
- odd function

How strong are you? Did you ever try to pick something up just to see if you could lift it? Often times, the weight a person can lift depends on that person's weight. People who weigh more tend to be able to lift more.

Powerlifting, a sport originating in the 1950's, developed separate weight classes for competitors in order to maintain a sense of fairness. Powerlifting consists of athletes competing in specific lifts: squat, bench press, and deadlift. The USA Powerlifting competition starts in high school, where young men in the 114 pound weight class are able to bench press over 250 pounds; while men in the 181 pound weight class have benched over 400 pounds. This competition is not only for men—high school women compete as well. Women in the 132 pound weight class have benched over 215 pounds.

PROBLEM 1   What Odd Behavior . . . or Is It Even?

You have studied linear functions, quadratic functions, and now you will explore more polynomial functions. A common type of polynomial function is a *power function*. A **power function** is a function of the form $P(x) = ax^n$, where n is a non-negative integer.

For the purpose of this lesson, you will only focus on power functions where $a = 1$ and -1. In the next lesson you will investigate power functions with various a-values.

1. Consider each power function and its graph in the sequence shown.

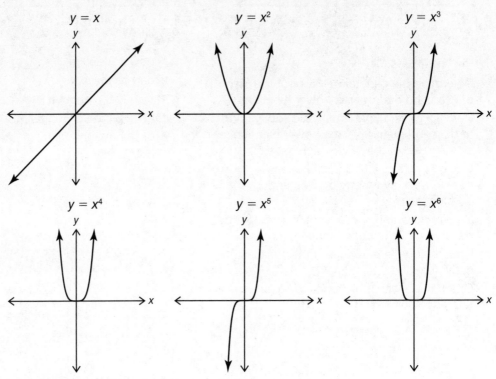

a. Sketch and label the next two graphs in the sequence.

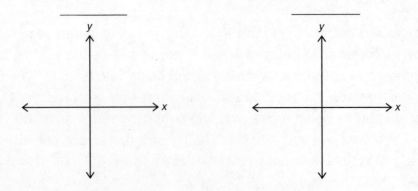

5

b. State any observations or patterns that you notice about the graphs in the sequence.

c. Make a general statement about the graph of a power function raised to an odd degree.

d. Make a general statement about the graph of a power function raised to an even degree.

2. Based on you work in Question 1, sketch the graph of x^n when:

a. $n = 12$

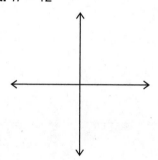

b. $n = 27$

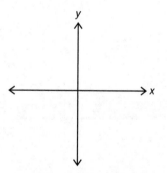

c. $n = 2m$, where m is an integer greater than 0

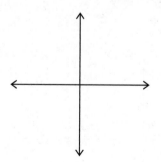

d. $n = 2m + 1$, where m is an integer greater than 0

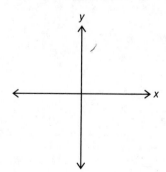

The **end behavior** of a graph of a function is the behavior of the graph as x approaches infinity and as x approaches negative infinity.

You can write the end behavior of this polynomial function using the notation:

As $x \rightarrow \infty$, $f(x) \rightarrow \infty$.

As $x \rightarrow -\infty$, $f(x) \rightarrow -\infty$.

3. Explain in words what the end behavior in the worked example means.

4. Consider the sequence of graphs shown.

$f_1(x) = x$　　　　　$f_2(x) = x^2$　　　　　$f_3(x) = x^3$

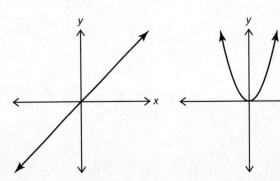

a. Write each function in terms of x, and then sketch it.

$-f_1(x) =$ _____　　　$-f_2(x) =$ _____　　　$-f_3(x) =$ _____

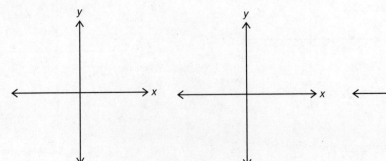

b. Complete the table to describe the end behavior for any polynomial function.

	Odd Degree Power Function	**Even Degree Power Function**
a > 0		
a < 0		

PROBLEM 2 If It's Flat, Then How Is It Rising?

1. The function, $f(x) = x^2$, has been graphed for you. Complete the tables for $g(x) = x^4$ and $h(x) = x^6$. Then use your knowledge of the axis of symmetry to graph and label each function on the same coordinate plane shown.

x	$g(x) = x^4$
0	
0.5	
1	

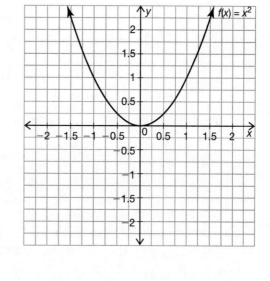

x	$h(x) = x^6$
0	
0.5	
1	

a. Notice how all 3 graphs intersect at (0, 0), therefore $f(0) = g(0) = h(0) = 0$. Describe any other intersection points using function notation.

b. As the even degree power increases, what do you notice about the graph?

c. Sketch the graph of $k(x) = x^{12}$ on the same coordinate plane as $g(x)$ and $h(x)$.

5

d. Explain why the graphs of the even degree functions flatten as the degree increases for values of x between -1 and 1.

e. Explain why the graphs of the greater even degree functions steepen when the distance from x exceeds 1.

2. The function, $f(x) = x^3$, has been graphed for you. Complete the tables for $g(x) = x^5$ and $h(x) = x^7$. Then use your knowledge of the axis of symmetry to graph and label each function on the same coordinate plane.

x	g(x) = x⁵
0	
0.5	
1	

x	h(x) = x⁷
0	
0.5	
1	

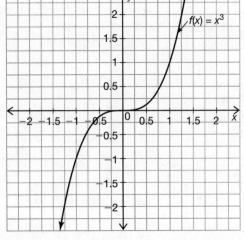

a. Notice how all 3 graphs intersect at (0, 0), therefore $f(0) = g(0) = h(0) = 0$. Describe any other intersection points using this function notation.

b. As the odd degree power increases, what do you notice about the graph?

c. Sketch and label the graph of $k(x) = x^{13}$ on the same coordinate plane as $g(x)$ and $h(x)$.

d. Explain why the graphs of the odd degree functions flatten as the degree increases for values of *x* between −1 and 1.

e. Explain why the graphs of the greater odd degree functions steepen when the distance from *x* exceeds 1.

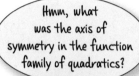

Hmm, what was the axis of symmetry in the function family of quadratics?

 Recall that the axis of symmetry divides the graph into two parts that are mirror images of each other. If you do a reflection across an axis and the graph looks exactly the same as the original, it means that the graph is symmetric with respect to that axis.

 1. Sketch 2 graphs that are symmetric to:

a. the *x*-axis

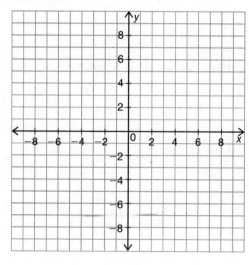

b. the line *y* = 0

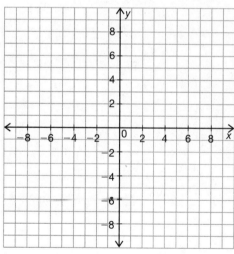

c. the line $x = 3$

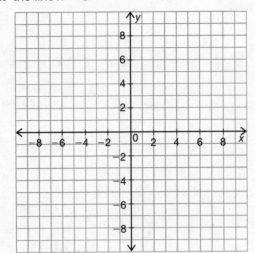

d. the line $y = 0$

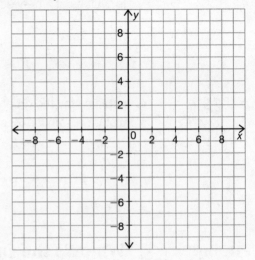

e. the line $x = -4$

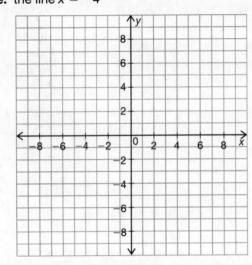

f. the line $y = 2$

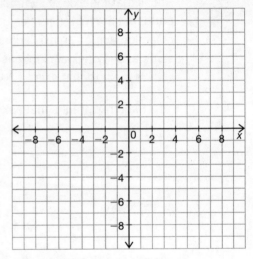

g. Is each of your sketches a function? Explain why or why not.

2. Analyze the graph shown.

   a. Identify 2 symmetric points.

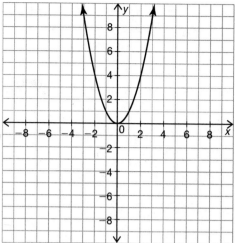

   b. If one point is (x, y) what are the coordinates of the other symmetric point?

   c. What do you notice about the y-values when you replace x with $-x$?

   d. Write a general statement to explain the relationship between any two points symmetrical to the line $x = 0$.

3. Analyze the graph shown.

   a. Identify 2 symmetric points.

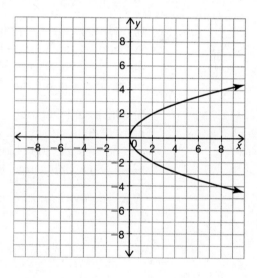

   b. If one point is (x, y) what are the coordinates of the other symmetric point?

   c. What do you notice about the x-values when you replace y with $-y$?

   d. Write a general statement to explain the relationship between any two points symmetrical to the line $y = 0$.

If a graph is **symmetric about a line**, the line divides the graph into two identical parts. Special attention is given to the line of symmetry when it is the *y*-axis as it tells you that the function is even.

4. Analyze the graph shown.

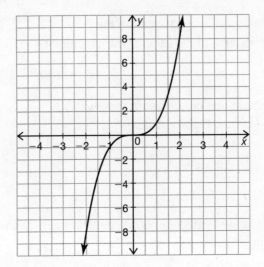

Olivia says that the graph has no line of symmetry because if she reflected the graph across the *x*- or *y*-axis, it would just change the graph to look like an odd degree power function with a negative *a*-value, thus not looking like a mirror image.

Randall says that the graph has no line of symmetry because if he looks at the *x*-value at 1 and −1, the *y*-value is not the same, so there can't be symmetry about the *y*-axis. Also if he looks at the *y*-value at 8 and −8, the *x*-value is not the same, so there can't be symmetry about the *x*-axis.

Shedrick said that there is some type of symmetry. He notices that if he looks at the point (2, 8) the point (−2, −8) is also on the graph. Likewise he looks at the point (1, 1) and notices that the point (−1, −1) is also on the graph. He concluded that it must have a reflection across the *x*- and *y*-axis at the same time.

Who's correct? Explain your reasoning.

The graph of an odd degree basic power function is *symmetric about a point*, in particular the origin. A function is **symmetric about a point** if each point on the graph has a point the same distance from the central point, but in the opposite direction. Special attention is given when the central point is the origin as it determines that the function is odd. When the point of symmetry is the origin, the graph is reflected across the *x*-axis and the *y*-axis. If you replace both (x, y) with $(-x, -y)$, the function remains the same.

You can think of the point of symmetry about the origin, as a double reflection.

$f_1(x) = x^3$

$f_2(x) = f_1(-x)^3$

$= (-x)^3$

$f_3(x) = -f_2(x)$

$= x^3$

The function $f_1(x)$ is shown.

The function $f_1(x)$ is reflected across the *y*-axis to produce f_2.

The function $f_2(x)$ is reflected across the *x*-axis to produce f_3.

An **even function** has a graph symmetric about the *y*-axis, thus $f(x) = f(-x)$.

An **odd function** has a graph symmetric about the origin, thus $f(x) = -f(-x)$.

5. Which graph in Questions 2 through 4 represents an even function? Explain your reasoning.

6. Which graph in Questions 2 through 4 represents an odd function? Explain your reasoning.

7. State whether the graph of each function shown is even, odd, or neither.

a.

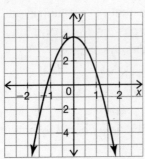

_____

b.

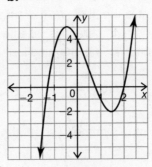

_____

c.

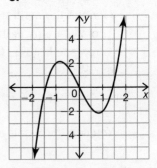

_____

Odd and even functions are NOT the same as odd and even degree functions.

8. Lillian and Destiny are working on the problem shown.

Determine algebraically whether the polynomial function $f(x) = 3x^4 - 2x^3 + 4x - 6$ is even, odd, or neither.

 Lillian

$f(x) = 3x^4 - 2x^3 + 4x - 6$

$f(x) = 3x^4 - 2x^3 + 4x - 6$
$f(-x) = 3(-x)^4 - 2(-x)^3 + 4(-x) - 6$
$f(-x) = 3x^4 + 2x^3 - 4x - 6$

$-f(x) = -(3x^4 - 2x^3 + 4x - 6)$
$-f(x) = -3x^4 + 2x^3 - 4x + 6$

$f(x) \neq f(-x)$ or $-f(x)$ thus
$f(x)$ is neither even or odd.

 Destiny

$f(x) = 3x^4 - 2x^3 + 4x - 6$

$f(x) = 3x^4 - 2x^3 + 4x - 6$
$f(-x) = 3(-x^4) - 2(-x^3) + 4(-x) - 6$
$f(-x) = -3x^4 + 2x^3 - 4x - 6$

$-f(x) = -(3x^4 - 2x^3 + 4x - 6)$
$-f(x) = -3x^4 + 2x^3 - 4x + 6$

$f(x) \neq f(-x)$ or $-f(x)$ thus
$f(x)$ is neither even or odd.

a. Explain why Destiny's work is incorrect.

 b. How can you use algebra to determine whether a function is even or odd?

9. Determine algebraically whether the functions are even, odd, or neither.

  a. $f(x) = 2x^3 - 3x$

Take your time and check your substitutions.

  b. $g(x) = 6x^2 + 10$

  c. $h(x) = x^3 - 3x^2 - 2x + 7$

Be prepared to share your solutions and methods.

Function Makeover

Transformations and Symmetry of Polynomial Functions

M.C. Escher is a well-known artist with a unique visual perspective. Many of his works display elusive connections, peculiar symmetry, and tessellations. Tessellations are symmetric designs with a repeated pattern.

You can find many images of Escher's work on the World Wide Web. Take a look and enjoy! Make sure to take a close look, because things may not be as straightforward as they seem.

Refer to the Reference Points

Recall that reference points are a set of points that are used to graph a basic function. Previously, you used reference points and the key characteristics of a parabola to graph the basic quadratic function. You learned that the reference points for the basic quadratic function are (0, 0), (1, 1), and (2, 4). The basic quadratic function is symmetric about the y-axis; that is, $f(x) = f(-x)$. Therefore, you can use symmetry to graph two other points of the basic function, $(-1, 1)$, $(-2, 4)$.

Let's consider a set of reference points and the property of symmetry to graph the basic cubic function.

To complete Questions 1 and 2, consider the basic cubic function, $f(x) = x^3$.

1. Complete the table for the given reference points. Then graph the points on the coordinate plane shown.

x	$f(x) = x^3$
0	
1	
2	

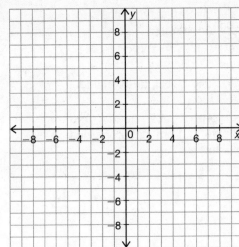

> The pattern for a basic cubic function is to cube the input value to get the output value. So, from the origin, move over 1 unit and up 1 unit. For the next point, start at the origin, move over 2 units and up 8 units.

2. The graph of the basic cubic function is symmetric about the origin. So, $f(x) = -f(-x)$. Use the property of symmetry to determine 2 other points from the reference points. Then, use these points to graph the basic cubic function on the coordinate plane shown.

Will Symmetry Prevail?

Transformations performed on a function $f(x)$ to form a new function $g(x)$ can be described by the transformational function:

$$g(x) = Af(B(x - C)) + D.$$

Previously, you graphed quadratic functions using this notation. You can use this notation to identify the transformations to perform on any function.

Recall that the constants A and D affect the *outside* of the function (the output values). For instance, if $A = 2$, then you can multiply each y-coordinate of $f(x)$ by 2 to determine the y-coordinates of $g(x)$.

The constants B and C affect the inside of the function (the input values). For instance, if $B = 2$, then you can multiply each x-coordinate of $f(x)$ by $\frac{1}{2}$ to determine the x-coordinates of $g(x)$.

Function Form	Equation Information	Description of Transformation of Graph
$y = Af(x)$	$|A| > 1$	vertical stretch of the graph by a factor of A units
	$0 < |A| < 1$	vertical compression of the graph by a factor of A units
	$A < 0$	reflection across the x-axis
$y = f(Bx)$	$|B| > 1$	compressed horizontally by a factor of $\frac{1}{|B|}$
	$0 < |B| < 1$	stretched horizontally by a factor of $\frac{1}{|B|}$
	$B < 0$	reflection across the y-axis
$y = f(x - C)$	$C > 0$	horizontal shift right C units
	$C < 0$	horizontal shift left C units
$y = f(x) + D$	$D > 0$	vertical shift up D units
	$D < 0$	vertical shift down D units

5

1. Complete the table to show the coordinates of $g(x) = Af(B(x - C)) + D$ after each type of transformation performed on $f(x)$.

Type of Transformation Performed on $f(x)$	Coordinates of $f(x) \rightarrow$ Coordinates of $g(x)$
Vertical Dilation by a Factor of A	$(x, y) \rightarrow ($ _____ , _____ $)$
Horizontal Dilation by a Factor of B	$(x, y) \rightarrow ($ _____ , _____ $)$
Horizontal Translation of C units	$(x, y) \rightarrow ($ _____ , _____ $)$
Vertical Translation of D units	$(x, y) \rightarrow ($ _____ , _____ $)$
All four transformations: A, B, C, and D	$(x, y) \rightarrow ($ _____ , _____ $)$

You are now ready to transform any function!

2. The graph of the basic cubic function $c(x) = x^3$ is shown.

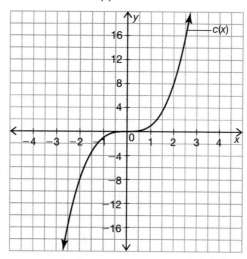

a. Suppose that $g(x) = 2c(x)$. Use reference points and properties of symmetry to complete the table of values for $g(x)$. Then, graph and label $g(x)$ on the same coordinate plane as $c(x)$.

Reference Points on $c(x)$	$\rightarrow$	Corresponding Points on $g(x)$
(0, 0)	$\rightarrow$	
(1, 1)	$\rightarrow$	
(2, 8)	$\rightarrow$	

b. Suppose that $h(x) = \frac{1}{2}c(x)$. Use reference points and properties of symmetry to complete the table of values for $h(x)$. Then, graph and label $h(x)$ on the same coordinate plane as $c(x)$ and $g(x)$.

Reference Points on $c(x)$	$\rightarrow$	Corresponding Points on $h(x)$
(0, 0)	$\rightarrow$	
(1, 1)	$\rightarrow$	
(2, 8)	$\rightarrow$	

c. Describe the symmetry of $g(x)$ and $h(x)$. How does the symmetry of $g(x)$ and $h(x)$ compare to the symmetry of $c(x)$?

d. Determine whether $g(x)$ and $h(x)$ are even functions, odd functions, or neither. Verify your answer algebraically.

3. The graph of the basic cubic function $c(x) = x^3$ is shown.

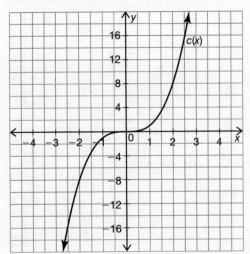

a. Suppose that $u(x) = c(2x)$. Use reference points and properties of symmetry to complete the table of values for $u(x)$. Then, graph and label $u(x)$ on the same coordinate plane as $c(x)$.

Reference Points on $c(x)$	$\rightarrow$	Corresponding Points on $u(x)$
(0, 0)	$\rightarrow$	
(1, 1)	$\rightarrow$	
(2, 8)	$\rightarrow$	

b. Suppose that $v(x) = c\left(\frac{1}{2}x\right)$. Use reference points and properties symmetry to complete the table of values for $v(x)$. Then, graph and label $v(x)$ on the same coordinate plane as $c(x)$ and $u(x)$.

Reference Points on $c(x)$	$\rightarrow$	Corresponding Points on $v(x)$
(0, 0)	$\rightarrow$	
(1, 1)	$\rightarrow$	
(2, 8)	$\rightarrow$	

c. Describe the symmetry of $u(x)$ and $v(x)$. How does the symmetry of $u(x)$ and $v(x)$ compare to the symmetry of $c(x)$?

d. Determine whether $u(x)$ and $v(x)$ are even functions, odd functions, or neither. Verify your answer algebraically.

4. The graph of the basic cubic function $c(x) = x^3$ is shown.

a. Suppose that $a(x) = -c(x)$. Use reference points and properties of symmetry to complete the table of values for $a(x)$. Then, graph and label $a(x)$ on the same coordinate plane as $c(x)$.

Reference Points on $c(x)$	→	Corresponding Points on $a(x)$
(0, 0)	→	
(1, 1)	→	
(2, 8)	→	

b. Suppose that $b(x) = c(-x)$. Use reference points and properties symmetry to complete the table of values for $b(x)$. Then, graph and label $b(x)$ on the same coordinate plane as $c(x)$ and $a(x)$.

Reference Points on $c(x)$	→	Corresponding Points on $b(x)$
(0, 0)	→	
(1, 1)	→	
(2, 8)	→	

c. Describe the symmetry of $a(x)$ and $b(x)$. How does the symmetry of $a(x)$ and $b(x)$ compare to the symmetry of $c(x)$?

d. Determine whether $a(x)$ and $b(x)$ are even functions, odd functions, or neither. Verify your answer algebraically.

5. The graph of the basic cubic function $c(x) = x^3$ is shown.

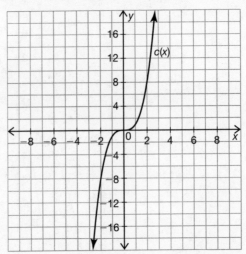

c(x)

a. Suppose that $m(x) = c(x - 5)$. Use reference points and properties of symmetry to complete the table of values for $m(x)$. Then, graph and label $m(x)$ on the same coordinate plane as $c(x)$.

Reference Points on c(x)	→	Corresponding Points on m(x)
(0, 0)	→	
(1, 1)	→	
(2, 8)	→	

b. Suppose that $n(x) = c(x + 5)$. Use reference points and properties of symmetry to complete the table of values for $n(x)$. Then, graph and label $n(x)$ on the same coordinate plane as $c(x)$ and $m(x)$.

Reference Points on c(x)	→	Corresponding Points on n(x)
(0, 0)	→	
(1, 1)	→	
(2, 8)	→	

c. Describe the symmetry of $m(x)$ and $n(x)$. How does the symmetry of $a(x)$ and $b(x)$ compare to the symmetry of $c(x)$?

d. Determine whether $m(x)$ and $n(x)$ are even functions, odd functions, or neither. Verify your answer algebraically.

6. The graph of the basic cubic function $c(x) = x^3$ is shown.

a. Suppose that $j(x) = c(x) + 5$. Use reference points and properties of symmetry to complete the table of values for $j(x)$. Then, graph and label $j(x)$ on the same coordinate plane as $c(x)$.

Reference Points on $c(x)$	$\rightarrow$	Corresponding Points on $j(x)$
(0, 0)	$\rightarrow$	
(1, 1)	$\rightarrow$	
(2, 8)	$\rightarrow$	

b. Suppose that $k(x) = c(x) - 5$. Use reference points and properties of symmetry to complete the table of values for $k(x)$. Then, graph and label $k(x)$ on the same coordinate plane as $c(x)$ and $j(x)$.

Reference Points on $c(x)$	$\rightarrow$	Corresponding Points on $k(x)$
(0, 0)	$\rightarrow$	
(1, 1)	$\rightarrow$	
(2, 8)	$\rightarrow$	

c. Describe the symmetry of $j(x)$ and $k(x)$. How does the symmetry of $j(x)$ and $k(x)$ compare to the symmetry of $c(x)$?

d. Determine whether $j(x)$ and $k(x)$ are even functions, odd functions, or neither. Verify your answer algebraically.

7. Complete the table to summarize the effects that transformations have on the basic cubic function $c(x) = x^3$. The first row has been completed for you.

Effects of Rigid Motions on the Basic Cubic Function $c(x) = x^3$			
Rigid Motion	**New Transformed Function $p(x)$ in Terms of $c(x)$**	**Description of Symmetry of $p(x)$**	**Is $p(x)$ Even, Odd, or Neither?**
Vertical Stretch Dilation	$p(x) = Ac(x),$ $\|A\| > 1$	Symmetric about the point $(0, 0)$	Odd
Vertical Compression Dilation			
Horizontal Stretch Dilation			
Horizontal Compression Dilation			
Reflection across x-axis			
Reflection across y-axis			
Vertical Translation			
Horizontal Translation			

8. Do you think that your results in Question 7 would be the same for *any* odd power function? Explain your reasoning.

9. The graph of the basic quartic function $q(x) = x^4$ and its reference points are shown. Use the graph to sketch the function after dilations, reflections, and translations. Pay special attention to the symmetry after the transformations. Record your conclusions by completing the table that follows. The first row has been completed for you.

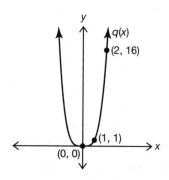

Effects of Rigid Motions on the Basic Cubic Function $q(x) = x^4$			
Rigid Motion	**New Transformed Function $p(x)$ in Terms of $q(x)$**	**Description of Symmetry of $p(x)$**	**Is $p(x)$ Even, Odd, or Neither?**
Vertical Stretch Dilation	$p(x) = Ac(x)$, $\|A\| > 1$	Symmetric about the y-axis	Even
Vertical Compression Dilation			
Horizontal Stretch Dilation			
Horizontal Compression Dilation			
Reflection across x-axis			
Reflection across y-axis			
Vertical Translation			
Horizontal Translation			

10. Do you think that your results in Question 9 would be the same for *any* even power function? Explain your reasoning.

11. Use the appropriate word from the box to complete each statement.

always	sometimes	never

a. If a dilation is performed on an odd function $f(x)$ to produce $g(x)$, then $g(x)$ will

_____ be an odd function.

b. If a reflection is performed on an even function $f(x)$ to produce $g(x)$, then $g(x)$ will

_____ be an even function.

c. If a translation is performed on an odd function $f(x)$ to produce $g(x)$, then $g(x)$ will

_____ be an odd function.

d. If a translation is performed on an even function $f(x)$ to produce $g(x)$, then $g(x)$ will

_____ be an even function.

PROBLEM 3 **Multiple Transformations**

1. Analyze the graphs of $f(x)$ and $g(x)$. Describe the transformations performed on $f(x)$ to create $g(x)$. Then, write an equation for $g(x)$ in terms of $f(x)$. For each set of points shown on $f(x)$, the corresponding points after the rigid motions are shown on $g(x)$.

a. $g(x) =$ _____

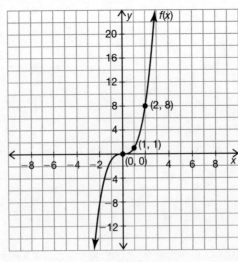

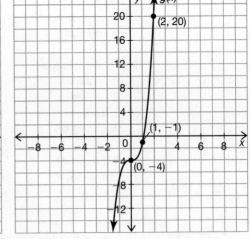

b. $g(x) =$ _____

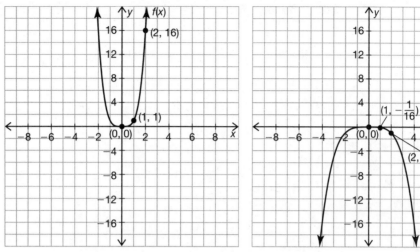

c. $g(x) =$ _____

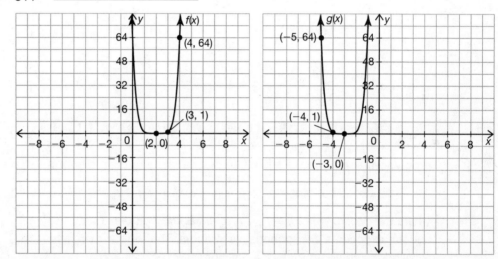

2. The equation for a polynomial function $p(x)$ is given. The equation for the transformed function $t(x)$ in terms of $p(x)$ is also given. Describe the transformation(s) performed on $p(x)$ that produced $t(x)$. Then, write an equation for $t(x)$ in terms of x.

a. $p(x) = x^5$

$t(x) = 0.5p(-x)$

b. $p(x) = x^4$

$t(x) = 2p(x + 3)$

c. $p(x) = x^3$

$t(x) = -p(x - 2) + 4$

When Transformations Just Don't Cut It

 A **polynomial function** is a function that can be written in the form

$$p(x) = a_nx^n + a_{n-1}x^{n-1} + \cdots + a_2x^2 + a_1x + a_0,$$

where the coefficients $a_n, a_{n-1}, \ldots a_2, a_1, a_0$ are complex numbers and the exponents are nonnegative integers. The form shown here is called the standard form of a polynomial.

You already know that a third-degree polynomial function has a special name—a cubic function. A **quartic function** is a fourth degree polynomial function, while a **quintic function** is a fifth degree polynomial function.

You can describe any linear or quadratic functions in terms of the transformations performed on the basic functions. Is this true for *any* polynomial function? That is, can you derive any polynomial function by transforming a basic function?

All of the polynomial functions in this course will have real number coefficients.

 1. Consider the polynomial function $p(x) = x^3 + 2x^2 - 3x$.

a. Predict what the graph of $p(x)$ looks like. Describe the number of x-intercepts and end behavior.

---

b. Use a graphing calculator to graph $p(x)$. Were your predictions accurate?

c. Can you describe which transformations were performed on $f(x) = x^3$ that results in the graph of $p(x)$?

Transformations on basic functions cannot be used to derive any polynomial. Therefore, you will need to consider another method.

Use each basic power function shown to complete Questions 2 through 6.

$$f(x) = x \qquad g(x) = x^2 \qquad h(x) = x^3 \qquad j(x) = x^4 \qquad k(x) = x^5$$

2. Consider the function $a(x)$, where $a(x) = h(x) + 2g(x)$.

   a. The functions $g(x)$ and $h(x)$ are shown. Complete the table of values and sketch $a(x)$ on the coordinate plane shown. The first row has been completed for you.

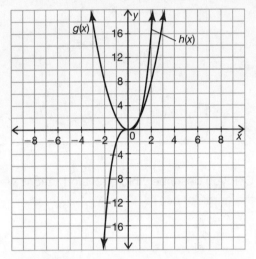

x	h(x)	g(x)	a(x)
−2	−8	4	−8 + 2(4) = 0
−1			
0			
1			
2			

   b. Write the equation for $a(x)$.

   c. Explain any differences between the graph of $a(x)$ and the graph of the basic power function of the same degree as $a(x)$.

Hmm . . . I wonder if the sum or difference of polynomials is still a polynomial? Let's find out!

$$f(x) = x \qquad g(x) = x^2 \qquad h(x) = x^3 \qquad j(x) = x^4 \qquad k(x) = x^5$$

3. Consider the function $b(x)$, where $b(x) = 2f(x) - h(x)$.

    a. The functions $f(x)$ and $h(x)$ are shown. Complete the table of values and sketch $b(x)$ on the coordinate plane.

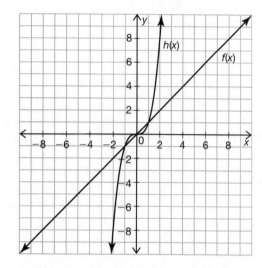

x	f(x)	h(x)	b(x)
−2			
−1			
0			
1			
2			

    b. Write the equation for $b(x)$.

    c. Explain any differences between the graph of $b(x)$ and the graph of the basic power function of the same degree as $b(x)$.

$$f(x) = x \qquad g(x) = x^2 \qquad h(x) = x^3 \qquad j(x) = x^4 \qquad k(x) = x^5$$

4. Consider the function $c(x)$, where $c(x) = j(x) + 0.5h(x) - 2g(x)$.

   a. The functions $g(x)$, $h(x)$, and $j(x)$ are shown. Complete the table of values and sketch $c(x)$ on the coordinate plane.

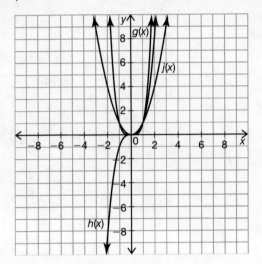

x	j(x)	h(x)	g(x)	c(x)
−2				
−1				
0				
1				
2				

   b. Write the equation for $c(x)$.

   c. Explain any differences between the graph of $c(x)$ and the graph of the basic power function of the same degree as $c(x)$.

$$f(x) = x \qquad g(x) = x^2 \qquad h(x) = x^3 \qquad j(x) = x^4 \qquad k(x) = x^5$$

5. Consider the function $d(x)$, where $d(x) = -j(x) + 3g(x) - 1$.

   a. The functions $g(x)$ and $j(x)$ are shown. Complete the table of values and sketch $d(x)$ on the coordinate plane.

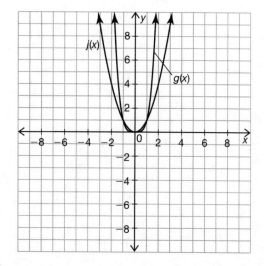

x	j(x)	g(x)	d(x)
−2			
−1			
0			
1			
2			

   b. Write the equation for $d(x)$. Is $d(x)$ a polynomial?

   c. Explain any differences between the graph of $d(x)$ and the graph of the basic power function of the same degree as $d(x)$.

$$f(x) = x \qquad g(x) = x^2 \qquad h(x) = x^3 \qquad j(x) = x^4 \qquad k(x) = x^5$$

6. Consider the function $z(x)$, where $z(x) = k(x) + 2j(x) - 4h(x) - 6g(x)$.

   a. The functions $g(x)$, $h(x)$, $j(x)$, and $k(x)$ are shown. Complete the table of values and sketch $z(x)$ on the coordinate plane.

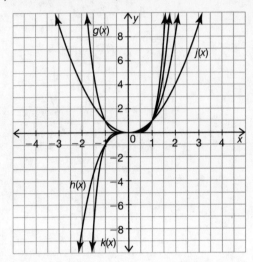

x	k(x)	j(x)	h(x)	g(x)	z(x)
−3					
−2					
−1					
0					
1					
2					
3					

   b. Write the equation for $z(x)$.

   c. Explain any differences between the graph of $z(x)$ and the graph of the basic power function of the same degree as $z(x)$.

Talk the Talk

The possible shapes of linear, quadratic, cubic, quartic, and quintic functions are shown.

Linear Functions

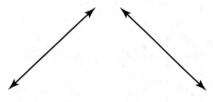

Quadratic Functions

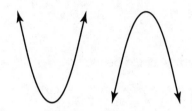

Cubic Functions

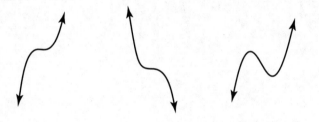

Quartic Functions

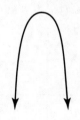
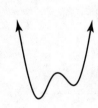

Quintic Functions

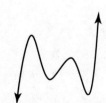
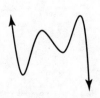

1. Choose the possible graph(s) for each given polynomial function $f(x)$.

a. Which graph(s) could be the graph of $f(x) = 2x^2$?

Graph A	Graph B	Graph C
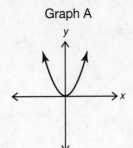	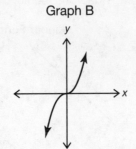	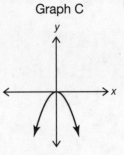

b. Which graph(s) could be the graph of $f(x) = -x^3 - x^2 + 6x$?

Graph A	Graph B	Graph C
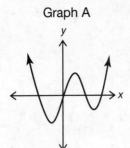	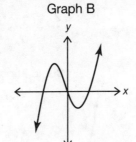	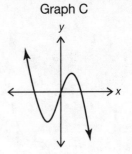

c. Which graph(s) could be the graph of $f(x) = x^4 + 1$?

Graph A	Graph B	Graph C
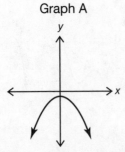	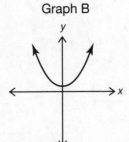	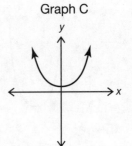

Be prepared to share your solutions and methods.

Polynomial DNA
Key Characteristics of Polynomial Functions

LEARNING GOALS

In this lesson, you will:

- Interpret polynomial key characteristics in the context of a problem situation.
- Generalize the key characteristics of polynomials.
- Sketch the graph of any polynomial given certain key characteristics.

KEY TERMS

- absolute maximum
- absolute minimum
- extrema

Children typically resemble their parents because of the inheritance of genes from parent to offspring. Scientists know of over 200 hereditary traits that are transmitted across generations of families. The genes that carry these traits are in specific strands of DNA. You can witness these traits by crossing your hands. Is your left thumb over your right thumb? If it is, you have the dominant trait. People with the recessive trait will cross their right thumb over their left thumb. Try it the opposite way, it feels awkward doesn't it?

Did you ever work with Punnett squares in biology to determine the probability of an offspring having a particular characteristic like blue eyes versus brown eyes or eyelash length? Being able to roll your tongue is actually a dominant genetic feature. Some other dominant genetic human traits are non-cleft chins, widow's peaks, broad eyebrows, freckles, dimples, and unattached ear lobes to name a few. When you look at the specific genotype of a species you can determine or predict what the offspring may look like.

The same thing is true for polynomials! If you know certain characteristics about the polynomial, you can predict what the graph will look like, as well as other key characteristics.

Math World vs. Real World

The data shown represents the population of a rare, endangered species of frog called the glass frog. In order to better understand the glass frog's fertilization habits, scientists performed a study and recorded the average number of frog eggs over the span of 44 months.

Month of Study	Average Number of Glass Frog Eggs	Month of Study	Average Number of Glass Frog Eggs
0	10,534	19	14,330.5
1	5500	20	13,845.1
2	5033	21	13,893.1
3	2600	22	14,546.3
4	239.4	23	11,815.8
6	137.3	23	13,086.2
7	108.4	24	15,966.9
8	667.1	29	9904.4
9	387.4	29	8257.3
12	4813.1	31	5297.5
14	9539.5	32	2494.1
15	11,318.6	33	1805.4
16	8953.3	34	665
18	15,402.5	43	4813

The data has been plotted for you and a quartic regression was used to generate the polynomial function to best represent the data. The quartic regression option calculates the best-fit equation of the form $y = ax^4 + bx^3 + cx^2 + dx + e$.

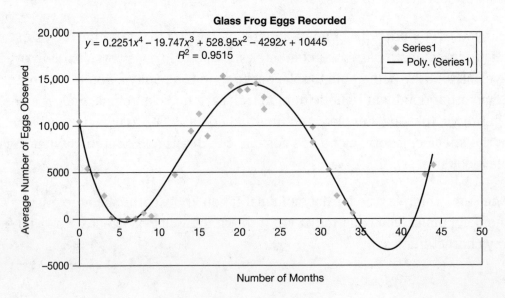

Glass Frog Eggs Recorded

$y = 0.2251x^4 - 19.747x^3 + 528.95x^2 - 4292x + 10445$
$R^2 = 0.9515$

Average Number of Eggs Observed

Number of Months

1. Consider the graph and equation to answer each question.

 a. What is the domain and range of the study?

 b. Explain what the domain and range represent in the context of this problem.

 c. What is the domain and range of the function?

 d. At what month in the study were the most frog eggs observed? How many eggs were recorded?

 e. At what month in the study were the least frog eggs observed? How many eggs were recorded?

 f. If the study lasted for 50 months, how many frog eggs would there be according to the function?

 g. If the study lasted forever, how many eggs would there be according to the function?

 h. How many frog eggs appeared between months 35 and 40?

 i. At what month(s) of the study were there approximately 4800 glass frog eggs observed?

2. Use a graphing calculator to determine the x-intercepts of the function. What do the x-intercepts mean in the context of this problem situation?

3. State the end behavior of the function. Does this make sense in the context of this problem scenario? Explain your reasoning.

4. How many frog eggs were observed at the beginning of the study? Explain the mathematical meaning of your answer.

5. Describe the interval when the frog's egg population is:

   a. increasing.

   b. decreasing.

PROBLEM 2 **A Polynomial is Born**

So far in this chapter, you have learned a great deal about polynomial functions. You have learned about minimums, maximums, zeros, end behavior, and the general shapes of their graphs. Now, you will combine all that information to generalize the key characteristics for any degree polynomial.

Recall the definition of a relative maximum is the highest point in a particular section of a function's graph, and a relative minimum is the lowest point in a particular section of the graph. Similarly, the **absolute maximum** is the highest point in the entire graph, and the **absolute minimum** is the lowest point in the entire graph. The set of absolute maximums, absolute minimums, relative maximums, and relative minimums may also be referred to as **extrema**. The extrema are also called extreme points and extremum.

1. Consider the graph that represents the average number of glass frog eggs in Problem 1.

   a. State all relative maximums and minimums.

   b. State all absolute maximums and minimums.

c. Do the absolute minimums and/or maximums make sense in the context of this problem situation? Explain your reasoning.

2. Determine the number of extrema in each polynomial.

$g_1(x) = x^4$

$g_2(x) = x^4 - 3x^2$

4th Degree Polynomials

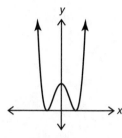

Don't forget to look for relationships!

Number of Extrema   _____   _____

$f_1(x) = x^5$

$f_2(x) = x^5 + 4x^2$

$f_3(x) = x^5 - 5x^3 + 5x + 1.18$

5th Degree Polynomials

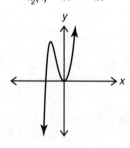

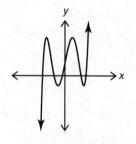

Number of Extrema   _____   _____   _____

$h_1(x) = x^6$

$h_2(x) = x^6 - 3x^2$

$h_3(x) = 2x^6 - 13x^5 + 26x^4 - 7x^3 - 2$

6th Degree Polynomials

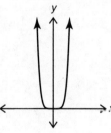

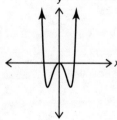

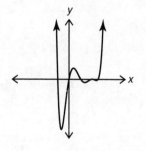

Number of Extrema   _____   _____   _____

5

3. List any observations you notice about the possible number of extrema and the degree of the polynomial.

4. List the possible number of extrema for the each polynomial.

   a. 9th degree polynomial

   b. 18th degree polynomial

   c. nth degree odd polynomial

   d. nth degree even polynomial

Use the knowledge you gained about 4th, 5th, and 6th degree polynomials to answer these questions.

5. Choose the appropriate word from the box to complete each statement. Justify your answer with a sketch or explanation.

always	sometimes	never

   a. An odd degree function will _____ have absolute extrema.

   b. An even degree function will _____ have relative extrema.

   c. An even degree function will _____ have 3 or more relative extrema.

d. An even degree function will _____ have absolute extrema.

e. An odd degree function will _____ have relative extrema.

f. An odd degree function will _____ one have relative extrema.

6. Analyze the graphs shown.

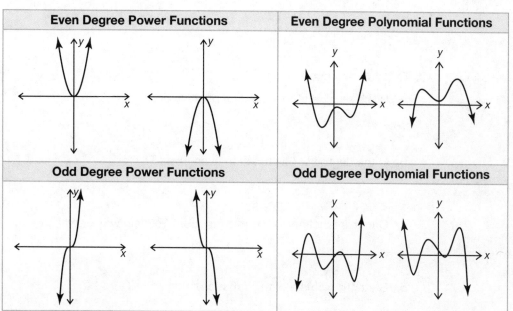

a. State the similarities and differences you notice between the power functions and the polynomial functions.

b. What conclusions can you make about the end behavior of all even degree polynomial functions?

c. What conclusions can you make about the end behavior of all odd degree polynomial functions?

d. What conclusions can you make about the domain and range of all even degree polynomial functions?

e. What conclusions can you make about the domain and range of all odd degree polynomial functions?

7. Consider the graph shown.

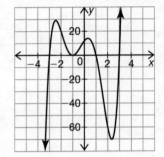

a. Is the *a*-value of this function positive or negative?

b. Is the degree of this function even or odd?

c. Can this function be a cubic function? Explain why or why not.

d. State the domain of this function.

e. State the range of this function.

f. Determine the number of relative extrema in this graph.

g. Determine the number of absolute extrema in this graph.

h. State the intervals where the graph is increasing.

8. Consider the graph shown.

   a. Is the *a*-value of this function positive or negative?

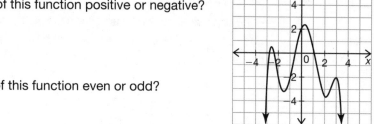

   b. Is the degree of this function even or odd?

   c. Can this function be a 6th degree polynomial function? Explain why or why not.

   d. State the domain of this function.

   e. State the range of this function.

   f. Determine the number of relative extrema in this graph.

   g. Determine the number of absolute extrema in this graph.

   h. State the intervals where the graph is decreasing.

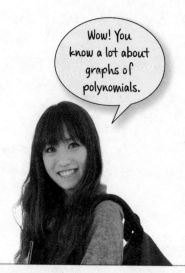

Wow! You know a lot about graphs of polynomials.

9. Complete the table on the next page to represent the graphs of various polynomials.

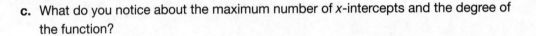

After you complete the table, answer parts (b) through (e).

a. Sketch the basic shape on each set of axes, given the number of zeros. If you cannot sketch the basic shape, explain why.

b. Compare your graphs with a partner. State the similarities and differences.

c. What do you notice about the maximum number of x-intercepts and the degree of the function?

d. Use your graphs to determine the greatest number of extrema (absolute and relative) in each degree polynomial.

Type of Polynomial Function	Number of Extrema
Linear	
Quadratic	
Cubic	
Quartic	
Quintic	

e. What do you notice about the number of extrema and the degree of a polynomial? Write a statement to generalize the possible number of extrema in any degree polynomial function.

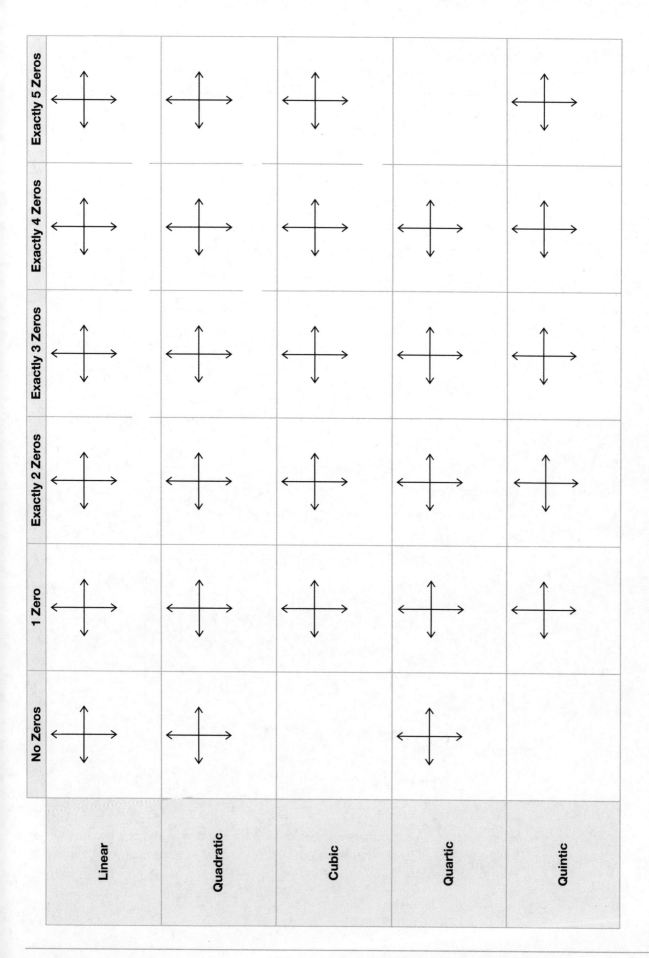

	No Zeros	1 Zero	Exactly 2 Zeros	Exactly 3 Zeros	Exactly 4 Zeros	Exactly 5 Zeros
Linear	✦	✦	✦	✦	✦	✦
Quadratic	✦	✦	✦	✦	✦	✦
Cubic		✦	✦	✦	✦	✦
Quartic	✦	✦	✦	✦	✦	
Quintic		✦	✦	✦	✦	✦

1. Use the coordinate plane to sketch a graph with the characteristics given. If the graph is not possible to sketch, explain why.

a. Characteristics:

- degree 4
- starts in quadrant III
- ends in quadrant IV
- relative maximum at $x = -4$
- absolute maximum at $x = 3$

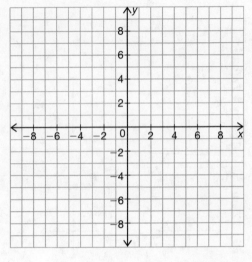

b. Characteristics:

- always increasing
- y-intercept at 5
- x-intercept at -1.7

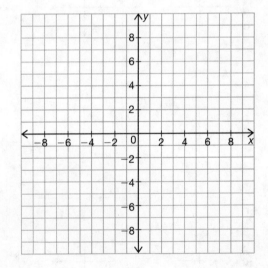

c. Characteristics:

- odd degree
- increases to $x = -3$, then decreases to $x = 3$, then increases
- absolute maximum at $y = 4$

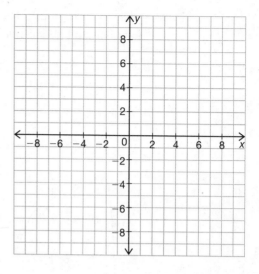

d. Characteristics:

- as $x \to \infty$, $f(x) \to \infty$
  as $x \to -\infty$, $f(x) \to \infty$
- 4 x-intercepts
- relative maximum at $y = 3$

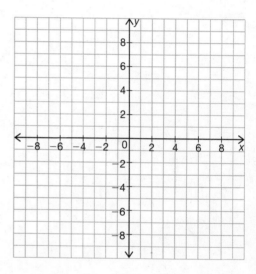

e. Characteristics:

- x-intercepts at -2, 2 and 5
- negative a value
- degree 2

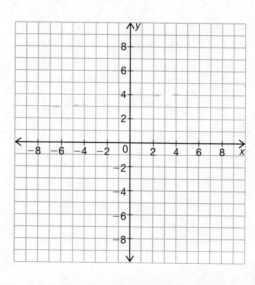

2. Analyze each graph. Circle the function(s) which could model the graph. Describe your reasoning to either eliminate or choose each function.

a.
$$f_1(x) = -3x^5 - 2x^2 + 4x + 7$$

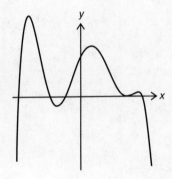

$$f_2(x) = -(x + 2)(x + 1.5)(x + 0.5)(x - 2.5)^2(x - 3)$$

$$f_3(x) = -3x^4 - 2x^2 + 4x + 7$$

b.
$$f_1(x) = 0.5(x + 7)(x + 1)(x - 5) - 3$$

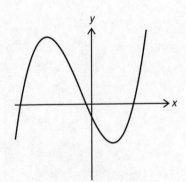

$$f_2(x) = -2(x + 7)(x + 1)(x - 5) - 3$$

$$f_3(x) = 2(x + 7)(x + 1)(x - 5)(x - 3)$$

Talk the Talk

Complete each table to summarize the key characteristics for quartics and quintics. The cubics table has been done for you.

	Cubics
All possible end behavior	As $x \to \infty$, $f(x) \to \infty$. As $x \to -\infty$, $f(x) \to -\infty$. As $x \to \infty$, $f(x) \to -\infty$. As $x \to -\infty$, $f(x) \to \infty$.
Possible number of x-intercept(s)	3, 2, or 1
Possible number of y-intercept(s)	1
Possible intervals of increase and decrease	• Always increasing • Always decreasing • Increasing, decreasing, increasing • Decreasing, increasing, decreasing
Number of possible relative extrema	2 or none
Number of possible absolute extrema	None

Quartics	
All possible end behavior	
Possible number of x-intercept(s)	
Possible number of y-intercept(s)	
Possible intervals of increase and decrease	
Number of possible relative extrema	
Number of possible absolute extrema	

Quintics	
All possible end behavior	
Possible number of x-intercept(s)	
Possible number of y-intercept(s)	
Possible intervals of increase and decrease	
Number of possible relative extrema	
Number of possible absolute extrema	

 Be prepared to share your solutions and methods.

That Graph Looks a Little Sketchy

Building Cubic and Quartic Functions

In this lesson, you will:

- Construct cubic functions graphically from three linear functions.
- Construct cubic functions graphically from one quadratic and one linear function.
- Connect graphical behavior of a cubic function to key characteristics of its factors.
- Construct quartic polynomial functions.
- Determine the number of real and imaginary roots for a polynomial function based on its factors.

People in the world today use a lot of energy, much more than previous generations. Consider modern conveniences people in the U.S. have in public spaces such as heating, air conditioning, lights, and electronic devices. Also, consider food products, clothes, and other goods that often travel halfway around the world on planes, ships, or trucks before ending up in U.S. shopping malls. Quite a bit of energy goes into getting these resources to you. People also travel much more these days than ever before. You may ride a bus to school and shop at a mall; adults may commute 30+ miles to work; business people may fly across the country to attend a conference. Compare this lifestyle to how people lived throughout the vast majority of history. People generally grew their own food, traveled on foot, and made their own clothes and wares. Is our lifestyle sustainable? In other words, can we continue using this much energy forever?

We use approximately 1.2 trillion gallons of gasoline each year. We also use tremendous amounts of coal and natural gas. The world's current energy consumption is so large that the numbers are difficult to even comprehend. The unit of measure Cubic Mile of Oil was developed to help make sense of it. A CMO is literally the amount of energy released by burning a cubic mile of oil. To visualize a cubic mile, imagine a huge cube-shaped container with length, width, and height of approximately 18 football fields. The energy from burning three of these containers of oil is the amount of energy we currently use in just one year. At this rate of consumption our natural gas reserves will be gone by 2080. Coal reserves will run out by 2150.

It is hard to imagine people voluntarily returning to a world without the conveniences we have today. However, natural resources are limited. What options do we have if we want our children to live a life filled with the conveniences that we currently enjoy?

So far in this chapter you've built a cubic function by multiplying three linear functions and by multiplying a linear function and a quadratic function. Let's explore how the properties of linear and quadratic functions determine the key characteristics of cubic functions.

1. Sketch a set of functions whose product builds a cubic function with the given characteristics. Explain your reasoning. Then list similarities and differences between your graphs and your classmates' graphs.

   a. zeros: $x = 0$, $x = 2$, and $x = -5$

   Explanation:

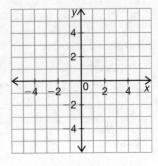

   Similarities/Differences:

Remember, you are not graphing the cubic—just the linear or quadratic functions that build it. Precise drawings aren't necessary here, just sketches with key characteristics.

You will learn more as you work through the lesson. At this point if you are unsure, experiment on your calculator, discuss with partners, and try a few things . . . that's how mathematicians work!

b. zeros: $x = -3$, $x = 4$ (multiplicity 2)

Explanation:

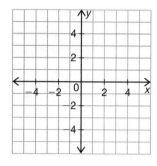

Which mathematical property guarantees that the zeros of a function must be the same as the zeros of its factors?

Similarities/Differences:

2. Alex and Derek disagree over which functions when multiplied together build a cubic function with zeros $x = 5$, $x = -1$ (multiplicity 2).

Alex

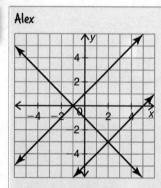

I sketched three linear functions, each with an x-intercept that matches the zero.

Derek

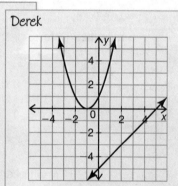

I sketched a parabola with vertex (−1, 0) and a line with x-intercept at (5, 0).

Who is correct? Explain your reasoning.

3. Sketch a set of functions whose product builds a cubic function with the given characteristics. Explain your reasoning. Then list similarities and differences between your graphs and your classmates' graphs.

    a. two imaginary zeros and a real zero

       Explanation:

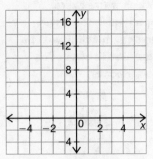

       Similarities/Differences:

    b. y-intercept of (0, 12)

       Explanation:

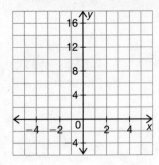

       Similarities/Differences:

    c. zero: $x = -4$ (multiplicity 3)

       Explanation:

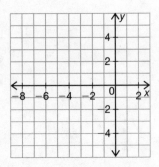

       Similarities/Differences:

5

d. The cubic function is in Quadrants II and IV only.

Explanation:

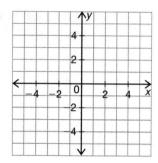

The product has to be in Quadrants II and IV, not necessarily the functions that build it. What determines direction? What determines the intercepts?

Similarities/Differences:

e. 3 imaginary roots

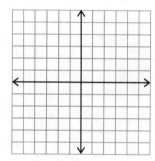

Explanation:

Similarities/Differences:

5

4. What are the possible combinations of real and imaginary roots that a cubic function can have? Explain your reasoning in terms of the functions that can build a cubic function.

Remember to include multiple roots.

5. Emily makes an observation about the number of imaginary zeros a cubic function may have.

Emily

A cubic function must have three zeros. I know this from the Fundamental Theorem. However, the number of real and imaginary zeros can vary. The function may have 0, 1, 2, or 3 imaginary zeros.

Explain the error in Emily's reasoning.

6. Augie, Kathryn, and Chili each wrote a cubic function with zeros at $x = 3$, $x = 1$, and $x = -4$.

Augie

The cubic function $f(x) = (x - 3)(x - 1)(x + 4)$ has the three zeros given. I can verify this by solving the equations $x - 3 = 0$, $x - 1 = 0$, and $x + 4 = 0$.

Kathryn

The cubic function $g(x) = 5(x - 3)(x - 1)(x + 4)$ has the three zeros given.

Chili

The cubic function $j(x) = (2x - 6)(3x - 3)(x + 4)$ has the three zeros given.

a. How does multiplying by a constant affect the graph of the function?

b. Why do the zeros remain the same after multiplying by a constant?

c. How many different cubic functions can you write from a given set of zeros?

7. Write two different cubic functions with the given characteristics.

a. zeros: $x = 2$, $x = 0$ and $x = -4$

b. zeros: $x = 0$, $x = 2i$, $x = -2i$

c. zeros: $x = 6$ (multiplicity 2) and $x = -5$

d. zeros: $x = 2$, $x = 3$, $x = 1$ and a y-intercept $(0, -24)$

e. the point $(1, 12)$ lies on the graph of the function

The factors and roots determine the general shape of a cubic function. The table summarizes all possible combinations of roots and factors for a cubic function.

Roots	Factors	Graph
1 real 2 imaginary	(linear factor) $\times$ (quadratic factor with 0 real roots)	
1 real (multiplicity 1) 1 real (multiplicity 2)	(linear factor) $\times$ (linear factor)^2	
1 real (multiplicity 3)	(linear factor)^3	
3 real distinct	(linear factor) $\times$ (linear factor) $\times$ (linear factor)	

Recall that the volume function $V(x) = x(18 - 2x)(12 - 2x)$ from Plant-A-Seed was built by multiplying three linear functions representing length, width, and height. It was also built from a quadratic function representing the area of the base and a linear function representing the height. You can sketch the graph of a cubic function by determining the *x*-intercepts and the intervals for which the output values of the factors are positive or negative.
The Plant-A-Seed example is shown.

The linear functions that represent the length, width, and height of the planter boxes from Plant-A-Seed are shown on the graph.

Description	Graphical Display
Graph each factor as an individual function. • The *x*-intercepts for each function are circled.	
Draw dashed vertical lines through the *x*-intercepts. • The coordinate plane is now divided into 4 sections: $(-\infty, 0)$, $(0, 6)$, $(6, 9)$ and $(9, \infty)$.	

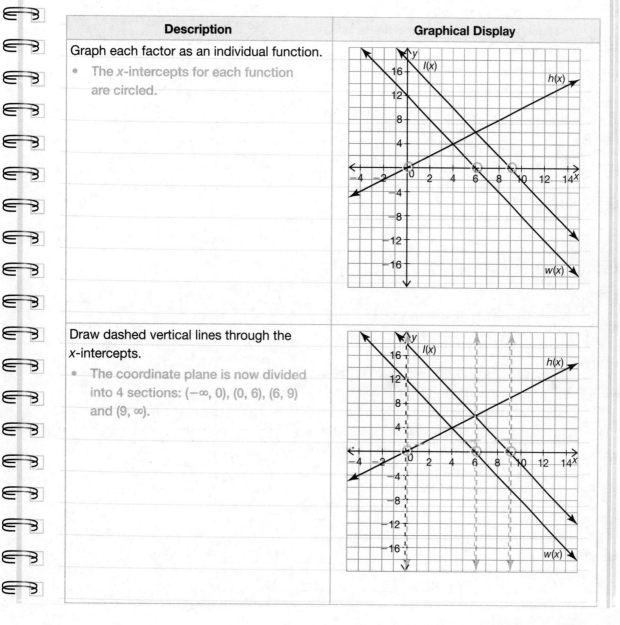

Determine whether the output values for each function in the interval are positive or negative.

- Values above the x-axis are positive.
- Values below the x-axis are negative.
- Determine the location of the cubic function by calculating whether the product of the factors is positive or negative over each interval.

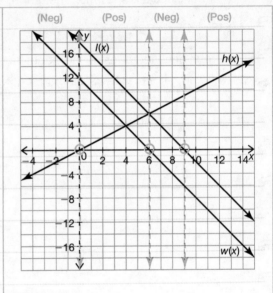

- Use the x-intercepts and the sign of the output value over each interval to sketch the graph.
- The new function will cross the x-axis at each of the x-intercepts as the factors.
- The graph will increase or decrease depending on whether the output is positive or negative as it moves from one interval to the next.

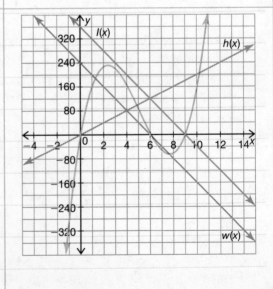

1. Analyze the worked example.

   a. Given the three functions $l(x)$, $w(x)$, and $h(x)$, summarize how to determine when $V(x)$ lies above or below the x-axis.

   b. Why must the volume function intersect the x-axis at $(0, 0)$, $(6, 0)$, $(9, 0)$?

   c. Is it possible for a function to have a zero that is different from its factors? Explain your reasoning.

2. Sketch the graph of the cubic function that is the product of the 3 linear functions shown. Show all work and explain your reasoning.

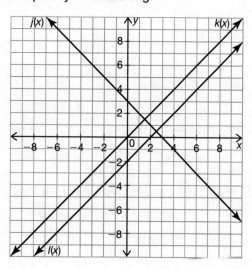

3. Sketch the graph of the cubic function that is the product of the quadratic and linear functions shown. Show all work and explain your reasoning.

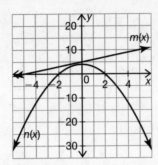

The process is the same as before. Focus on the zeros and the intervals over which the output is positive or negative.

4. In Question 2 you graphically determined the product of the functions $f(x) = 3 - x$, $g(x) = x$ and $h(x) = x - 2$.

    a. Determine the product of the functions algebraically.

    b. Verify your sketch by graphing the product on a graphing calculator.

5. In Question 3 you graphically determined the product of the functions $j(x) = 4 - x^2$ and $k(x) = x + 5$

    a. Determine the product of the functions algebraically.

    b. Verify your sketch by graphing the product on a graphing calculator.

Anyone Have Change for a Quartic?

 In Problems 1 and 2, you determined that a cubic function has 3 zeros. The zeros may be real, imaginary, or have multiplicity depending on the key characteristics of the functions that built it. Similarly, the Fundamental Theorem of Algebra guarantees that a quartic function has 4 zeros. The key characteristics of the quartic function also vary depending on the functions that built it.

 1. Analyze the linear, quadratic, and cubic functions that are shown.

$$f(x) = x \qquad g(x) = -x + 2 \qquad m(x) = x^2 - 2x - 5$$

$$p(x) = x^2 + 4 \qquad r(x) = (x + 2)^2 \qquad w(x) = x^3$$

a. List the number and type of zeros for each function provided.

b. List 5 possible sets of functions from the list that multiply to build a quartic function.

You may use a function more than once.

5

2. Complete each statement with *always*, *sometimes*, or *never*. Explain your reasoning.

   a. A quartic function _____ has 4 real roots.

   b. A function of the nth degree _____ has n roots.

   c. The number of x-intercepts _____ matches the number of roots of a function.

   d. A function _____ has imaginary roots.

   e. A function _____ has an odd number of imaginary roots.

3. Analyze the table shown. The function $h(x)$ is the product of $f(x)$ and $g(x)$.

x	$f(x)$	$g(x)$	$h(x) = f(x) \cdot g(x)$
−2	8	4	32
−1	5	1	5
0	4	0	0
1	5	1	5
2	8	4	32
3	13	9	117

   a. Determine whether $h(x)$ is a quartic function. Explain your reasoning.

   b. Determine the number of real and imaginary zeros of $h(x)$. Explain your reasoning.

   c. Describe the end behavior of $h(x)$. How does this help you determine whether the function is quartic or not?

4. Analyze the table shown. The function $m(x)$ is the product of $j(x)$ and $k(x)$.

x	j(x)	k(x)	m(x) = j(x) · k(x)
−2	4	−1	−4
−1	0	0	0
0	−2	1	−2
1	−2	2	−4
2	0	3	0
3	4	4	16

a. Determine whether $m(x)$ is a quartic function. Explain your reasoning.

b. Determine the number of real and imaginary zeros for the function $m(x)$. Explain your reasoning.

c. Describe the end behavior of $m(x)$. How does this help you determine whether the function is quartic or not?

5

5. Gavin explains the relationship between the imaginary zeros of a polynomial function and the table of values for that function. Henry disagrees.

> **Gavin**
>
> A polynomial function with imaginary zeros has imaginary numbers in the table of values. For example, the function $x^2 + 4$ has 2 imaginary zeros. These values appear in the table.

> **Henry**
>
> It is impossible for a polynomial function to have imaginary numbers in the table of values. A real input value must have a real output value.

Who is correct? Explain your reasoning.

6. Sketch a set of functions whose product builds a quartic function with the given characteristics. Explain your reasoning. Determine similarities and differences between your graphs and your classmates' graphs.

a. two imaginary roots and a double root

Explanation:

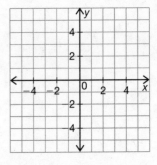

Similarities/Differences:

b. four distinct roots and a *y*-intercept of (0, −24)

Explanation:

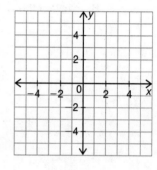

Similarities/Differences:

c. located in Quadrants III and IV only

Explanation:

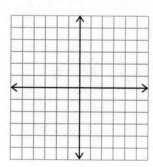

Similarities/Differences:

d. located in quadrants II and IV only

Explanation:

Similarities/Differences:

7. What function types can be multiplied together to build a new function of degree 5? How many total zeros will the function have? How many can be imaginary?

8. Explain the possible ways to build a function of degree *n*?

 Be prepared to share your solutions and methods.

Closing Time
The Closure Property

LEARNING GOALS

In this lesson, you will:

- Compare functions that are closed under addition, subtraction, and multiplication to functions that are not closed under these operations.
- Analyze the meaning for polynomials to be closed under an operation.
- Compare integer and polynomial operations.

KEY TERM

- closed under an operation

The word "closure" can mean many things depending on the context.

- In business, closure is a process in which an organization can no longer operate. For instance, closure for a business may be caused by an organization going bankrupt.
- In psychology, closure is a person's emotional need for the conclusion of a difficult event in their life.
- In government, closure, which is also referred to as "cloture," is a procedure by which the Senate can vote to place a time limit on consideration of a bill.

Closure is also an important term in mathematics. Can you think of any other meanings for the word closure?

In this chapter you have learned the properties of polynomials in different representations.

Graphically, polynomials are:	Algebraically, polynomials are:	In a table of values, polynomials are:
• smooth • continuous • increase or decrease to infinity as x approaches positive or negative infinity	• written in the form $ax^n + bx^{n-1} + \cdots$	• made up of real numbers • increase or decrease to infinity as x approaches positive or negative infinity

You have studied many different types of functions. A function has a unique output for every input value. However, a function does not necessarily have to be a polynomial function.

1. Sketch the graphs of two functions that are not polynomial functions. Explain your reasoning.

   a.

   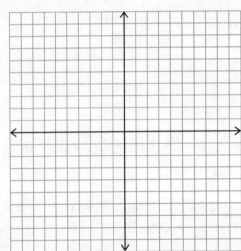

   b.

   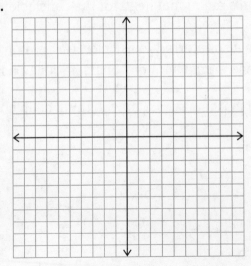

2. Analyze the graphs of the functions shown. Describe why each function is not a polynomial function.

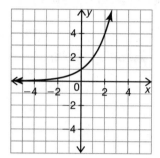

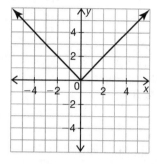

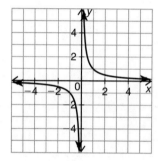

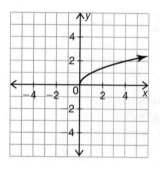

Throughout this chapter you added, subtracted, or multiplied two or more polynomial functions to build a new polynomial function. You did this using a graph, algebra, and a table of values. When an operation is performed on any number or expression in a set and the result is in the same set, it is said to be **closed under that operation**. Are polynomials closed under addition, subtraction, and multiplication? In other words, when you add, subtract, or multiply polynomial functions, will you *always* create another polynomial function?

Before answering this question, let's analyze closure within the real number system.

Recall how it is a useful mathematical practice to compare abstract topics to what we already know about real numbers.

5

3. Determine whether each set within the Real Number System is closed under addition, subtraction, multiplication, and division.

    a. Complete the table. If a set is not closed under a given operation, provide a counterexample.

	Addition	Subtraction	Multiplication	Division
Natural Numbers {1, 2, 3, 4, . . .}				
Whole Numbers {0, 1, 2, 3, . . .}	Yes	No 2 − 3 = −1		
Integers {. . . −2, −1, 0, 1, 2 . . .}				
Rational Can be represented as the ratio of two integers				
Irrational Cannot be represented as the ratio of two integers				

    b. What patterns do you notice?

The sum of 2 whole numbers is always another whole number. Therefore, whole numbers are closed under addition. Whole numbers are not closed under subtraction. The counterexample is 2 − 3 = −1, since −1 is not a whole number. Experiment with other sets of numbers to determine whether they are closed.

4. Determine whether polynomial functions are closed under addition, subtraction, multiplication, and division?

a. Write 5 polynomials with various degrees that you will use to explore closure.

$$y_1 = \underline{\hspace{2cm}} \qquad\qquad y_2 = \underline{\hspace{2cm}}$$

$$y_3 = \underline{\hspace{2cm}}$$

$$y_4 = \underline{\hspace{2cm}} \qquad\qquad y_5 = \underline{\hspace{2cm}}$$

b. Determine whether the polynomials are closed under addition, subtraction, multiplication, and division. Show all work and explain your reasoning.

Take some time to explore closure by performing operations with various polynomials. Experiment algebraically and graphically and see what happens, then make a conjecture – that's what mathematicians do!

c. How do you know when a polynomial is not closed under a given operation? Explain your reasoning in terms of the graph, table, and algebraic representation.

d. Have you proven that polynomials are closed under a given operation? Have you proven that polynomials are not closed under a given operation? Explain your reasoning.

Okay Then, Prove It!

 In the previous problem, *Closed For Business*, you conjectured that integers and polynomials are both closed under addition, subtraction, and multiplication. You also determined through counterexamples that integers and polynomials are not closed under division.

1. Similarities between integer and polynomial operations are shown in the table.

	Integer Example	**Polynomial Example**
Addition	$\begin{array}{r} 400 + 30 + 7 \\ +\quad\ 20 + 5 \\ \hline 400 + 50 + 12 \end{array}$	$\begin{array}{r} 4x^2 + 3x + 7 \\ +\quad 2x + 5 \\ \hline 4x^2 + 5x + 12 \end{array}$
Subtraction	$\begin{array}{r} 400 + 30 + 7 \\ -\quad (20 + 5) \\ \hline 400 + 10 + 2 \end{array}$	$\begin{array}{r} 4x^2 + 3x + 7 \\ -\quad (2x + 5) \\ \hline 4x^2 + x + 2 \end{array}$
Multiplication	$\begin{array}{r} 400 + 30 + 7 \\ \times\quad\ 20 + 5 \\ \hline 2000 + 150 + 35 \\ 8000 + 600 + 140\quad\ \\ \hline 8000 + 2600 + 290 + 35 \end{array}$	$\begin{array}{r} 4x^2 + 3x + 7 \\ \times\quad\ 2x + 5 \\ \hline 20x^2 + 15x + 35 \\ 8x^3 + 6x^2 + 14x\quad\ \\ \hline 8x^3 + 26x^2 + 29x + 35 \end{array}$
Division	$\dfrac{437}{25} = 17\ R12$	$\dfrac{4x^2 + 3x + 7}{2x + 5} = (2x - 3)\ R(-x + 22)$

 a. Describe the similarities between polynomial and integer operations.

b. In what ways is the distributive property essential to performing operations with integers and polynomials?

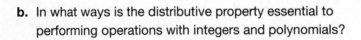 

For part d, consider the integer example. How would you verify that $\dfrac{437}{25} = 17\ R12$?

c. How does this example demonstrate that polynomials are not closed under division?

 d. Verify that the polynomial division was performed correctly.

You have explored operations under various polynomials. It appears as though polynomials are closed under addition, subtraction, and multiplication, but these examples do not constitute a proof. The real number system is closed, but discovering that polynomials are analogous to the real number system does not allow you to assume that polynomials are also closed. The worked example shows you how to formally prove that polynomials are closed under addition.

Consider the two polynomial functions $f(x)$ and $g(x)$.

$f(x) = a_n x^n + a_{n-1} x^{n-1} + \cdots + a_1 x + a_0$

$g(x) = b_n x^n + b_{n-1} x^{n-1} + \cdots + b_1 x + b_0$

You can show that the polynomials are closed under addition.

Step 1: Write the sum $f(x) + g(x)$. Because the polynomials have multiple terms, it is best to arrange the sum vertically.

$$a_n x^n + a_{n-1} x^{n-1} + \cdots + a_1 x + a_0$$
$$+\ b_n x^n + b_{n-1} x^{n-1} + \cdots + b_1 x + b_0$$

Step 2: Add the polynomials by combining like terms.

$$a_n x^n + a_{n-1} x^{n-1} + \cdots + a_1 x + a_0$$
$$+\ b_n x^n + b_{n-1} x^{n-1} + \cdots + b_1 x + b_0$$
$$(a_n + b_n)x^n + (a_{n-1} + b_{n-1})x^{n-1} + \cdots + (a_1 + b_1)x + (a_0 + b_0)$$

Step 3: In the sum, each coefficient is of the form $a_n + b_n$.
A coefficient $a_n + b_n$ is a real number because a_n and b_n are real numbers, and the real numbers are closed under addition.

Step 4: The sum of the polynomials $f(x)$ and $g(x)$ is in the form of a polynomial function with a real coefficient. Therefore, polynomials are closed under addition.

> Remember, like terms are terms that have identical variables and exponents.

2. Consider the two polynomial functions $f(x)$ and $g(x)$.

$$f(x) = a_n x^n + a_{n-1} x^{n-1} + \cdots + a_1 x + a_0$$

$$g(x) = b_n x^n + b_{n-1} x^{n-1} + \cdots + b_1 x + b_0$$

a. Prove that polynomials are closed under subtraction.

b. Use the multiplication table to prove that polynomials are closed under multiplication.

$\bullet$	$a_n x^n$	$a_{n-1} x^{n-1}$	$\cdots$	$a_1 x$	a_0
$b_n x^n$					
$b_{n-1} x^{n-1}$					
$\vdots$					
$b_1 x$					
b_0					

Be prepared to share your solutions and methods.

Chapter 5 Summary

- relative maximum (5.1)
- relative minimum (5.1)
- cubic function (5.1)
- multiplicity (5.1)
- power function (5.2)
- end behavior (5.2)

- symmetric about a line (5.2)
- symmetric about a point (5.2)
- even function (5.2)
- odd function (5.2)
- polynomial function (5.3)

- quartic function (5.3)
- quintic function (5.3)
- absolute maximum (5.4)
- absolute minimum (5.4)
- extrema (5.4)
- closed under an operation (5.6)

5.1 Representing Cubic Functions Using Words, Tables, and Equations and Identifying Key Characteristics

The formula for volume: $V = l \cdot w \cdot h$ can represent a cubic function when length and width are given in terms of height. Each value can be shown in a table and the final formula as a function of one variable. The key characteristics of a function may be different within a given domain. As the input values for height increase, the output values for volume approach infinity. Therefore, the function doesn't have a maximum. But, it can have a relative maximum, or a highest point in a particular section of a graph. Similarly, as the values for height decrease, the output values approach negative infinity. Therefore, a relative minimum can occur at the lowest point in that particular section of a graph.

Example

The relative maximum is circled.

Height of Box (in.)	Width of Box (in.)	Length of Box (in.)	Volume of Box (cu. in.)
0	6	12	0
1	5	11	55
2	4	10	80
3	3	9	81
4	2	8	64
5	1	7	35
6	0	6	0
h	$6 - h$	$12 - h$	$h(6 - h)(12 - h)$

5

5.1 Building Cubic Functions From Linear and Quadratic Functions

A cubic function is a polynomial function of degree three. When multiplying three linear factors, the result is always a cubic function. First choose two of the factors to multiply and combine like terms. Then, multiply that product with the remaining factor and combine like terms. The original expression and the new expression can be graphed to verify that they are equivalent.

Example

$$\begin{aligned}(2x - 1)(3x + 2)(x - 5) &= (6x^2 + 4x - 3x - 2)(x - 5)\\ &= (6x^2 + x - 2)(x - 5)\\ &= 6x^3 - 30x^2 + x^2 - 5x - 2x + 10\\ &= 6x^3 - 29x^2 - 7x + 10\end{aligned}$$

The graph of the original expression and the final expression are the same, so the product is correct.

$$\begin{aligned}(12 - 5x - x^2)(3x + 1) &= 36x + 12 - 15x^2 - 5x - 3x^3 - x^2\\ &= -3x^3 - 16x^2 + 31x + 12\end{aligned}$$

The graph of the original expression and the final expression are the same, so the product is correct.

5.2 Determining the General Behavior of the Graph of Even and Odd Degree Power Functions

A power function is a function of the form $P(x) = ax^n$, where n is a non-negative integer. The graph of a power function raised to an odd degree increases from left to right (or right to left if $a < 0$), flattening near the origin, as the absolute value of the power increases. The graph of a power function raised to an even degree is a concave up (or down if $a < 0$) parabola, flattening near the origin as the absolute value of the power increases. The end behavior for even and odd degree power functions can be described as:

	Odd Degree Power Function	Even Degree Power Function
$a > 0$	As $x \to \infty$, $f(x) \to \infty$. As $x \to -\infty$, $f(x) \to -\infty$.	As $x \to \infty$, $f(x) \to \infty$. As $x \to -\infty$, $f(x) \to \infty$.
$a < 0$	As $x \to \infty$, $f(x) \to -\infty$. As $x \to -\infty$, $f(x) \to \infty$.	As $x \to \infty$, $f(x) \to -\infty$. As $x \to -\infty$, $f(x) \to -\infty$.

Example

x^{12}

As $x \to \infty$, $f(x) \to \infty$.

As $x \to -\infty$, $f(x) \to \infty$.

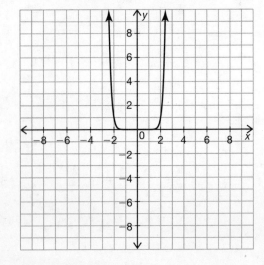

Using a Graph to Determine the Symmetry of Even and Odd Functions

If a graph is symmetric about a line, the line divides the graph into two identical parts. Special attention is given to the line of symmetry when it is the y-axis, as it tells you that the function is even. The graph of an odd degree basic power function is symmetric about a point, in particular the origin. A function is symmetric about a point if each point on the graph has a point the same distance from the central point but in the opposite direction. Special attention is given when the central point is the origin as it determines that the function is odd. When the point of symmetry is the origin, the graph is reflected across the x-axis and the y-axis. If you replace both (x, y) with $(-x, -y)$, the function remains the same. You can think of the point of symmetry about the origin, as a double reflection. An even function has a graph symmetric about the y-axis, thus $f(x) = f(-x)$. An odd function has a graph symmetric about the origin, thus $f(x) = -f(-x)$.

Example

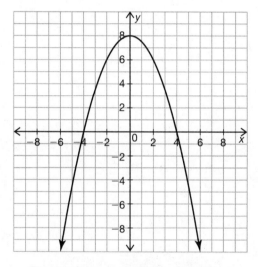

The function is even because it is symmetrical about the y-axis.

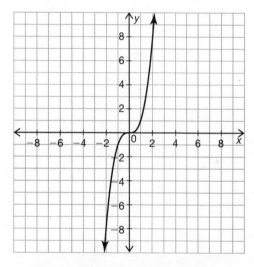

The function is odd because it is symmetrical about the origin.

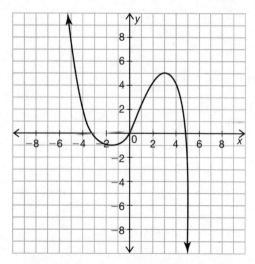

The function is neither even nor odd because it is not symmetrical.

Determining Whether a Function Is Even or Odd Based on an Algebraic Function

An even function has a graph symmetric about the y-axis, thus $f(x) = f(-x)$. An odd function has a graph symmetric about the origin, thus $f(x) = -f(-x)$. So, solve $f(x)$ for $-x$ and solve for $-f(x)$ and compare.

Example

$m(x) = 4x^5 - 2x^2$

$m(-x) = 4(-x)^5 - 2(-x)^2$

$m(-x) = -4x^5 + 2x^2$

$-m(x) = -(4x^5 - 2x^2)$

$-m(x) = -4x^5 + 2x^2$

$m(-x) = -m(x)$ thus $m(x)$ is odd.

Using Reference Points to Dilate, Reflect, and Translate Cubic and Quartic Functions

Reference points are a set of points of a basic function that are used to graph the function. The graph of the basic cubic function is symmetric about the origin. So, $f(x) = -f(-x)$. Use symmetry to determine two other points from the reference points. Rigid motions performed on a function $f(x)$ to form a new function $g(x)$ can be described by $g(x) = Af(B(x - C)) + D$. The table shows the coordinates of $g(x)$ after each type of rigid motion performed on $f(x)$.

Type of Rigid Motion Performed on $f(x)$	Coordinates of $f(x) \rightarrow$ Coordinates of $g(x)$
Vertical Dilation by a Factor of A	$(x, y) \rightarrow (x, Ay)$
Horizontal Dilation by a Factor of B	$(x, y) \rightarrow \left(\frac{1}{B}x, y\right)$
Horizontal Translation of C units	$(x, y) \rightarrow (x + C, y)$
Vertical Translation of D units	$(x, y) \rightarrow (x, y + D)$
All four rigid motions (A, B, C, and D)	$(x, y) \rightarrow \left(\frac{1}{B}x + C, Ay + D\right)$

Example

$m(x) = x^4$

$p(x) = -m(x) + 2$

Reference Points on $m(x)$	$\rightarrow$	Corresponding Points on $p(x)$
(0, 0)	$\rightarrow$	(0, 2)
(1, 1)	$\rightarrow$	(1, 1)
(2, 16)	$\rightarrow$	(2, −14)

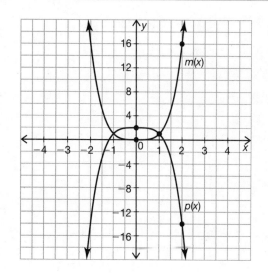

The line of reflection is $y = 2$.
The function $p(x)$ is an even function.

5.3 Describing the Rigid Motions and Writing Cubic and Quartic Functions That Have Been Dilated, Reflected, or Translated

The table shows the effects of rigid motions on basic cubic and quartic functions. Rigid motions performed on a function $f(x)$ to form a new function $g(x)$ can be described by $g(x) = Af(B(x - C)) + D$. Observe how corresponding points have changed on a graph and use the data to write the new function. Or, describe the rigid motions based on the equation of the transformed function in terms of the original function.

Rigid Motion	New Transformed Function $p(x)$ in Terms of $q(x)$
Vertical Stretch Dilation	$p(x) = Aq(x)$, $|A| > 1$
Vertical Compression Dilation	$p(x) = Aq(x)$, $0 < |A| < 1$
Horizontal Stretch Dilation	$p(x) = q(Bx)$, $0 < |B| < 1$
Horizontal Compression Dilation	$p(x) = q(Bx)$, $|B| > 1$
Reflection across x-axis	$p(x) = -q(x)$
Reflection across y-axis	$p(x) = q(-x)$
Vertical Translation	$p(x) = q(x) + D$
Horizontal Translation	$p(x) = q(x - C)$

Example

$g(x) = x^3$

$f(x) = 0.5g(x - 1) + 2$

$A = 0.5$
$C = 1$
$D = 2$

$(x, y) \rightarrow (x + 1, 0.5y + 2)$

The graph of the function $g(x)$ has been vertically compressed by a factor of 0.5, translated 1 unit to the right, and 2 units up.

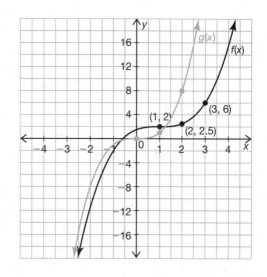

$f(x) = 0.5g(x - 1) + 2$

$\quad = 0.5(x - 1)^3 + 2$

$\quad = 0.5(x^3 - 3x^2 + 3x - 1) + 2$

$\quad = 0.5x^3 - 1.5x^2 + 1.5x + 1.5$

5.3 Using Power Functions to Build Cubic, Quartic, and Quintic Functions

A polynomial function is a function that can be written in the form

$$p(x) = a_n x^n + a_{n-1} x^{n-1} + \cdots + a_2 x^2 + a_1 x + a_0$$

where the coefficients a_n, a_{n-1}, ... a_2, a_1, a_0 are complex numbers and the exponents are nonnegative integers. The form shown here is called the standard form of a polynomial. A third degree polynomial function has a special name—a cubic function. A quartic function is a fourth degree polynomial function. A quintic function is a fifth degree polynomial function. Basic power functions, such as $f(x) = x^2$, $f(x) = x^3$, $f(x) = x^4$, etc, can be transformed and combined to create more complex polynomial functions.

Example

$f(x) = x$; $g(x) = x^2$

$a(x) = 2g(x) - 3f(x)$

x	g(x)	f(x)	a(x)
−2	4	−2	14
−1	1	−1	5
0	0	0	0
1	1	1	−1
2	4	2	2

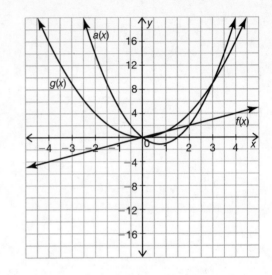

$a(x) = 2x^2 - 3x$

5.4 Determining the Number of Possible Extrema for a Polynomial

The relative maximum and minimum are the highest and lowest point in a particular section of a graph. Similarly, absolute maximum is the highest point in the entire graph, and absolute minimum is the lowest point in the entire graph. The set of absolute maximums, absolute minimums, relative maximums, and relative minimums may also be referred to as extrema. The extrema are also called extreme points and extremum. The maximum number of extrema is one less than the degree of the polynomial. The possible number of extrema is always a difference of 2. The possible number of extrema for an odd degree polynomial is even. The possible number of extrema for an even degree polynomial is odd.

Example

A 9th degree polynomial can have 0, 2, 4, 6, or 8 extrema.

Determining the Correct Graph and Function of a Polynomial Given Key Characteristics

Key characteristics of polynomial function such as the number and kind of extrema, the end behavior, the a-value, degree of the function, intercepts, etc., can be used to sketch the graph of the polynomial. These characteristics can also be gleaned from the function and the correct polynomial function matched to the graph.

Example

Characteristics:

- even degree polynomial
- negative a-value
- y-intercept of -2
- x-intercepts of 1 and 2

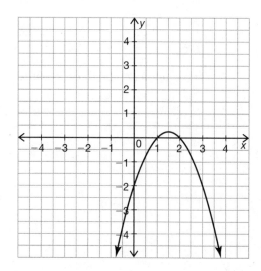

Circle the possible function(s) to represent the graph:

$f_1(x) = (x - 1)(x - 2)$

This function can be eliminated because it does not have a negative a-value.

$f_2(x) = -x^2 + 3x - 2$

This function matches the graph because it has a negative a-value, an even degree, a y-intercept of -2, and can be factored into $(-x + 1)(x - 2)$ which gives x-intercepts of 1 and 2.

$f_3(x) = -x^3 + 2x^2 - x + 1$

This function can be eliminated because it has an odd degree.

5

Determining Linear and Quadratic Functions That Would Construct a Cubic Function With Key Characteristics

Cubic functions can be built by multiplying three linear functions or by multiplying a linear function and a quadratic function. Key characteristics of cubic functions, such as zeros and y-intercepts can be used to determine the linear and quadratic functions whose product builds that cubic function.

Example

zeros are $x = 0$, $x = -4$, and $x = 2$

The graphs can be three linear functions or one linear and one quadratic.

The following functions represent one possible solution.

$f(x) = x$

$g(x) = (x + 4)$

$h(x) = (x - 2)$

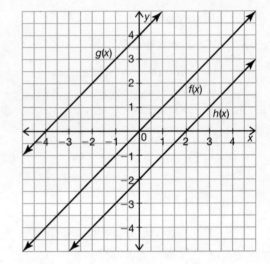

Constructing Cubic Functions Graphically From Linear and Quadratic Functions

The graph of a cubic function can be sketched by graphing the linear and quadratic factors of the function. Divide the graph into vertical sections at the x-intercepts. Determine whether the output values for each function in the interval are positive or negative. Values above the x-axis are positive. Values below the x-axis are negative. Determine the location of the cubic function by calculating whether the product of the factors is positive or negative over each interval. Use the x-intercepts and the sign of the output value over each interval to sketch the graph. The new function will cross the x-axis at each of the x-intercepts as the factors. The graph will increase or decrease depending on whether the output is positive or negative as it moves from one interval to the next.

Example

$h(x) = -x^2 + 1$

$g(x) = x - 3$

$m(x) = h(x) \cdot g(x)$

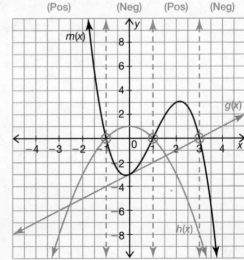

5.5 Graphing Linear and Quadratic Functions That Would Construct a Quartic Function With Key Characteristics

Quartic functions can be built by multiplying two quadratic functions, four linear functions, or a linear function and a cubic function. Key characteristics of quartic functions, such as zeros and y-intercepts can be used to determine the linear and quadratic functions whose product builds that quartic function.

Example

zeros are $x = 0$, $x = 1$, and $x = 2$ (multiplicity 2)

The graphs can be 4 linear functions, 1 quadratic and 2 linear functions, 1 linear and 1 cubic, or two quadratics. The following functions represent one possible solution.

$f(x) = (x^2 - x)$

$g(x) = (x - 2)^2$

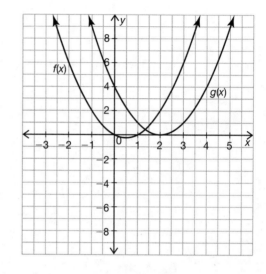

5.6 Determining Whether a Graph Represents a Polynomial or Not

The graph of a polynomial function is smooth, continuous, and increases or decreases to infinity as x approaches positive or negative infinity.

Example

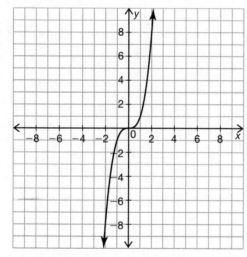

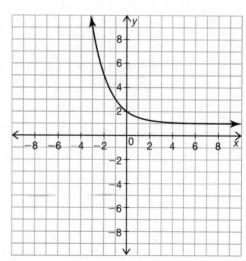

The graph is a polynomial function because it is continuous and increases as x approaches positive infinity and decreases as x approaches negative infinity.

The graph is not of a polynomial function because as x approaches positive infinity, the graph approaches 0 instead of positive or negative infinity.

Determining Whether a Set Is Closed or Not Under Multiple Operations

When an operation is performed on any number or expression in a set and the result is in the same set, it is said to be closed under that operation.

Example

Is the set of integers closed under subtraction?

$-4 - 8 = -12$

Yes. The set of integers is closed under subtraction.

Determining Whether Polynomials Are Closed or Not Under Multiple Operations

Polynomials are closed under addition, subtraction, and multiplication. The sum, difference, and product is always another polynomial. They are not closed under division: the algebraic and graphical representations are not polynomials, the graph is not a smooth, continuous curve that approaches positive or negative infinity as x increases or decreases to infinity, and the algebraic representation is not in the correct form.

Example

Is the set of polynomials closed under addition?

$y_1 = -4x^3 + 2x^2 - x + 3$
$y_2 = 5x^3 - 2x^2 - 4$

$$\begin{array}{r} -4x^3 + 2x^2 - x + 3 \\ +5x^3 - 2x^2 \quad\quad - 4 \\ \hline x^3 \quad\quad - x - 1 \end{array}$$

Yes. The set is polynomials are closed under addition because the sum is a polynomial.

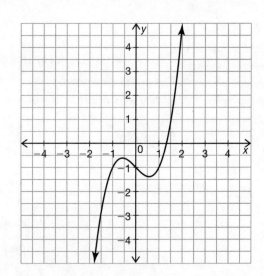

Polynomial Expressions and Equations

6

This is a really close-up picture of rain. Really. The picture represents falling water broken down into molecules, each with two hydrogen atoms connected to one oxygen atom: H_2O!

423

Don't Take This Out of Context

Analyzing Polynomial Functions

The *kill screen* is a term for a stage in a video game where the game stops or acts oddly for no apparent reason. More common in classic video games, the cause may be a software bug, a mistake in the program, or an error in the game design. A well-known kill screen example occurs in the classic game *Donkey Kong*. When a skilled player reaches level 22, the game stops just seconds into Mario's quest to rescue the princess. Game over even though the player did not do anything to end the game!

Video game technology has advanced dramatically over the last several decades, so these types of errors are no longer common. Games have evolved from simple movements of basic shapes to real-time adventures involving multiple players from all over the globe.

How do you think video games will change over the next decade?

Play Is Our Work

The polynomial function $p(x)$ models the profits of Zorzansa, a video game company, from its original business plan through its first few years in business.

Zorzansa's Profits

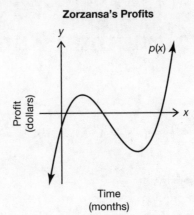

1. Label the portion(s) of the graph that model each of the memorable events in the company's history by writing the letter directly on the graph. Explain your reasoning.

    a. The Chief Executive Officer anxiously meets with her accountant.

    Several answers may be correct as long as you can defend your reasoning. The events are not necessarily written in chronological order.

    b. The highly anticipated game, *Rage of Destructive Fury II*, is released.

    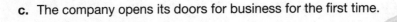

    c. The company opens its doors for business for the first time.

    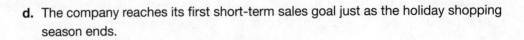

    d. The company reaches its first short-term sales goal just as the holiday shopping season ends.

6

e. The company breaks even.

f. Members of the Board of Directors get in a heated debate over the next move the company should make.

g. The game design team is fired after their 2 game releases, *Leisurely Sunday Drive* and *Peaceful Resolution*, delight many parents but sell poorly.

No model is perfect for real data, though some are more appropriate than others. In what ways does this cubic model make sense? In what ways does it not make sense?

h. A large conglomerate buys the company.

2. Do you think this cubic function is an appropriate model for this scenario? Explain your reasoning.

6

PROBLEM 2   **There's Nothing "Average" About This Rate of Change**

 The cubic function $p(x)$ models Zorzansa's total profits over the first five years of business.

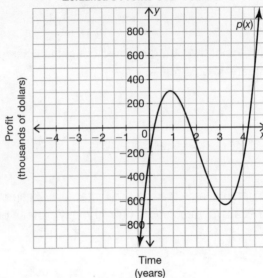

Zorzansa's Profits Over Years 0 – 5

 1. Use the graph to estimate when Zorzansa's achieved each profit. Then explain how you determined your estimate.

a. $800,000

What is the maximum number of solutions for a given profit?

b. $200,000

c. greater than $200,000

6

d. the company is losing money

e. the company is making a profit.

2. Avi and Ariella disagree about the end behavior of the function.

Avi

The end behavior is incorrect. As time increases, profit approaches infinity. It doesn't make sense that the profits are increasing before the company even opens.

Ariella

The end behavior is correct. The function is cubic with a positive a-value. This means as x approaches infinity, y approaches infinity. As x approaches negative infinity, y also approaches negative infinity.

Who is correct? Explain your reasoning.

The **average rate of change** of a function is the ratio of the change in the dependent variable to the change in the independent variable over a specific interval. The formula for average rate of change is $\frac{f(b) - f(a)}{b - a}$ for the interval (a, b). The expression $b - a$ represents the change in the input values of the function f. The expression $f(b) - f(a)$ represents the change in the output values of the function f as the input values change from a to b.

You've already calculated average rates of change when determining slope, miles per hour, or miles per gallon. It's the change in y divided by the change in x.

You can determine the average rate of change of Zorzansa's profit for the time interval (3.25, 4.25).

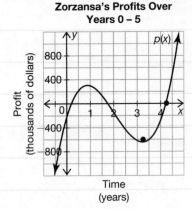

Zorzansa's Profits Over Years 0 – 5

Profit (thousands of dollars)

Time (years)

Substitute the input and output values into the average rate of change formula.

$$\frac{f(b) - f(a)}{b - a} = \frac{f(4.25) - f(3.25)}{4.25 - 3.25}$$

Simplify the expression.

$$= \frac{0 - (-600)}{1}$$

$$= \frac{600}{1} = 600$$

The average rate of change for the time interval (3.25, 4.25) is approximately $600,000 per year.

3. Analyze the worked example.

    a. Explain why the average rate of change is $600,000 per year, and not $600 per year.

    b. Explain why the average rate of change is positive over this interval.

    c. What does the average rate of change represent in this problem situation?

4. Determine the average rate of change of Zorzansa's profits for the time interval (1, 3).

5. Sam has a theory about the average rate of change.

> **Sam**
>
> I can quickly estimate the average rate of change for intervals that are above and below the x-axis because they add to zero. For example, at year 1, the profit is about $300,000 and at year 2.25 the profit is about −$300,000. Therefore, the average rate of change for the time interval (1, 2.25) is approximately $0.

Describe the error in Sam's reasoning.

6. After 4.5 years, would you consider Zorzansa a successful business? Explain your reasoning.

  Be prepared to share your solutions and methods.

The Great Polynomial Divide

Polynomial Division

Did you ever notice how little things can sometimes add up to make a huge difference? Consider something as small and seemingly insignificant as a light bulb. For example, a compact fluorescent lamp (CFL) uses less energy than "regular" bulbs. Converting to CFLs seems like a good idea, but you might wonder: how much good can occur from changing one little light bulb? The answer is a lot—especially if you convince others to do it as well. According to the U.S. Department of Energy, if each home in the United States replaced one light bulb with a CFL, it would have the same positive environmental effect as taking 1 million cars off the road!

If a new product such as the CFL can have such a dramatic impact on the environment, imagine the effect that other new products can have. A group of Canadian students designed a car that gets over 2,500 miles per gallon, only to be topped by a group of French students whose car gets nearly 7,000 miles per gallon! What impacts on the environment can you describe if just 10% of the driving population used energy efficient cars? Can all of these impacts be seen as positive?

The previous function-building lessons showed how the factors of a polynomial determine its key characteristics. From the factors, you can determine the type and location of a polynomial's zeros. Algebraic reasoning often allows you to reverse processes and work backwards. Specifically in this problem, you will determine the factors from one or more zeros of a polynomial from a graph.

1. Analyze the graph of the function $h(x) = x^3 + x^2 + 3x + 3$.

Recall the habit of mind comparing polynomials to real numbers. What does it mean to be a factor of a real number?

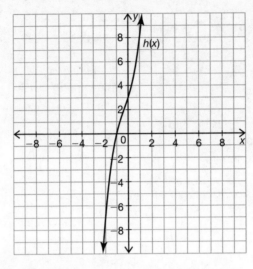

a. Describe the number and types of zeros of $h(x)$.

b. Write the factor of $h(x)$ that corresponds to the zero at $x = -1$.

c. What does it mean to be a factor of $h(x) = x^3 + x^2 + 3x + 3$?

d. How can you write any zero, r, of a function as a factor?

In Question 1 you determined that $(x + 1)$ is a factor of $h(x)$. One way to determine another factor of $h(x)$ is to analyze the problem algebraically through a table of values.

2. Analyze the table of values for $d(x) \cdot q(x) = h(x)$.

x	$d(x) = (x + 1)$	$q(x)$	$h(x) = x^3 + x^2 + 3x + 3$
-3	-2		-24
-2	-1		-7
-1	0		0
0	1		3
1	2		8
2	3		21

a. Complete the table of values for $q(x)$. Explain your process to determine the values for $q(x)$.

b. Two students, Tyler and McCall, disagree about the output $q(-1)$.

Tyler

The output value $q(-1)$ can be any integer. I know this because $d(-1) = 0$. Zero times any number is 0, so I can complete the table with any value for $q(-1)$.

McCall

I know $q(x)$ is a function so only one output value exists for $q(-1)$. I have to use the key characteristics of the function to determine that exact output value.

Who is correct? Explain your reasoning, including the correct output value(s) for $q(-1)$.

6

c. How can you tell from the table of values that $d(x)$ is a factor of $h(x)$?

3. Describe the key characteristics of $q(x)$. Explain your reasoning.

Recall that key characteristics include: vertex, line of symmetry, end behavior, and zeros. How do these key characteristics help you determine the algebraic representation?

4. What is the algebraic representation for $q(x)$? Verify algebraically that $d(x) \cdot q(x)$ is equivalent to $h(x)$.

5. Determine the zeros of $q(x)$. Then rewrite $h(x)$ as a product of its factors.

PROBLEM 2 · Long Story Not So Short

The Fundamental Theorem of Algebra states that every polynomial equation of degree n must have n roots. This means that every polynomial can be written as the product of n factors of the form $(ax + b)$. For example, $2x^2 - 3x - 9 = (2x + 3)(x - 3)$.

You know that a factor of an integer divides into that integer with a remainder of zero. This process can also help determine other factors. For example, knowing 5 is a factor of 115, you can determine that 23 is also a factor since $\frac{115}{5} = 23$. In the same manner, factors of polynomials also divide into a polynomial without a remainder. Recall that $a \div b$ is $\frac{a}{b}$, where $b \neq 0$.

Polynomial long division is an algorithm for dividing one polynomial by another of equal or lesser degree. The process is similar to integer long division.

Notice in the dividend of the polynomial example, there is a gap in the degrees of the terms; every power must have a placeholder. The polynomial $8x^3 - 12x - 7$ does not have an x^2 term.

Integer Long Division	Polynomial Long Division	Description
$4027 \div 12$ or $\dfrac{4027}{12}$	$(8x^3 - 12x - 7) \div (2x + 3)$ or $\dfrac{8x^3 - 12x - 7}{2x + 3}$	
$\begin{array}{r} 335 \\ 12\,\overline{\smash{)}\,4027} \\ -36 \\ \hline 42 \\ -36 \\ \hline 67 \\ -60 \\ \hline ⑦ \text{ Remainder} \end{array}$	$\begin{array}{r} Ⓑ\,4x^2 - Ⓔx + Ⓗ3 \\ 2x + 3\,\overline{\smash{)}\,8x^3 + ⒜0x^2 - 12x - 7} \\ Ⓒ-(8x^3 + 12x^2) \qquad ⒟↓ \\ \hline Ⓕ-12x^2 - 12x \\ -(-12x^2 - 18x) \qquad ⒢↓ \\ \hline ⒤6x - 7 \\ -(6x + 9) \\ \hline \text{Remainder } ⊖16 \end{array}$	A. Rewrite the dividend so that each power is represented. Insert $0x^2$. B. Divide $\dfrac{8x^3}{2x} = 4x^2$. C. Multiply $4x^2(2x + 3)$, and then subtract. D. Bring down $-12x$. E. Divide $\dfrac{-12x^2}{2x} = -6x$. F. Multiply $-6x(2x + 3)$, and then subtract. G. Bring down -7. H. Divide $\dfrac{6x}{2x} = 3$. I. Multiply $3(2x + 3)$, and then subtract.
$\dfrac{4027}{12} = 335 \text{ R } 7$	$\dfrac{8x^3 - 12x - 7}{2x + 3} =$ $4x^2 - 6x + 3 \text{ R } -16$	Rewrite
$4027 = (12)(335) + 7$	$8x^3 - 12x - 7 =$ $(2x + 3)(4x^2 - 6x + 3) - 16$	Check

1. Analyze the worked example that shows integer long division and polynomial long division.

   a. In what ways are the integer and polynomial long division algorithms similar?

To determine another factor of $x^3 + x^2 + 3x + 3$ in Problem I, you completed a table, divided output values, and then determined the algebraic expression of the result. Polynomial Long Division is a more efficient way to calculate.

   b. Is $2x + 3$ a factor of $f(x) = 8x^3 - 12x - 7$? Explain your reasoning.

2. Determine the quotient for each. Show all of your work.

   a. $x\overline{)4x^3 - 0x^2 + 7x}$

   b. $x - 4\overline{)x^3 + 2x^2 - 5x + 16}$

   c. $(4x^4 + 5x^2 - 7x + 9) \div (2x - 3)$

   d. $(9x^4 + 3x^3 + 4x^2 + 7x + 2) \div (3x + 2)$

3. Consider Question 2 parts (a) through (d) to answer each.

    a. Why was the term $0x^2$ included in the dividend in part (a)? Why was this necessary?

    b. When there was a remainder, was the divisor a factor of the dividend? Explain your reasoning.

    c. Describe the remainder when you divide a polynomial by a factor.

4. Determine whether $m(x) = 2x + 1$ is a factor of each function. Explain your reasoning.

    a. $j(x) = 2x^3 + 3x^2 + 7x + 5$

    b.

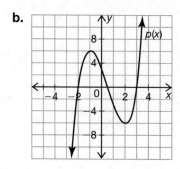

6

c.

x	k(x)
−2	−9
−1	−4
0	5
1	18
2	35

5. Determine the unknown in each.

  a. $\dfrac{x}{7} = 18$ R 2. Determine x.

  b. $\dfrac{p(x)}{x + 3} = 3x^2 + 14x + 15$ R 3. Determine the function $p(x)$.

  c. Describe the similarities and differences in your solution strategies.

  d. Use a graphing calculator to analyze the graph and table of $\dfrac{p(x)}{x + 3}$ over the interval (−10, 10). What do you notice?

6. Calculate the quotient using long division. Then write the dividend as the product of the divisor and the quotient plus the remainder.

Don't forget every power in the dividend must have a placeholder.

a. $f(x) = x^2 - 1$

$g(x) = x - 1$

Calculate $\dfrac{f(x)}{g(x)}$.

b. $f(x) = x^3 - 1$

$g(x) = x - 1$

Calculate $\dfrac{f(x)}{g(x)}$.

6

c. $f(x) = x^4 - 1$

$g(x) = x - 1$

Calculate $\dfrac{f(x)}{g(x)}$.

d. $f(x) = x^5 - 1$

$g(x) = x - 1$

Calculate $\dfrac{f(x)}{g(x)}$.

Do you see a pattern? Can you determine the quotient in part (d) without using long division?

7. Analyze the table of values. Then determine if $q(x)$ is a factor of $p(x)$. If so, explain your reasoning. If not, determine the remainder of $\frac{p(x)}{q(x)}$. Use the last column of the table to show your work.

x	q(x)	p(x)	
0	1	5	
1	2	7	
2	3	9	
3	4	11	
4	5	13	

8. Look back at the various polynomial division problems you have seen so far. Do you think polynomials are closed under division? Explain your reasoning.

PROBLEM 3   **Improve Your Efficiency Rating**

Although dividing polynomials through long division is analogous to integer long division, it can still be inefficient and time consuming. **Synthetic division** is a shortcut method for dividing a polynomial by a linear factor of the form $(x - r)$. This method requires fewer calculations and less writing by representing the polynomial and the linear factor as a set of numeric values. After the values are processed, you can then use the numeric outputs to construct the quotient and the remainder.

Notice in the form of the linear factor $(x - r)$, the x has a coefficient of 1. Also, just as in long division, when you use synthetic division, every power of the dividend must have a placeholder.

6

To use synthetic division to divide a polynomial $ax^2 + bx + c$ by a linear factor $x - r$, follow this pattern.

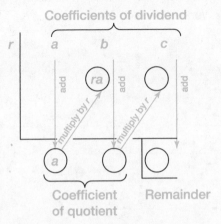

Coefficients of dividend

Coefficient of quotient   Remainder

You can use synthetic division in place of the standard long division algorithm to determine the quotient for $(2x^2 - 3x - 9) \div (x - 3)$.

Long Division	Synthetic Division
$$\begin{array}{r} 2x + 3 \\ x - 3{\overline{\smash{\big)}\,2x^2 - 3x - 9}} \\ \underline{2x^2 - 6x} \\ 3x - 9 \\ \underline{3x - 9} \\ 0 \end{array}$$	$r = 3$

$(2x^2 - 3x - 9) \div (x - 3) = 2x + 3$

1. Analyze the worked example.

   a. Write the dividend as the product of its factors.

   b. Why does the synthetic division algorithm work?

Notice when you use synthetic division, you are multiplying and adding, as opposed to multiplying and subtracting when you use long division.

2. Two examples of synthetic division are provided. Perform the steps outlined for each problem:

   i. Write the dividend.

   ii. Write the divisor.

   iii. Write the quotient.

   iv. Write the dividend as the product of the divisor and the quotient plus the remainder.

a.

$$
\begin{array}{c|ccccc}
2 & 1 & 0 & -4 & -3 & 6 \\
  &   & 2 & 4 & 0 & -6 \\
\hline
  & 1 & 2 & 0 & -3 & 0
\end{array}
$$

   i.

   ii.

   iii.

   iv.

How can you tell by looking at the synthetic division process if the divisor is a factor of the polynomial?

b.

$$
\begin{array}{c|ccccc}
-3 & 2 & -4 & -4 & -3 & 6 \\
   &   & -6 & 30 & -78 & 243 \\
\hline
   & 2 & -10 & 26 & -81 & 249
\end{array}
$$

   i.

   ii.

   iii.

   iv.

3. Calculate each quotient using synthetic division. Then write the dividend as the product of the divisor and the quotient plus the remainder.

   a. $g(x) = x^3 + 1$

   $r(x) = x + 1$

   Calculate $\dfrac{g(x)}{r(x)}$.

   b. $g(x) = x^3 + 8$

   $r(x) = x + 2$

   Calculate $\dfrac{g(x)}{r(x)}$.

   c. $g(x) = x^3 + 27$

   $r(x) = x + 3$

   Calculate $\dfrac{g(x)}{r(x)}$.

   Do you see a pattern? Can you determine the quotient in part (d) without using synthetic division?

   d. $g(x) = x^3 + 64$

   $r(x) = x + 4$

   Calculate $\dfrac{g(x)}{r(x)}$.

4. Use a graphing calculator to compare the graphs and table of values for each pair of functions.

Group 1: $g(x) = \dfrac{x^3 + 1}{x + 1}$ and $j(x) = x^2 - x + 1$

Group 2: $g(x) = \dfrac{x^3 + 8}{x + 2}$ and $j(x) = x^2 - 2x + 4$

Group 3: $g(x) = \dfrac{x^3 + 27}{x + 3}$ and $j(x) = x^2 - 3x + 9$

Remember to use parenthesis when entering the functions in your graphing calculator.

a. Describe the similarities and differences in the graphs and tables of values within each pair of functions.

b. Are the functions within each pair equivalent? Explain your reasoning.

6

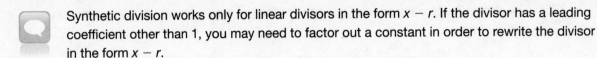
Synthetic division works only for linear divisors in the form $x - r$. If the divisor has a leading coefficient other than 1, you may need to factor out a constant in order to rewrite the divisor in the form $x - r$.

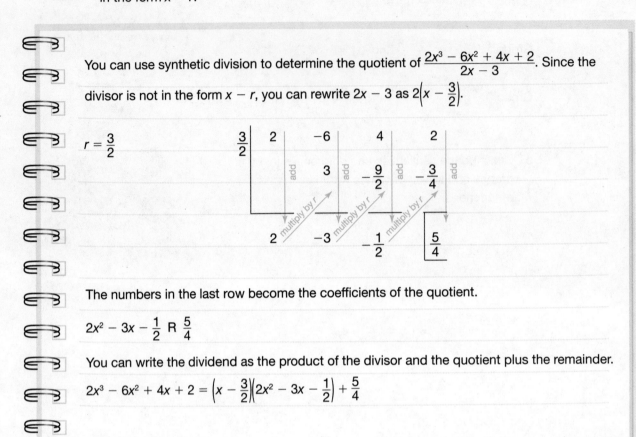

You can use synthetic division to determine the quotient of $\dfrac{2x^3 - 6x^2 + 4x + 2}{2x - 3}$. Since the divisor is not in the form $x - r$, you can rewrite $2x - 3$ as $2\left(x - \dfrac{3}{2}\right)$.

$r = \dfrac{3}{2}$

The numbers in the last row become the coefficients of the quotient.

$2x^2 - 3x - \dfrac{1}{2}$ R $\dfrac{5}{4}$

You can write the dividend as the product of the divisor and the quotient plus the remainder.

$2x^3 - 6x^2 + 4x + 2 = \left(x - \dfrac{3}{2}\right)\left(2x^2 - 3x - \dfrac{1}{2}\right) + \dfrac{5}{4}$

5. Verify $(3x - 2)(x^2 + x + 1) = 3x^3 + x^2 + x - 2$ using synthetic division. Show all work and explain your reasoning.

6

6. Analyze each division problem given $f(x) = x^3 - 3x^2 - x + 3$.

$$g(x) = \frac{f(x)}{x - 1} \qquad h(x) = \frac{f(x)}{2x - 2} \qquad j(x) = \frac{f(x)}{3x - 3}$$

a. Determine the quotient of each function.

b. Use function notation to write $h(x)$ and $j(x)$ in terms of $g(x)$.

6

c. Use a graphing calculator to compare the graphical representations of $g(x)$, $h(x)$, and $j(x)$. What are the similarities and differences in the key characteristics? Explain your reasoning.

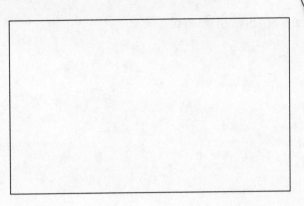

Before you start calculating, think about the structure of the three functions and how they are similar or different.

d. Given the function $g(x)$, describe the transformation(s) that occurred to produce $h(x)$ and $j(x)$.

7. Is the function $q(x) = (x + 2)$ a factor of the function $p(x) = (x + 2)(x - 4)(x + 3) + 1$? Show all work and explain your reasoning.

8. The lesson opener discussed efficiency. Describe patterns and algorithms learned in this lesson that made your mathematical work more efficient.

Be prepared to share your solutions and methods.

The Factors of Life

The Factor Theorem and Remainder Theorem

LEARNING GOALS

In this lesson, you will:

- Use the Remainder Theorem to evaluate polynomial equations and functions.
- Use the Factor Theorem to determine if a polynomial is a factor of another polynomial.
- Use the Factor Theorem to calculate factors of polynomial equations and functions.

KEY TERMS

- Remainder Theorem
- Factor Theorem

When you hear the word *remainder*, what do you think of? Leftovers? Fragments? Remnants?

The United States, as a country, produces a great deal of its own "leftovers." The amount of paper product leftovers per year is enough to heat 50,000,000 homes for 20 years. The average household disposes of over 13,000 pieces of paper each year, most coming from the mail. Some studies show that 2,500,000 plastic bottles are used every hour, most being thrown away, while 80,000,000,000 aluminum soda cans are used every year. Aluminum cans that have been disposed of and not recycled will still be cans 500 years from now.

There are certain things you can do to help minimize the amount of leftovers you produce. For example, recycling one aluminum can save enough energy to watch TV for three hours. Used cans can be recycled into "new" cans in as little as 60 days from when they are recycled. If just $\frac{1}{10}$ of the daily newspapers were recycled, 25,000,000 trees could be saved per year. Recycling plastic uses half the amount of energy it would take to burn it.

You learned that the process of dividing polynomials is similar to the process of dividing integers. Sometimes when you divide two integers there is a remainder, and sometimes there is not a remainder. What does each case mean? In this lesson, you will investigate what the remainder means in terms of polynomial division.

Remember from your experiences with division that:

$$\frac{\text{dividend}}{\text{divisor}} = \text{quotient} + \frac{\text{remainder}}{\text{divisor}}$$

or

$$\text{dividend} = (\text{divisor})(\text{quotient}) + \text{remainder}.$$

It follows that any polynomial, $p(x)$, can be written in the form:

$$\frac{p(x)}{\text{linear factor}} = \text{quotient} + \frac{\text{remainder}}{\text{linear factor}}$$

or

$$p(x) = (\text{linear factor})(\text{quotient}) + \text{remainder}.$$

 Generally, the linear factor is written in the form $(x - r)$, the quotient is represented by $q(x)$, and the remainder is represented by R, meaning:

$$p(x) = (x - r)q(x) + R.$$

1. Given $p(x) = x^3 + 8x - 2$ and $\dfrac{p(x)}{(x - 3)} = x^2 + 3x + 17$ R 49.

   a. Verify $p(x) = (x - r)q(x) + R$.

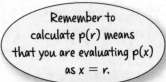

Remember to calculate $p(r)$ means that you are evaluating $p(x)$ as $x = r$.

   b. Given $x - 3$ is a linear factor of $p(x)$, evaluate $p(3)$.

2. Given $p(x) = (x - r)q(x) + R$, calculate $p(r)$.

3. Explain why $p(r)$, where $(x - r)$ is a linear factor, will always equal the remainder R, regardless of the quotient.

6

4. What conclusion can you make about any polynomial evaluated at r?

The **Remainder Theorem** states that when any polynomial equation or function, $f(x)$, is divided by a linear factor $(x - r)$, the remainder is R $= f(r)$, or the value of the equation or function when $x = r$.

5. Given $p(x) = x^3 + 6x^2 + 5x - 12$ and $\dfrac{p(x)}{(x - 2)} = x^2 + 8x + 21$ R 30,

Rico says that $p(-2) = 30$ and Paloma says that $p(2) = 30$.

Without performing any calculations, who is correct? Explain your reasoning.

6. The function, $f(x) = 4x^2 + 2x + 9$ generates the same remainder when divided by $(x - r)$ and $(x - 2r)$, where r is not equal to 0. Calculate the value(s) of r.

6

Factors to Consider

Consider the factors of 24: 1, 2, 3, 4, 6, 8, 12, 24.

Notice that when you divide 24 by any of its factors the remainder is 0. This same principle holds true for polynomial division.

The **Factor Theorem** states that a polynomial has a linear polynomial as a factor if and only if the remainder is zero; or, in other words, $f(x)$ has $(x - r)$ as a factor if and only if $f(r) = 0$.

1. Haley and Lillian each prove that $(x - 7)$ is a factor of the polynomial $f(x) = x^3 - 10x^2 + 11x + 70$.

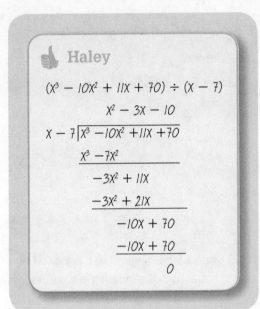

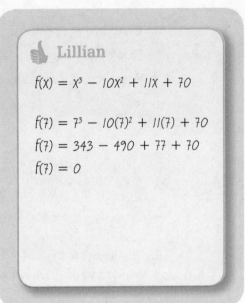

Haley

$$(x^3 - 10x^2 + 11x + 70) \div (x - 7)$$

$$\begin{array}{r} x^2 - 3x - 10 \\ x - 7 \overline{\smash{)}\, x^3 - 10x^2 + 11x + 70} \\ \underline{x^3 - 7x^2} \\ -3x^2 + 11x \\ \underline{-3x^2 + 21x} \\ -10x + 70 \\ \underline{-10x + 70} \\ 0 \end{array}$$

Lillian

$$f(x) = x^3 - 10x^2 + 11x + 70$$

$$f(7) = 7^3 - 10(7)^2 + 11(7) + 70$$
$$f(7) = 343 - 490 + 77 + 70$$
$$f(7) = 0$$

Explain why each student's method is correct.

6

You can continue to factor the polynomial $f(x) = x^3 - 10x^2 + 11x + 70$.

From Haley and Lillian's work, you know that $f(x) = (x - 7)(x^2 - 3x - 10)$.

The quadratic factor can also be factored.

$$f(x) = (x - 7)(x^2 - 3x - 10)$$

$$f(x) = (x - 7)(x + 2)(x - 5)$$

2. Use the Factor Theorem to prove each factor shown in the worked example is correct.

3. What other method(s) could you use to verify that the factors shown in the worked example are correct?

6

4. Use the Factor Theorem to prove that $f(x) = (x + 1 - 3i)(x + 1 + 3i)$ is the factored form of $f(x) = x^2 + 2x + 10$.

5. Determine the unknown coefficient, a, in each function.

a. $f(x) = 2x^4 + x^3 - 14x^2 - ax - 6$ if $(x - 3)$ is a linear factor.

b. $f(x) = ax^4 + 25x^3 + 21x^2 - x - 3$ if $(x + 1)$ is a linear factor.

Talk the Talk

Given the information:

$$p(x) = x^3 + 6x^2 + 11x + 6, \text{ and}$$
$$p(x) \div (x + 4) = x^2 + 2x + 3 \text{ R} -6$$

Determine whether each statement is true or false. Explain your reasoning.

1. $p(-4) = 6$

2. $p(x) = (x + 4)(x^2 + 2x + 3) - 6$

3. -4 is not a zero of $p(x)$

4. -2 is a zero of $p(x)$

Be prepared to share your solutions and methods.

6

Break It Down
Factoring Higher Order Polynomials

In this lesson, you will:

- Factor higher order polynomials using a variety of factoring methods.

Factoring in mathematics is similar to the breakdown of physical and chemical properties in chemistry.

For example, the chemical formula of water is H_2O. This formula means that 2 molecules of hydrogen (H) combined with one molecule of oxygen (O) creates water. The formula for water gives us insight into its individual parts or factors.

Although the general idea is the same between factoring in mathematics, and the breakdown of chemicals, there are some big differences. When factoring polynomials, the factored form does not change any of the characteristics of the polynomial; they are two equivalent expressions. The decomposition of chemicals, however, can sometimes cause an unwanted reaction.

If you have ever taken prescription medication, you might have read the warning labels giving specific directions on how to store the medication, including temperature and humidity. The reason for these directions: if the temperature is too hot or too cold, or if the air is too humid or too dry, the chemicals in the medication may begin to decompose, thus changing its properties.

What other reasons might people want to break down the chemical and physical components of things? How else can these breakdowns be beneficial to people?

In this lesson, you will explore different methods of factoring. To begin factoring any polynomial, always look for a greatest common factor (GCF). You can factor out the greatest common factor of the polynomial, and then factor what remains.

> Remember, a greatest common factor can be a variable, constant, or both.

1. Ping and Shalisha each attempt to factor $3x^3 + 12x^2 - 36x$ by factoring out the greatest common factor.

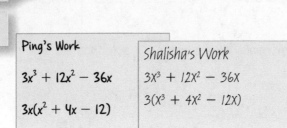

Ping's Work

$3x^3 + 12x^2 - 36x$

$3x(x^2 + 4x - 12)$

Shalisha's Work

$3x^3 + 12x^2 - 36x$

$3(x^3 + 4x^2 - 12x)$

Analyze each student's work. Determine which student is correct and explain the inaccuracy in the other student's work.

2. If possible, completely factor the expression that Ping and Shalisha started.

3. Factor each expression over the set of real numbers. Remember to look for a greatest common factor first. Then, use the factors to sketch the graph of each polynomial.

Remember to think of the end behavior when sketching the function.

a. $3x^3 - 3x^2 - 6x$

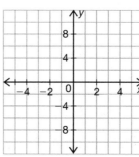

b. $x^3 - x^2 - 20x$

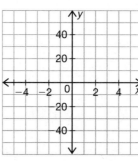

c. $2x^2 + 6x$

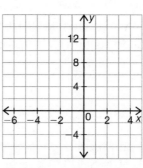

d. $3x^2 - 3x - 6$

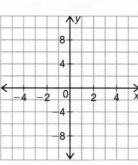

e. $10x^2 - 50x - 60$

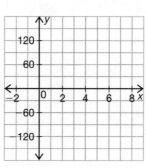

6

4. Analyze the factored form and the corresponding graphs in Question 3. What do the graphs in part (a) through part (c) have in common that the graphs of part (d) and part (e) do not? Explain your reasoning.

5. Write a statement about the graphs of all polynomials that have a monomial GCF that contains a variable.

PROBLEM 2 Continue Parsing

Some polynomials in quadratic form may have common factors in some of the terms, but not all terms. In this case, it may be helpful to write the terms as a product of 2 terms. You can then substitute the common term with a variable, z, and factor as you would any polynomial in quadratic form. This method of factoring is called *chunking*.

You can use chunking to factor $9x^2 + 21x + 10$.

Notice that the first and second terms both contain the common factor, $3x$.

$$9x^2 + 21x + 10 = (3x)^2 + 7(3x) + 10 \qquad \text{Rewrite terms as a product of common factors.}$$
$$= z^2 + 7z + 10 \qquad \text{Let } z = 3x.$$
$$= (z + 5)(z + 2) \qquad \text{Factor the quadratic.}$$
$$= (3x + 5)(3x + 2) \qquad \text{Substitute } 3x \text{ for } z.$$

The factored form of $9x^2 + 21x + 10$ is $(3x + 5)(3x + 2)$.

1. Use chunking to factor $49x^2 + 35x + 6$.

2. Given $z^2 + 2z - 15 = (z - 3)(z + 5)$, write another polynomial in standard form that has a factored form of $(z - 3)(z + 5)$ with different values for z.

Using a similar method of factoring, you may notice, in polynomials with 4 terms, that although not all terms share a common factor, pairs of terms might share a common factor. In this situation, you can *factor by grouping*.

3. Colt factors the polynomial expression $x^3 + 3x^2 - x - 3$.

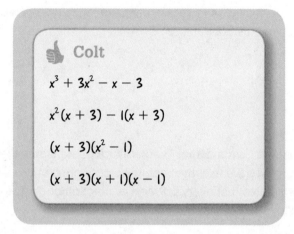

Colt

$x^3 + 3x^2 - x - 3$

$x^2(x + 3) - 1(x + 3)$

$(x + 3)(x^2 - 1)$

$(x + 3)(x + 1)(x - 1)$

Explain the steps Colt took to factor the polynomial expression.

$x^3 + 3x^2 - x - 3$

$x^2(x + 3) - 1(x + 3)$ Step 1: _____

_____

$(x + 3)(x^2 - 1)$ Step 2: _____

_____

$(x + 3)(x + 1)(x - 1)$ Step 3: _____

_____

4. Use factor by grouping to factor the polynomial expression $x^3 + 7x^2 - 4x - 28$.

6

5. Braxton and Kenny both factor the polynomial expression $x^3 + 2x^2 + 4x + 8$.

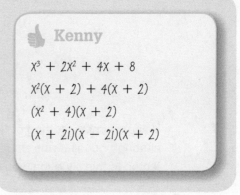

Braxton

$x^3 + 2x^2 + 4x + 8$

$x^2(x + 2) + 4(x + 2)$

$(x^2 + 4)(x + 2)$

Kenny

$x^3 + 2x^2 + 4x + 8$

$x^2(x + 2) + 4(x + 2)$

$(x^2 + 4)(x + 2)$

$(x + 2i)(x - 2i)(x + 2)$

Analyze the set of factors in each student's work. Describe the set of numbers over which each student factored.

Recall that the Fundamental Theorem of Algebra states that any polynomial equation of degree n must have exactly n complex roots or solutions. Also, the Fundamental Theorem of Algebra states that every polynomial function of degree n must have exactly n complex zeros.

This implies that any polynomial function of degree n must have exactly n complex factors:

$f(x) = (x - r_1)(x - r_2) \ldots (x - r_n)$ where $r \in \{complex\ numbers\}$.

Some 4th degree polynomials, written as a trinomial, look very similar to quadratics as they have the same form, $ax^4 + bx^2 + c$. When this is the case, the polynomial may be factored using the same methods you would use to factor a quadratic. This is called *factoring by using quadratic form*.

Factor the quartic polynomial by using quadratic form.

$x^4 - 29x^2 + 100$

$(x^2 - 4)(x^2 - 25)$

$(x - 2)(x + 2)(x - 5)(x + 5)$

- Determine whether you can factor the given trinomial into 2 factors.

- Determine if you can continue to factor each binomial.

6. Factor each polynomial expression over the set of complex numbers.

    a. $x^4 - 4x^3 - x^2 + 4x$ **b.** $x^4 - 10x^2 + 9$

PROBLEM 3   Still Parsing

1. Factor each polynomial function over the set of real numbers.

    a. $f(x) = x^3 - 8$

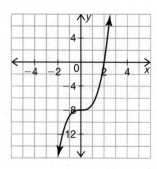

b.

x	$f(x) = x^3 + 27$
−4	−37
−3	0
−2	19
−1	26
0	27
1	28

You may have noticed that all the terms in the polynomials from Question 1 are perfect cubes. You can rewrite the expression $x^3 - 8$ as $(x)^3 - (2)^3$, and $x^3 + 27$ as $(x)^3 + (3)^3$. When you factor sums and differences of cubes, there is a special factoring formula you can use, which is similar to the difference of squares for quadratics.

To determine the formula for the difference of cubes, generalize the difference of cubes as $a^3 - b^3$.

To determine the factor formula for the difference of cubes, factor out $(a - b)$ by considering $(a^3 - b^3) \div (a - b)$.

$$
\begin{array}{r}
a^2 + ab + b^2 \\
a - b \overline{)a^3 + 0 + 0 - b^3} \\
\underline{a^3 - a^2b} \\
a^2b + 0 \\
\underline{a^2b - ab^2} \\
ab^2 - b^3 \\
\underline{ab^2 - b^3} \\
0
\end{array}
$$

Therefore, the difference of cubes can be rewritten in factored form:
$a^3 - b^3 = (a - b)(a^2 + ab + b^2)$.

2. Determine the formula for the sum of cubes by dividing $a^3 + b^3$ by $(a + b)$.

Remember that you can factor a binomial that has perfect square a- and c-values and no middle value using the difference of squares.

You can use the difference of squares when you have a binomial of the form $a^2 - b^2$.

The binomial $a^2 - b^2 = (a + b)(a - b)$.

3. Use the difference of squares to factor each binomial over the set of real numbers.

   a. $x^2 - 64$ **b.** $x^4 - 16$

   c. $x^8 - 1$ **d.** $x^4 - y^4$

6

Another special form of polynomial is the perfect square trinomials. Perfect square trinomials occur when the polynomial is a trinomial, and where the first and last terms are perfect squares and the middle term is equivalent to 2 times the product of the first and last term's square root.

Factoring a perfect square trinomial can occur in two forms:

$$a^2 - 2ab + b^2 = (a - b)^2$$
$$a^2 + 2ab + b^2 = (a + b)^2$$

 4. Determine which of the polynomial expression(s) is a perfect square trinomial and write it as a sum or difference of squares. If it is not a perfect square trinomial, explain why.

a. $x^4 + 14x^2 - 49$

b. $16x^2 - 40x + 100$

 c. $64x^2 - 32x + 4$

d. $9x^4 + 6x^2 + 1$

Talk the Talk

 You have used many different methods of factoring:

- Factoring Out the Greatest Common Factor

- Chunking

- Factoring by Grouping

- Factoring in Quadratic Form

- Sum or Difference of Cubes

- Difference of Squares

- Perfect Square Trinomials

Depending on the polynomial, some methods of factoring will prove to be more efficient than others.

1. Based on the form and characteristics, match each polynomial with the method of factoring you would use from the bulleted list given. Every method from the bulleted list should be used only once. Explain why you choose the factoring method for each polynomial. Finally, write the polynomial in factored form over the set of real numbers.

Polynomial	Method of Factoring	Reason	Factored Form
$3x^4 + 2x^2 - 8$			
$9x^2 - 16$			
$x^2 - 12x + 36$			
$x^3 - 64$			
$x^3 + 2x^2 + 7x + 14$			
$25x^2 - 30x - 7$			
$2x^4 + 10x^3 + 12x^2$			

Be prepared to share your solutions and methods.

6

6

Getting to the Root of It All

Rational Root Theorem

Out of the many vegetables there are to eat, root vegetables are unique. Root vegetables are distinguishable because the root is the actual vegetable that is edible, not the part that grows above ground. These roots would provide the plant above ground the nourishment they need to survive, just like the roots of daisies, roses, or trees; however, we pull up the roots of particular plants from the ground to provide our own bodies with nourishment and vitamins. Although root vegetables should only pertain to those edible parts below the ground, the category of root vegetables includes corms, rhizomes, tubers, and any vegetable that grows underground. Some of the most common root vegetables are carrots, potatoes, and onions.

Root vegetables were a very important food source many years ago before people had the ability to freeze and store food at particular temperatures. Root vegetables, when stored between 32 and 40 degrees Fahrenheit, will last a very long time. In fact, people had root cellars to house these vegetable types through cold harsh winters. In fact, some experts believe people have been eating turnips for over 5000 years! Now that's one popular root vegetable! So, what other root vegetables can you name? What root vegetables do you like to eat?

Consider the product and sum of each set of roots.

Polynomial	Roots	Product of Roots	Sum of Roots
$x^2 + 4x - 1 = 0$	$-2 \pm \sqrt{5}$	-1	-4
$x^3 + 2x^2 - 5x - 6 = 0$	$-1, 2, -3$	6	-2
$2x^3 + 5x^2 - 8x - 20 = 0$	$\pm 2, -\dfrac{5}{2}$	10	$-\dfrac{5}{2}$
$4x^3 - 3x^2 + 4x - 3 = 0$	$\pm i, \dfrac{3}{4}$	$\dfrac{3}{4}$	$\dfrac{3}{4}$
$36x^3 + 24x^2 - 43x + 86 = 0$	$\dfrac{2}{3} \pm \dfrac{\sqrt{3}}{2} i, -2$	$-\dfrac{43}{18}$	$-\dfrac{2}{3}$
$4x^4 - 12x^3 + 13x^2 - 2x - 6 = 0$	$1 \pm i, -\dfrac{1}{2}, \dfrac{3}{2}$	$-\dfrac{3}{2}$	3

1. Compare the sums of the roots to the first two coefficients of each polynomial equation. What conclusion can you draw?

2. Compare the products of the roots to the first and last coefficients of each odd degree polynomial equation. What conclusion can you draw?

3. Compare the products of the roots to the first and last coefficients of each even degree polynomial equation. What conclusion can you draw?

These patterns will help you factor higher-order polynomials.

Up until this point, in order to completely factor a polynomial with a degree higher than 2, you needed to know one of the factors or roots. Whether that was given to you, taken from a table, or graph and verified by the Factor Theorem, you started out with one factor or root. What if you are not given any factors or roots? Should you start randomly choosing numbers and testing them to see if they divide evenly into the polynomial? This is a situation when the *Rational Root Theorem* becomes useful.

The **Rational Root Theorem** states that a rational root of a polynomial equation $a_nx^n + a_{n-1}x^{n-1} + \cdots + a_2x^2 + a_1x + a_0x^0 = 0$ with integer coefficients is of the form $\frac{p}{q}$, where p is a factor of the constant term, a_0, and q is a factor of the leading coefficient, a_n.

> Go back and check out your answers to Questions 2 and 3. Did you identify the ratio $\frac{p}{q}$?

4. Beyonce and Ivy each list all possible rational roots for the polynomial equation they are given.

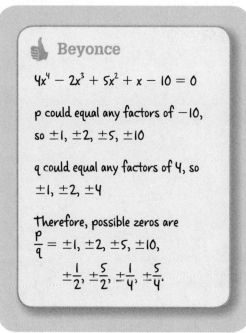

Beyonce

$4x^4 - 2x^3 + 5x^2 + x - 10 = 0$

p could equal any factors of -10, so $\pm1, \pm2, \pm5, \pm10$

q could equal any factors of 4, so $\pm1, \pm2, \pm4$

Therefore, possible zeros are
$\frac{p}{q} = \pm1, \pm2, \pm5, \pm10,$

$\pm\frac{1}{2}, \pm\frac{5}{2}, \pm\frac{1}{4}, \pm\frac{5}{4}.$

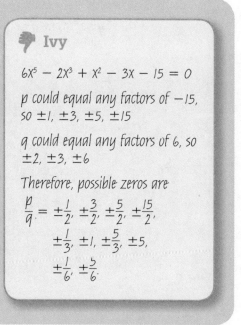

Ivy

$6x^5 - 2x^3 + x^2 - 3x - 15 = 0$

p could equal any factors of -15, so $\pm1, \pm3, \pm5, \pm15$

q could equal any factors of 6, so $\pm2, \pm3, \pm6$

Therefore, possible zeros are
$\frac{p}{q} = \pm\frac{1}{2}, \pm\frac{3}{2}, \pm\frac{5}{2}, \pm\frac{15}{2},$

$\pm\frac{1}{3}, \pm1, \pm\frac{5}{3}, \pm5,$

$\pm\frac{1}{6}, \pm\frac{5}{6}.$

Explain why Ivy is incorrect and correct her work.

5. Complete each step to factor and solve $x^4 + x^3 - 7x^2 - x + 6 = 0$.

    a. Determine all the possible rational roots.

    b. Use synthetic division to determine which of the possible roots are actual roots.

    c. Rewrite the polynomial as a product of its quotient and linear factor.

    d. Repeat steps $a-c$ for the cubic expression.

    e. Factor completely and solve.

6. Determine all roots for $x^4 - 7x^2 - 18 = 0$.

    a. Determine the possible roots.

    b. Use synthetic division to determine one of the roots.

    c. Rewrite the original polynomial as a product.

    d. Determine the possible rational roots of the quotient.

    e. Use synthetic division to determine one of the roots.

    f. Rewrite the original polynomial as a product.

g. Determine the possible rational roots of the quotient.

h. Determine the remaining roots.

i. Rewrite the original polynomial as a product.

What Bulbs are in Your Garden?

You have learned many different ways to solve higher order polynomials. To determine all the roots or solutions of a polynomial equation:

- Determine the possible rational roots.
- Use synthetic division to determine one of the roots.
- Rewrite the original polynomial as a product.
- Determine the possible rational roots of the quotient.
- Repeat the process until all the rational roots are determined.
- Factor the remaining polynomial to determine any irrational or complex roots.
- Recall that some roots may have a multiplicity.

1. Solve each equation over the set of complex numbers.

   a. $x^3 + 1 = 0$

If a quadratic is not factorable, you might want to use the quadratic formula:
$$x = \frac{-b \pm \sqrt{b^2 - 4ac}}{2a}.$$

b. $x^4 + 3x^2 - 28 = 0$

c. $x^4 - 5x^2 - 6x - 2 = 0$

2. Determine the zeros of each function.

a. $f(x) = x^3 + 11x^2 + 37x + 42$

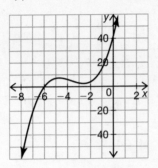

b. $f(x) = x^3 - 4.75x^2 + 3.125x - 0.50$

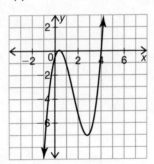

 Be prepared to share your solutions and methods.

Identity Theft
Exploring Polynomial Identities

LEARNING GOALS

In this lesson, you will:

- Use polynomial identities to rewrite numeric expressions.
- Use polynomial identities to generate Pythagorean triples.
- Identify patterns in numbers generated from polynomial identities.
- Prove statements involving polynomials.

KEY TERM

- Euclid's Formula

Have you or someone you know ever been the victim of identity theft? With more and more tasks being performed through the use of technology, identity theft is a growing problem throughout the world. Identity theft occurs when someone steals another person's name or social security number in hopes of accessing that person's money or to make fraudulent purchases.

There are many different ways a person can steal another person's identity. Just a few of these methods are:

- rummaging through a person's trash to obtain personal information and bank statements,
- computer hacking to gain access to personal data,
- pickpocketing to acquire credit cards and personal identification, such as passports or drivers' licenses,
- browsing social networking sites to obtain personal details and photographs.

How important is it to you to secure your identity? What actions would you take to ensure that your identity is not stolen?

PROBLEM 1   Check Your Calculator at the Door

You have learned about many different equivalent polynomial relationships. These relationships are also referred to as polynomial identities.

Some of the polynomial identities that you have used so far are shown.

- $(a + b)^2 = a^2 + 2ab + b^2$

- $(a - b)^2 = a^2 - 2ab + b^2$

- $a^2 - b^2 = (a + b)(a - b)$

- $(a + b)^3 = (a + b)(a^2 + 2ab + b^2)$

- $(a - b)^3 = (a - b)(a^2 - 2ab + b^2)$

- $a^3 + b^3 = (a + b)(a^2 - ab + b^2)$

- $a^3 - b^3 = (a - b)(a^2 + ab + b^2)$

Polynomial identities can help you perform calculations. For instance, consider the expression 46^2. Most people cannot calculate this value without the use of a calculator. However, you can use a polynomial identity to write an equivalent expression that is less difficult to calculate.

You can use the polynomial identity $(a + b)^2 = a^2 + 2ab + b^2$ to calculate 46^2.

$46^2 = (40 + 6)^2$	Write 46 as the sum of 40 and 6.
$= 40^2 + 2(40)(6) + 6^2$	Apply the polynomial identity $(a + b)^2 = a^2 + 2ab + b^2$.
$= 1600 + 2(40)(6) + 36$	Apply exponents.
$= 1600 + 480 + 36$	Perform multiplication.
$= 2116$	Perform addition.

The value of 46^2 is 2116.

---

1. Calculate 46^2 in a different way by writing 46 as the difference of two integers squared.

2. Use polynomial identities and number properties to perform each calculation. Show your work.

    a. 112^2

    b. 27^3

    c. 55^3

Remember that a Pythagorean triple is a set of three positive integers, a, b, and c, such that $a^2 + b^2 = c^2$.

1. Determine whether each set of numbers is a Pythagorean triple. Explain your reasoning.

   a. 4, 5, 9

   b. 0.4, 0.5, 0.3

   c. 89, 80, 39

You have just determined whether three positive numbers make up a Pythagorean triple, but suppose that you wanted to *generate* integers that are Pythagorean triples.

2. Describe a process you could use to calculate integers that are Pythagorean triples.

There is an efficient method to generate Pythagorean triples that involves a polynomial identity called *Euclid's Formula*.

Euclid's Formula is a formula used to generate Pythagorean triples given any two positive integers. Given positive integers r and s, where $r > s$, Euclid's Formula is shown.

$$(r^2 + s^2)^2 = (r^2 - s^2)^2 + (2rs)^2$$

The expressions in Euclid's Formula represent the side lengths of a right triangle, a, b, and c, as shown.

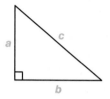

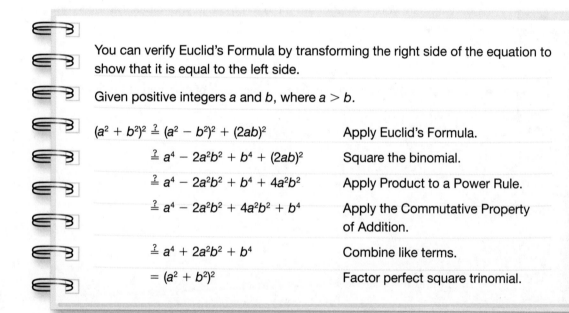

You can verify Euclid's Formula by transforming the right side of the equation to show that it is equal to the left side.

Given positive integers a and b, where $a > b$.

$(a^2 + b^2)^2 \stackrel{?}{=} (a^2 - b^2)^2 + (2ab)^2$	Apply Euclid's Formula.
$\stackrel{?}{=} a^4 - 2a^2b^2 + b^4 + (2ab)^2$	Square the binomial.
$\stackrel{?}{=} a^4 - 2a^2b^2 + b^4 + 4a^2b^2$	Apply Product to a Power Rule.
$\stackrel{?}{=} a^4 - 2a^2b^2 + 4a^2b^2 + b^4$	Apply the Commutative Property of Addition.
$\stackrel{?}{=} a^4 + 2a^2b^2 + b^4$	Combine like terms.
$= (a^2 + b^2)^2$	Factor perfect square trinomial.

3. Use Euclid's Formula to generate a Pythagorean triple.

   a. Choose two integers and use them to generate a Pythagorean triple. Explain your choice in integers.

   b. Compare your Pythagorean triple to others in your class. Did everyone get the same triple?

4. Generate a Pythagorean triple using each pair of given numbers and Euclid's Formula.

   a. 4 and 7

   b. 11 and 5

   c. 15 and 20

5. Did any of the Pythagorean triples you generated have a common factor? If so, identify them, and explain why you think this happened.

Do you think that there is only one r-value and only one s-value that will generate each Pythagorean triple?

6. The integers 5, 12, 13 make up a fairly well-known Pythagorean triple. What two integers generate this triple? Show your work.

After learning that Euclid's Formula generates numbers that are Pythagorean triples, Danielle and Mike wonder what other formulas they could use to generate interesting patterns. Each came up with their own sets of numbers.

Danielle named her numbers the "Danielle numbers." She defined them as shown.

The Danielle numbers are any numbers that can be generated using the formula $a^2 + b^2$, where a and b are positive integers and $a > b$.

Following suit, Mike named his numbers the "Mike numbers," and he defined his numbers as shown.

The Mike numbers are any numbers that can be generated using the formula $a^2 - b^2$, where a and b are positive integers and $a > b$.

 1. Complete each table to determine the first few Danielle numbers and the first few Mike numbers. Shade the corresponding cell if a is not greater than b.

Danielle Numbers: $a^2 + b^2$

		b				
		1	2	3	4	5
a	1					
	2					
	3					
	4					
	5					

Mike Numbers: $a^2 - b^2$

		b				
		1	2	3	4	5
a	1					
	2					
	3					
	4					
	5					

2. Describe any and all patterns you see in each table in Question 1.

3. Determine whether each number is a Danielle number, a Mike number, both, or neither. Explain your reasoning.

    a. 13

    b. 3

    c. 2

After hearing about Danielle and Mike's numbers, Dave and Sandy decide to create their own numbers as well. Their definitions are shown.

The Dave numbers are any numbers that can be generated using the formula $a^3 + b^3$, where a and b are positive integers and $a > b$.

The Sandy numbers are any numbers that can be generated using the formula $a^3 - b^3$, where a and b are positive integers and $a > b$.

4. Complete the tables to determine the first few Dave numbers, and the first few Sandy numbers. Shade the corresponding cell if a is not greater than b.

Dave Numbers: $a^3 + b^3$

		b				
		1	2	3	4	5
a	1					
	2					
	3					
	4					
	5					

Sandy Numbers: $a^3 - b^3$

		b				
		1	2	3	4	5
a	1					
	2					
	3					
	4					
	5					

5. Describe any and all patterns you see in each table in Question 4.

6. Determine whether each number is a Dave number, a Sandy number, both, or neither. Explain your reasoning.

    a. 35

    b. 5

7. Write a rule that defines your own set of numbers. What interesting patterns do you see with your numbers?

Verify each algebraic statement by transforming one side of the equation to show that it is equivalent to the other side of the equation.

1. $v^6 - w^6 = (v^2 - w^2)(v^2 - vw + w^2)(v^2 + vw + w^2)$

2. $(p^4 + q^4)^2 = (p^4 - q^4)^2 + (2p^2q^2)^2$

6

3. $m^9 + n^9 = (m + n)(m^2 - mn + n^2)(m^6 - m^3n^3 + n^6)$

 Be prepared to share your solutions and methods.

6

The Curious Case of Pascal's Triangle

Pascal's Triangle and the Binomial Theorem

LEARNING GOALS

In this lesson, you will:

- Identify patterns in Pascal's Triangle.
- Use Pascal's Triangle to expand powers of binomials.
- Use the Binomial Theorem to expand powers of binomials.
- Extend the Binomial Theorem to expand binomials of the form $(ax + by)^n$.

KEY TERM

- Binomial Theorem

Some sets of numbers are given special names because of the interesting patterns they create. A *polygonal number* is a number that can be represented as a set of dots that make up a regular polygon. For example, the number 3 is considered a polygonal number because it can be represented as a set of dots that make up an equilateral triangle, as shown.

More specifically, the polygonal numbers that form equilateral triangles are called the *triangular numbers*. The first four triangular numbers are shown. (Note that polygonal numbers always begin with the number 1.)

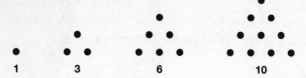

1 3 6 10

The *square numbers* are polygonal numbers that form squares. The first four square numbers are shown.

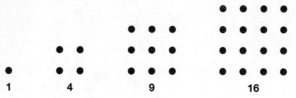

1 4 9 16

Can you determine the first four pentagonal numbers? How about the first four hexagonal numbers?

There is an interesting pattern of numbers that makes up what is referred to as Pascal's Triangle.

The first six rows of Pascal's Triangle are shown, where $n = 0$ represents the first row, $n = 1$ represents the second row, and so on.

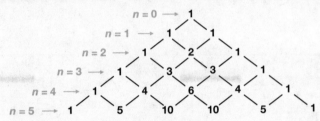

 1. Analyze the patterns in Pascal's Triangle.

   a. Describe all the patterns you see in Pascal's Triangle.

> Remember the types of numbers discussed in the lesson opener? Maybe you can see some of those patterns here!

 b. Complete the rows for $n = 6$ and $n = 7$ in the diagram of Pascal's Triangle. Describe the pattern you used.

2. Brianna loves hockey. In fact, Brianna is so obsessed with hockey that she drew "hockey sticks" around the numbers in Pascal's Triangle. Lo and behold, she found a pattern! Her work is shown.

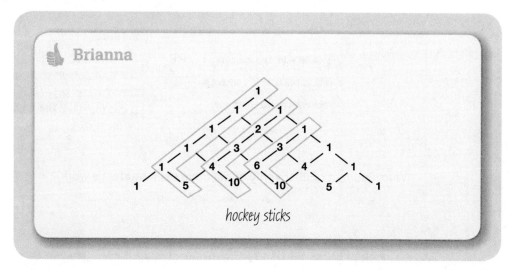

a. Describe the pattern shown by the numbers inside the hockey sticks that Brianna drew.

I'll give you a hint. Analyze the numbers along the longer part of the "stick." Then, look at the lone number at the end of the shorter part of the stick.

b. Sketch two more hockey sticks that include numbers that have the same pattern described in part (a).

3. Drew and Latasha analyzed Pascal's Triangle, and each described a pattern.

Drew

The sum of the numbers in each row is equal to 2^n, where $n = 0$ represents the first row.

Latasha

If I alternate the signs of the numbers in any row after the first row and then add them together, their sum is 0.

Who's correct? Either verify or disprove each student's work.

4. Consider the numbers along the dashed lines shown.

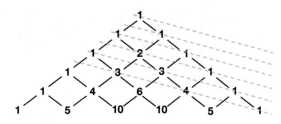

a. Write the sequence for the sum of numbers along each dashed line.

b. Explain how the sums of numbers along the dashed lines in Pascal's Triangle can be linked to a well-known sequence of numbers.

The patterns shown in Pascal's Triangle have many uses. For instance, you may have used Pascal's Triangle to calculate probabilities. Let's explore how you can use Pascal's Triangle to raise a binomial to a positive integer.

5. Multiply to expand each binomial. Write your final answer so that the powers of *a* are in descending order.

a. $(a + b)^0 =$

b. $(a + b)^1 =$

c. $(a + b)^2 =$

d. $(a + b)^3 =$

e. $(a + b)^4 =$

6. Analyze your answers to Question 5.

    a. Compare the coefficients of each product with the numbers shown in Pascal's Triangle. What do you notice?

    b. What do you notice about the exponents of the a- and b-variables in each expansion?

    c. What do you notice about the sum of the exponents of the a- and b-variables in each expansion?

7. Use Pascal's Triangle to expand each binomial.

    a. $(a + b)^5 =$

    b. $(a + b)^6 =$

    c. $(a + b)^7 =$

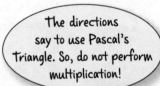

The directions say to use Pascal's Triangle. So, do not perform multiplication!

6

Binomial Theorem Delirium!

What if you want to expand a binomial such as $(a + b)^{15}$? You could take the time to draw that many rows of Pascal's Triangle, but there is a more efficient way.

Recall that the factorial of a whole number n, represented as $n!$, is the product of all numbers from 1 to n.

> You are going to see another method for expanding binomials. But, let's get some notation out of the way first.

1. Perform each calculation and simplify.

   a. $5! =$

   b. $2!3! =$

> You may remember that the value of 0! is 1. This is because the product of zero numbers is equal to the multiplicative identity, which is 1.

   c. $\frac{5!}{3!} =$

You may have seen the notation $\binom{n}{k}$ or $_nC_k$ when calculating probabilities in another course. Both notations represent the formula for a *combination*. Recall that a combination is a selection of objects from a collection in which order does not matter. The formula for a combination of k objects from a set of n objects for $n \geq k$ is shown.

$$\binom{n}{k} = {_nC_k} = \frac{n!}{k!(n - k)!}$$

Calculate $\begin{pmatrix} 4 \\ 2 \end{pmatrix}$, or $_4C_2$.

$$\begin{pmatrix} n \\ k \end{pmatrix} = {_nC_k} = \frac{n!}{k!(n-k)!}$$ Write the formula for a combination.

$n = 4$ and $k = 2$ Identify n and k.

$$\begin{pmatrix} 4 \\ 2 \end{pmatrix} = \frac{4!}{2!(4-2)!}$$ Substitute the values for n and k into the formula.

$$= \frac{4 \cdot 3 \cdot 2 \cdot 1}{(2 \cdot 1)(2 \cdot 1)}$$ Write each factorial as a product.

$$= \frac{4 \cdot 3 \cdot \cancel{2} \cdot \cancel{1}}{(2 \cdot 1)(\cancel{2} \cdot \cancel{1})}$$ Divide out common factors.

$$= \frac{12}{2} = 6$$ Simplify.

2. Explain why n must be greater than or equal to k in the formula for a combination.

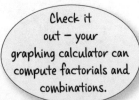

3. Perform each calculation and simplify.

   a. $\begin{pmatrix} 5 \\ 1 \end{pmatrix} =$

   b. $_7C_4 =$

Check it out – your graphing calculator can compute factorials and combinations.

4. Sarah and Montel's teacher asks each student to use Pascal's Triangle to calculate $_6C_3$. Their answers and explanations are shown.

> **Sarah**
>
> I can calculate $_nC_k$ by looking at the kth number (from left to right) in the nth row of Pascal's Triangle. So, $_6C_3$ is equal to 20.

> **Montel**
>
> I can calculate $_nC_k$ by looking at the (k + 1)th number (from left to right) in the (n + 1)th row of Pascal's Triangle. So, $_6C_3$ is equal to 35.

Who is correct? Explain your reasoning.

The **Binomial Theorem** states that it is possible to extend any power of $(a + b)$ into a sum of the form shown.

$$(a + b)^n = \binom{n}{0}a^n b^0 + \binom{n}{1}a^{n-1}b^1 + \binom{n}{2}a^{n-2}b^2 + \cdots + \binom{n}{n-1}a^1 b^{n-1} + \binom{n}{n}a^0 b^n$$

5. Use the Binomial Theorem to expand $(a + b)^{15}$. You can use your calculator to determine the coefficients.

$(a + b)^{15} =$

Suppose you have a binomial with coefficients other than one, such as $(2x + 3y)^5$. You can use substitution along with the Binomial Theorem to expand the binomial.

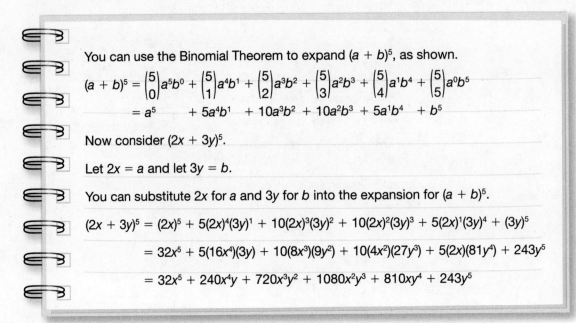

You can use the Binomial Theorem to expand $(a + b)^5$, as shown.

$$(a + b)^5 = \binom{5}{0}a^5b^0 + \binom{5}{1}a^4b^1 + \binom{5}{2}a^3b^2 + \binom{5}{3}a^2b^3 + \binom{5}{4}a^1b^4 + \binom{5}{5}a^0b^5$$

$$= a^5 \quad + 5a^4b^1 \quad + 10a^3b^2 + 10a^2b^3 + 5a^1b^4 \quad + b^5$$

Now consider $(2x + 3y)^5$.

Let $2x = a$ and let $3y = b$.

You can substitute $2x$ for a and $3y$ for b into the expansion for $(a + b)^5$.

$$(2x + 3y)^5 = (2x)^5 + 5(2x)^4(3y)^1 + 10(2x)^3(3y)^2 + 10(2x)^2(3y)^3 + 5(2x)^1(3y)^4 + (3y)^5$$

$$= 32x^5 + 5(16x^4)(3y) + 10(8x^3)(9y^2) + 10(4x^2)(27y^3) + 5(2x)(81y^4) + 243y^5$$

$$= 32x^5 + 240x^4y + 720x^3y^2 + 1080x^2y^3 + 810xy^4 + 243y^5$$

6. Use the Binomial Theorem and substitution to expand each binomial.

   a. $(3x + y)^4$

   b. $(x - 2y)^6$

Be prepared to share your solutions and methods.

Chapter 6 Summary

KEY TERMS

- average rate of change (6.1)
- polynomial long division (6.2)
- synthetic division (6.2)
- Euclid's Formula (6.6)

THEOREMS

- Remainder Theorem (6.3)
- Factor Theorem (6.3)
- Rational Root Theorem (6.5)
- Binomial Theorem (6.7)

6.1 Analyzing Graphs

A graph can be analyzed over certain intervals or at certain points.

Example

- From point C to point A the graph is increasing.

- From point A to point B the graph is decreasing.

- From point B to point F the graph is increasing.

- Points C, D, and E have a y-value of 0.

- Point A has a local maximum value of about 15.

- Point B has a local minimum value of about -5.

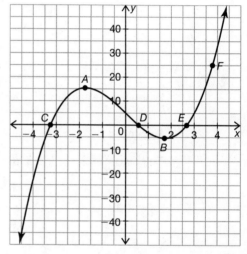

6.1 Determining the Average Rate of Change

The formula for average rate of change is $\dfrac{f(b) - f(a)}{b - a}$ for an interval (a, b).

Example

The average rate of change over
the interval $(-1, 4)$ is

$f(4) \approx 100$, $f(-1) \approx -200$

$$= \frac{f(b) - f(a)}{b - a}$$

$$= \frac{f(4) - f(-1)}{4 - (-1)}$$

$$= \frac{100 - (-200)}{5}$$

$$= \frac{300}{5}$$

$$= 60$$

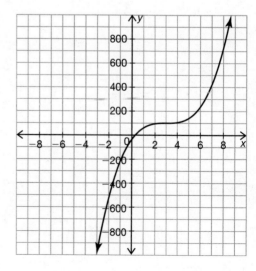

6

503

Using Polynomial Long Division

One polynomial can be divided by another of equal or lesser degree using a process similar to integer division. This process is called polynomial long division. To perform polynomial long division, every power in the dividend must have a placeholder. If there is a gap in the degrees of the dividend, rewrite it so that each power is represented.

Example

The quotient of $3x^3 - 4x^2 + 5x - 3$ divided by $3x + 2$ is $x^2 - 2x + 3$ R -9.

$$
\begin{array}{r}
x^2 - 2x + 3 \\
3x + 2 \overline{)3x^3 - 4x^2 + 5x - 3} \\
\underline{3x^3 + 2x^2} \\
-6x^2 + 5x \\
\underline{-6x^2 - 4x} \\
9x - 3 \\
\underline{9x + 6} \\
-9
\end{array}
$$

6.2 **Determining Factors Using Long Division**

When the remainder of polynomial long division is 0, the divisor is a factor of the dividend.

Example

The binomial $2x - 1$ is a factor of $2x^4 + 5x^3 - x^2 + x - 1$ since the remainder is 0.

$$
\begin{array}{r}
x^3 + 3x^2 + x + 1 \\
2x - 1 \overline{)2x^4 + 5x^3 - x^2 + x - 1} \\
\underline{2x^4 - x^3} \\
6x^3 - x^2 \\
\underline{6x^3 - 3x^2} \\
2x^2 + x \\
\underline{2x^2 - x} \\
2x - 1 \\
\underline{2x - 1} \\
0
\end{array}
$$

6

6.3 Using Synthetic Division

Synthetic division is a shortcut method for dividing a polynomial by a binomial $x - r$. To use synthetic division, follow the pattern:

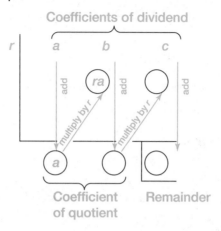

Example

$4x^3 + 3x^2 - 2x + 1$ divided by $x + 3$ is $4x^2 - 9x + 25$ R $\dfrac{-74}{x + 3}$.

$$
\begin{array}{c|cccc}
-3 & 4 & 3 & -2 & 1 \\
   &   & -12 & 27 & -75 \\
\hline
   & 4 & -9 & 25 & -74
\end{array}
$$

6.3 Using the Remainder Theorem

The Remainder Theorem states that when any polynomial equation or function, $f(x)$, is divided by a linear factor $(x - r)$, the remainder is $R = f(r)$, or the value of the equation or function when $x = r$.

Example

Let $f(x) = 6x^3 - 2x^2 - x + 1$. When $f(x)$ is divided by $x - 3$, the remainder is 142 since $f(3) = 142$.

$f(3) = 6(3)^3 - 2(3)^2 - 3 + 1$

$\qquad = 162 - 18 - 3 + 1$

$\qquad = 142$

6

Using the Factor Theorem

The Factor Theorem states that a polynomial has a linear polynomial as a factor if and only if the remainder is 0; $f(x)$ has $(x - r)$ as a factor if and only if $f(r) = 0$.

Examples

Let $f(x) = 2x^3 + 5x^2 - 15x - 12$.

The binomial $(x + 4)$ is a factor of $f(x)$ since $f(-4) = 0$.

$$f(-4) = 2(-4)^3 + 5(-4)^2 - 15(-4) - 12$$

$$= -128 + 80 + 60 - 12$$

$$= 0$$

The binomial $(x - 5)$ is not a factor of $f(x)$ since $f(5) \neq 0$.

$$f(5) = 2(5)^3 + 5(5)^2 - 15(5) - 12$$

$$= 250 + 125 - 75 - 12$$

$$= 288$$

6

Factoring Polynomials

There are different methods to factor a polynomial. Depending on the polynomial, some methods of factoring are more efficient than others.

Examples

Factoring out the Greatest Common Factor:
$6x^2 - 36x$
$6x(x - 6)$

Chunking:
$64x^2 + 24x - 10$
$(8x)^2 + 3(8x) - 10$

Let $z = 8x$.
$z^2 + 3z - 10$
$(z - 2)(z + 5)$
$(8x - 2)(8x + 5)$

Factoring by Grouping
$x^3 + 3x^2 + 2x + 6$
$x^2(x + 3) + 2(x + 3)$
$(x^2 + 2)(x + 3)$

Sum or Difference of Cubes
$x^3 - 27$
$(x - 3)(x^2 + 3x + 9)$

$x^3 + 8$
$(x + 2)(x^2 - 2x + 4)$

Difference of Squares
$x^2 - 25$
$(x + 5)(x - 5)$

Perfect Square Trinomials
$9x^2 - 12x + 4$
$(3x - 2)(3x - 2)$

Using the Rational Root Theorem

The Rational Root Theorem states that a rational root of a polynomial $a_nx^n + a_{n-1}x^{n-1} + \cdots + a_1x^1 + a_0x^0$ with integer coefficients will be of the form $\frac{p}{q}$ where p is a factor of the constant term a_0 and q is a factor of the leading coefficient a_n.

Example

Given the polynomial: $3x^2 + 2x - 6$

$p = \pm1, \pm2, \pm3, \pm6$

$q = \pm1, \pm3$

The possible rational roots are ±1, ±2, ±3, ±6, $\pm\frac{1}{3}$, and $\pm\frac{2}{3}$.

6.5 Solving Polynomials Equations

To determine all roots of a polynomial:

- Determine the possible rational roots.

- Use synthetic division to determine one of the roots.

- Rewrite the original polynomial as a product.

- Determine the possible rational roots of the quotient.

- Repeat the process until all the rational roots are determined.

- Factor the remaining polynomial to determine any irrational or complex roots.

- Recall that some roots may have a multiplicity.

Example

Solve $2x^3 - 9x^2 + 7x + 6 = 0$.

The possible rational roots of $2x^3 - 9x^2 + 7x + 6$ are $\pm\frac{1}{2}$, ± 1, $\pm\frac{3}{2}$, ± 2, ± 3, and ± 6 since $p = 6$ and $q = 2$.

Use synthetic division to divide the polynomial by $(x - 3)$.

$$
\begin{array}{r|rrrr}
3 & 2 & -9 & 7 & 6 \\
  &   & 6 & -9 & -6 \\
\hline
  & 2 & -3 & -2 & 0
\end{array}
$$

$2x^3 - 9x^2 + 7x + 6 = 0$

$(x - 3)(2x^2 - 3x - 2) = 0$

$(x - 3)(2x + 1)(x - 2) = 0$

$x - 3 = 0 \qquad 2x + 1 = 0 \qquad x - 2 = 0$

$\qquad x = 3 \qquad\qquad x = -\frac{1}{2} \qquad\qquad x = 2$

6

6.6 Using Polynomial Identities for Numerical Calculations

Some of the polynomial identities are shown. Polynomial identities can be used to perform calculations.

- $(a + b)^2 = a^2 + 2ab + b^2$
- $(a - b)^2 = a^2 - 2ab + b^2$
- $a^2 - b^2 = (a + b)(a - b)$
- $(a + b)^3 = (a + b)(a^2 + 2ab + b^2)$
- $(a - b)^3 = (a - b)(a^2 - 2ab + b^2)$
- $a^3 + b^3 = (a + b)(a^2 - ab + b^2)$
- $a^3 - b^3 = (a - b)(a^2 + ab + b^2)$

Example

To calculate 13^3, use the identity $(a + b)^3 = (a + b)(a^2 + 2ab + b^2)$.

$13^3 = (10 + 3)^3$

$= (10 + 3)(10^2 + 2(10)(3) + 3^2)$

$= 13(100 + 60 + 9)$

$= 13(100) + 13(60) + 13(9)$

$= 1{,}300 + 780 + 117$

$= 2{,}197$

6.6 Using Euclid's Formula to Generate Pythagorean Triples

Euclid's Formula is a formula used to generate Pythagorean triples given any two positive integers.

Given positive integers r and s, where $r > s$, Euclid's Formula is $(r^2 + s^2)^2 = (r^2 - s^2)^2 + (2rs)^2$.

Example

Generate a Pythagorean Triple using the numbers 6 and 13.

Let $r = 13$ and $s = 6$.

$(13^2 + 6^2) = (13^2 - 6^2) + (2(13)(6))^2$

$(205)^2 = (133)^2 + (156)^2$

$42{,}025 = 42{,}025$

So 133, 156, 205 is a Pythagorean triple.

6.7 Using Pascal's Triangle to Expand Binomials

The coefficients for the expansion of $(a + b)^n$ are the same as the numbers in the row of Pascal's Triangle where n is equal to the power of the original binomial.

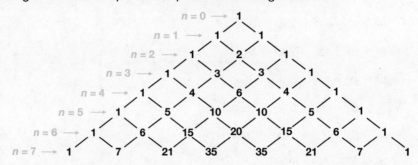

Example

$(a + b)^5 = a^5 + 5a^4b + 10a^3b^2 + 10a^2b^3 + 5ab^4 + b^5$

6.7 Using the Binomial Theorem to Expand Binomials

The Binomial Theorem states that it is possible to expand any power of $(a + b)$ into a sum in the following form:

$$(a + b)^n = \binom{n}{0}a^nb^0 + \binom{n}{1}a^{n-1}b^1 + \binom{n}{2}a^{n-2}b^2 + \cdots + \binom{n}{n-1}a^1b^{n-1} + \binom{n}{n}a^0b^n.$$

Example

Expand $(2x - y)^6$.

$$(a + b)^6 = \binom{6}{0}a^6b^0 + \binom{6}{1}a^5b^1 + \binom{6}{2}a^4b^2 + \binom{6}{3}a^3b^3 + \binom{6}{4}a^2b^4 + \binom{6}{5}a^1b^5 + \binom{6}{6}a^0b^6$$

$$= a^6 + 6a^5b + 15a^4b^2 + 20a^3b^3 + 15a^2b^4 + 6ab^5 + b^6$$

Let $a = 2x$ and $b = -y$.

$$(2x - y)^6 = (2x)^6 + 6(2x)^5(-y) + 15(2x)^4(-y)^2 + 20(2x)^3(-y)^3 + 15(2x)^2(-y)^4 + 6(2x)(-y)^5 + (-y)^6$$

$$= 64x^6 - 6(32)x^5y + 15(16)x^4y^2 - 20(8)x^3y^3 + 15(4)x^2y^4 - 12xy^5 + y^6$$

$$= 64x^6 - 192x^5y + 240x^4y^2 - 160x^3y^3 + 60x^2y^4 - 12xy^5 + y^6$$

Polynomial Models

Price changes for unleaded and diesel gas are difficult to model with simple functions from year to year. But no matter what year it is, a lot of people would agree that they pay a lot of money to fill up their tanks!

511

Unequal Equals
Solving Polynomial Inequalities

In this lesson, you will:

- Determine all roots of polynomial equations.
- Determine solutions to polynomial inequalities algebraically and graphically.

Income Inequality is a term used to describe the gap or difference between the amount of money that wealthy people possess as compared to the amount people without wealth possess. From the 1950s through the 1970s, the trend in the United States was toward *more* income equality. In other words, non-wealthy people earned money at a faster rate than the wealthiest segment of the population, creating a smaller gap between these two social classes. Many economists attribute this trend towards equality to the industrial boom leading up to and following World War II. Millions of soldiers returning from active war duty after World War II received low interest loans for housing, and money for college and career-training. This helped non-wealthy people earn a greater share of the country's wealth. In the 1970s the wealthiest 1% of the population owned approximately 9% of America's total wealth.

Since the 1970s, the United States has become a nation with much more income inequality. Wages in the middle and lower classes have remained fairly stagnant while the wealth of the top 1% has increased from 9% in the 1970s to nearly 25% today.

Why do you think the income inequality changed after the 1970s? Do you think this trend will continue for the foreseeable future? What factors play a part in determining wealthy and non-wealthy classes?

PROBLEM 1 Analyzing Profits

Lawn Enforcement is a small landscaping company. It has a profit model that can be represented by the function,

$$p(x) = -x^4 + 19.75x^3 - 133.25x^2 + 351.25x - 280.75$$

where profit, in thousands of dollars, is a function of time, in years, the company has been in business. Let's analyze $p(x)$ represented on a graph.

The graph shown represents the change in profit as a function of the number of years that Lawn Enforcement has been in business.

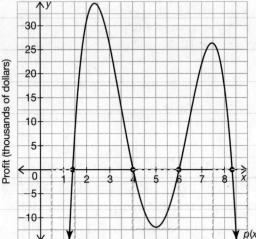

Years in Business

The points identified on the graph represent the zeros of the function where Lawn Enforcement's profit was 0.

Each point on the number line represents the years in business when Lawn Enforcement's profit was 0.

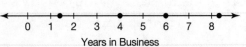

Years in Business

The function $p(x) = 0$ when $x = 1.4, 4, 6, 8.3$.

The regions enclosed in dashed boxes on the coordinate plane represent Lawn Enforcement's profit less than 0.

The regions on the number line enclosed in dashed boxes represent the years in business when Lawn Enforcement's profit was less than 0.

Years in Business

The function $p(x) < 0$ when $\begin{cases} x < 1.4 \\ 4 < x < 6 \\ x > 8.3 \end{cases}$.

1. Analyze the worked example.

   a. Why were the points changed to open circles on the number line to represent the years in business when $p(x) < 0$.

   b. Circle the parts of the graph on the coordinate plane that represent where $p(x) > 0$. Then circle the intervals on the number line that represent the years in business where $p(x) > 0$. Finally identify the set of x-values to complete the sentence and explain your answer in terms of this problem situation.

      The function $p(x) > 0$ when _____.

   c. Draw a solid box around the segment(s) where $p(x) > 35,000$. Then identify the set of x-values to complete the sentence. Finally, explain your answer in terms of this problem situation.

      The function $p(x) > 35,000$ when _____.

In this lesson, you will solve polynomial inequalities, which are very similar to solving linear inequalities. Recall from your experience of solving linear inequalities graphically, that < or > is represented with a dotted line, and ≤ or ≥ is represented with a solid line. Also remember that when you are determining which region(s) to shade, look at y-values above or below the boundary line depending on the inequality sign. It is always a good idea to check your work by selecting test points as well.

 1. Samson, Kaley, Paco, and Sal each solved the quadratic inequality $-24 > 2x^2 + 14x$.

Samson

I graphed both sides of the inequality.

$y_1 = -24$

$y_2 = 2x^2 + 14x$

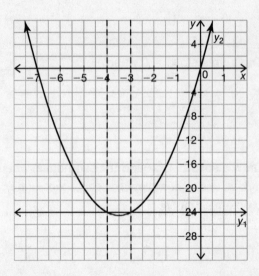

I drew vertical dashed lines at the two points where the graphs intersect.

I can then determine from the graph that the x-values of $2x^2 + 14x$ that generate values less than -24 are between -4 and -3.

Therefore the solution to the inequality is $-4 < x < -3$.

Paco

I added 24 to both sides of the inequality because I wanted one side to be equal to 0. Then, I graphed that inequality.

$y_1 = 2x^2 + 14x + 24$

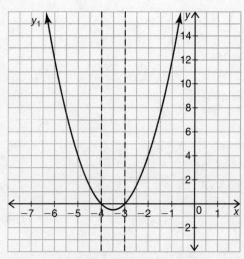

I drew vertical dashed lines where the graph crosses the x-axis.

I can then determine from the graph that the x-values of $2x^2 + 14x$ that generate values less than 0 are between -4 and -3.

Therefore the solution to the inequality is $-4 < x < -3$.

a. Explain why the graphs of Samson and Paco are different, yet generate the same answers.

b. Explain the error in Sal's work.

 Kaley

I remember from solving linear inequalities that I can first treat the inequality as an equation and solve:

$0 = 2x^2 + 14x + 24$
$0 = 2(x^2 + 7x + 12)$
$0 = 2(x + 3)(x + 4)$
$x = -4, -3$

This means that the x-intercepts are -4 and -3. Breaking up the number line into 3 parts and testing each section in the original inequality $-24 > 2x^2 + 14x$, I can determine the solution:

Test $x = -3.5$
$-24 > 2(-3.5)^2 + 14(-3.5)$
$-24 > -24.5$

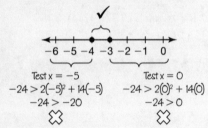

Test $x = -5$
$-24 > 2(-5)^2 + 14(-5)$
$-24 > -20$
✗

Test $x = 0$
$-24 > 2(0)^2 + 14(0)$
$-24 > 0$
✗

The only section that satisfies the original inequality is when x is between -4 and -3 so the solution to the inequality is $-4 < x < -3$.

 Sal

I remember from solving linear inequalities that I can treat the inequality as an equation and solve:

$2x^2 + 14x = -24$
$2x(x + 7) = -24$
$2x = -24 \quad (x + 7) = -24$
$x = -12 \quad\quad x = -31$

This means that the x-intercepts are -12 and -31, so the solution to the inequality is $-31 < x < -12$.

7

c. Compare Samson's method to Kaley's method. List advantages and disadvantages of each method.

2. Solve $18 \leq 3x^2 + x$ using any method. Explain why you chose the method.

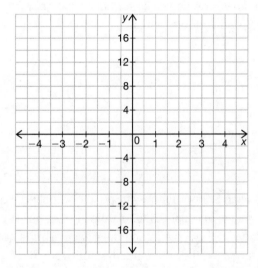

Polynomial inequalities can be used to represent everyday situations. Write and solve each real-world inequality.

1. Get Your Kicks is an indoor soccer complex. The roof's height at the facility is 80 feet. If a soccer ball is kicked and touches the ceiling during a game, the team that kicked the ball must have a player sit out for two minutes. Michael kicks a ball straight up in the air with an initial velocity of 73 feet per second.

    a. Write an inequality to represent this problem situation.

    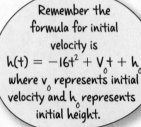

    Remember the formula for initial velocity is
    $$h(t) = -16t^2 + v_0 t + h_0$$
    where v_0 represents initial velocity and h_0 represents initial height.

    b. Use your inequality to determine whether Michael's team will be penalized for hitting the ceiling. Explain your reasoning.

2. Glen High School's student council is hosting a dance to raise money for panda bears. The dance will cost $2250. At the current ticket price of $10, the council knows that they will have 185 people attend the dance. This is not enough people to cover the cost of the dance, so they estimate that for every $0.25 decrease in ticket price, 15 more people will attend the dance.

    a. Write an equation that will represent the profit that the dance will make.

    b. Write an inequality to represent the dance making a profit.

c. Determine the maximum price the council can charge for tickets and still make a profit.

d. Determine the price of the ticket that will maximize profit. What is the maximum profit?

3. Use a graphing calculator to solve each inequality.

   a. $-5 \geq x^3 - 9x$ **b.** $0 < 2x^3 - 3x^2 - 3x + 2$

4. The average blood sugar (also known as glucose) levels in a person's blood should be between 70 and 100 mg/dL (milligrams per deciliter) one hour after eating. A person with Type 2 diabetes strives to keep glucose levels under 120 mg/dL with diet and exercise in order to avoid insulin injections. Glucose levels of one individual over the span of 72 hours can be represented with the polynomial function,

$$b(t) = 0.000139x^4 - 0.0188x^3 + 0.8379x^2 - 13.55x + 176.51$$

where glucose levels is a function of the number of hours.

a. For what hours were the glucose levels greater than 120 mg/dL?

b. For what hours were the glucose levels less than 120 mg/dL?

5. Solve each inequality by factoring and sketching. Use the coordinate plane to sketch the general graph of the polynomial in order to determine which values satisfy the inequality.

a. $2x^3 - 8x^2 - 8x + 32 > 0$

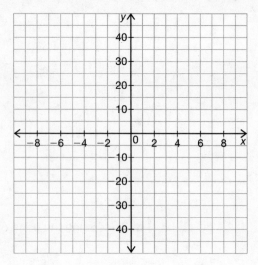

Think about the inequality sign when graphing the polynomial. Will it be a dashed or solid smooth curve?

b. $6x^3 - 21x^2 - 12x > 0$

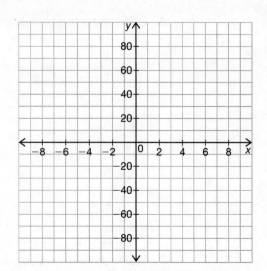

c. $x^4 - 13x^2 + 36 \leq 0$

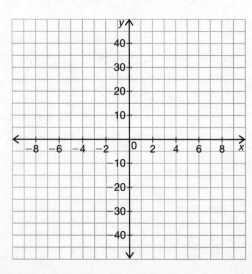

Be prepared to share your solutions and methods.

America's Next Top Polynomial Model

Modeling with Polynomials

Transportation plans are an essential part of any large urban development project. Whether designing residential blocks, shopping districts, or stadiums, part of the planning process is determining how to move large groups of people in and out of an area quickly. Building new highways, bus stations, bike lanes, or railways may be necessary for some large-scale developments.

Part of urban development projects is monitoring existing conditions in a specific area. Planners must determine how well the current traffic infrastructure meets the community's needs before modeling and predicting what transportation processes may work best for a future project.

What things do you consider when planning projects? What type of predictions or considerations do you make when planning projects?

City planners consider building a new stadium on several acres of land close to the downtown of a large city. They monitored the number of cars entering and exiting downtown from a major highway between 1:00 PM and 7:00 PM to determine current traffic conditions.

1. Analyze the table of values that represent the average number of cars entering and exiting downtown during the given hours of a typical weekday. The value for time represents the start-time for the full hour over which the vehicles were monitored.

Time (PM)	Average Number of Vehicles on a Typical Weekday (thousands)
1:00	7.0
2:00	10.8
3:00	14.5
4:00	21.1
5:00	23.9
6:00	19.0
7:00	10.0

When entering the data into your calculator, enter 1:00 as 1, 2:00 as 2, 3:00 as 3, etc.

a. Describe any patterns you notice. Explain the patterns in the context of this problem situation.

b. Predict the type of polynomial that best fits the data. Explain your reasoning.

7

2. Create a scatter plot of the data.

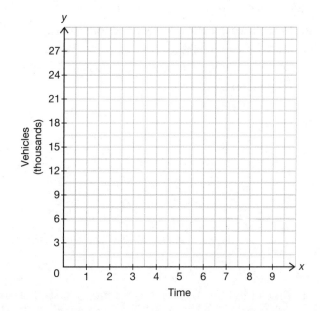

Recall that a **regression equation** is a function that models the relationship between two variables in a scatter plot. The regression equation can be used to make predictions about future events. Any degree polynomial can model a scatter plot, but data generally has one curve that best fits the data. You may also recall that the **coefficient of determination** (R^2) measures the "strength" of the relationship between the original data and its regression equation. The value ranges from 0 to 1 with a value of 1 indicating a perfect fit between the regression equation and the original data.

3. Use a graphing calculator to determine the regression equation for the average number of cars entering and exiting downtown on a typical weekday. Sketch the regression equation on the coordinate plane in Question 2. How well does the regression equation model the data? Was your prediction about the type of polynomial that best fits the data correct? Explain your reasoning.

4. Use the regression equation that best models the data to make predictions.

   a. Downtown is congested when more than 20,000 cars are on the streets and highway. Predict when the downtown will be congested. Explain your reasoning.

Use what you know about polynomials to work efficiently. Predict which degree function is the best fit first, then check to see if it has an R^2 value close to 1.

   b. Predict the hours when the number of cars that enter and exit downtown is less than 10,000. Explain your reasoning.

   c. Predict the number of vehicles that enter or exit downtown during the hour starting at noon.

   d. Predict the number of vehicles that enter or exit downtown during the hour starting at 9 PM.

   e. Predict the number of cars that enter or exit downtown during the hour starting at midnight the previous evening.

5. Consider the data and your regression equation.

    a. For what intervals is the model appropriate for this problem situation? For what intervals is the model inappropriate? Explain your reasoning.

    b. Sketch a curve that you believe accurately predicts the number of vehicles on the road over a 2-day period. Explain your reasoning.

When are more drivers on the road? When are fewer drivers on the road? Will the graph follow any patterns?

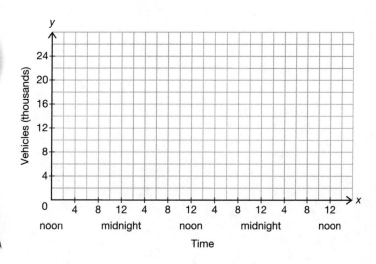

6. Do you think a polynomial function could accurately model this problem situation over the next 2 months before the next planning phase? Explain your reasoning.

PROBLEM 2 Keep It to a Minimum

Although the minimum wage may vary from state to state, the U.S. federal government sets an absolute minimum wage for the nation every few years.

1. Analyze the table of values that shows the absolute minimum wage, and the years they were enacted by Congress.

Time Since 1950 (years)	Absolute Minimum Wage (dollars)
5	0.75
6	1.00
11	1.15
13	1.25
17	1.40
18	1.60
24	2.00
25	2.10
28	2.65
29	2.90
30	3.10
31	3.35
40	3.80
41	4.25
46	4.75
47	5.15
57	5.85
58	6.55
59	7.25

Make sure you are comfortable with the data before analyzing the problem. How would you represent 1975? 1950? 1945?

a. Describe any patterns you notice.

b. Predict the type of polynomial that best fits this data. Explain your reasoning.

7

2. Analyze the data graphically.

   a. Use a graphing calculator to determine the best regression function $f(x)$ to model the changes in the minimum wage over the years since 1950. Sketch the regression equation on the coordinate plane.

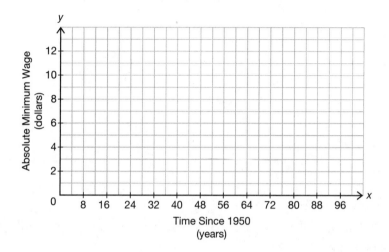

   b. How well does the regression function model this data? Explain your reasoning.

All of the decimal places are important in your regression equation, so don't round your answer when entering it into your graphing calculator.

3. Use the regression equation that best models the data to make predictions.

   a. Predict the absolute minimum wage in 2020. Explain your reasoning.

b. Predict the minimum wage in 1945. Explain your reasoning.

c. Predict when the minimum wage is greater than $12.50. Explain your reasoning.

4. Use the regression function to make predictions about events in the distant past and distant future.

   a. According to the regression equation, what was the minimum wage when the Civil War ended in 1865? Explain your reasoning.

   b. Predict the years when the minimum wage will be greater than $15.00. Explain your reasoning.

   c. Do you think that a cubic model is appropriate to predict minimum wages in the distant past and future? Explain your reasoning.

Let's take a closer look at the minimum wage in the early part of the 20th Century. A minimum wage did not exist until 1938 under the Fair Labor Standards Act. Before this time, employers could pay employees any hourly wage that employees were willing to accept. The initial hourly minimum wage in 1938 was $0.25 per hour. The wage increased steadily before reaching $0.75 in 1955.

5. Consider the minimum wage from 1900 to 1955.

   a. Sketch a graph that you believe accurately models the minimum wage for the time interval (1900, 1955). Explain your reasoning.

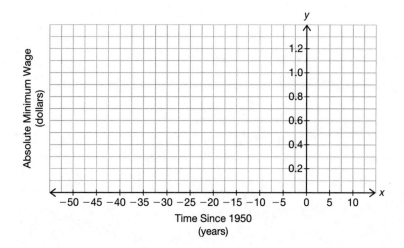

   b. Do you think a polynomial function can accurately model the changes in minimum wage in the 20th Century? Explain your reasoning.

Be prepared to share your solutions and methods.

7

Connecting Pieces
Piecewise Functions

In this lesson, you will:

- Write a piecewise function to model data.
- Graph a piecewise function.
- Determine intervals for a piecewise function to best model data.

- piecewise function

Some of the most popular children's books from the 1980s and 1990s had an interesting format: the reader controlled the action of the story! At various key moments throughout the text, the reader was given an opportunity to make a decision about the main character's next move. Each choice led to a different outcome.

For example, in a dragon adventure, the reader may have to decide whether the knight should run and hide from a dragon, or grab a sword and try to slay the beast. One set of conditions led to one outcome, while another set of conditions led to a different outcome.

This idea is fairly common today, but at the time it was revolutionary for the same book to have multiple story lines and endings.

Have you ever read a book like this? If so, what did you like or dislike about it?

Recall the minimum wage problem from the previous lesson.

The table shows the absolute minimum wage during various years. A scatter plot of this data is also shown.

Time Since 1950 (years)	Absolute Minimum Wage (dollars)
5	0.75
6	1.00
11	1.15
13	1.25
17	1.40
18	1.60
24	2.00
25	2.10
28	2.65
29	2.90
30	3.10
31	3.35
33	3.35
35	3.35
38	3.35
39	3.35
40	3.80
41	4.25
46	4.75
47	5.15
48	5.15
50	5.15
53	5.15
56	5.15
57	5.85
58	6.55
59	7.25

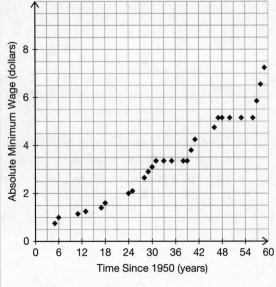

Sometimes, a single polynomial function is not the best model for a set of data. Analyze the graph of the minimum wage data. Instead of using a single polynomial function to model this data, consider separating the data into "pieces," where each piece is modeled by a single polynomial function.

To determine the pieces, look for breaks in the patterns that you see in the data. For example, the data in one part of the graph may appear to be linear, but then it may appear to be cubic in another part of the graph. Therefore, you can model these two parts of the graph with two different polynomial functions.

7

The number of pieces, or functions, that model the data can vary. For example, one person may look at the data and determine that it can be represented with two polynomial functions, while another person may see three, four, or even more functions.

Let's model the absolute minimum wage data by dividing it into five pieces, where each piece is modeled by a different polynomial function.

1. How do you think the data should be divided so that there are five pieces? Circle each piece on the given graph.

2. Consider the data from the years 1955 through 1981.

   a. Describe the type of polynomial function that best models the data over this interval. Explain your reasoning.

   Your graphing calculator is limited in that it can only calculate linear, quadratic, cubic, and quartic polynomial regressions. So, choose one of these for each regression equation.

   b. Write the regression equation that best models the data over this interval.

   c. What is the coefficient of determination for the regression equation? Is the model you chose a good fit for the data over this interval? Explain why or why not.

3. Consider the data after the year 1981 and before the year 1989.

   a. Describe the type of polynomial function that best models the data over this interval. Explain your reasoning.

   b. Determine a regression equation for this data over this interval.

   c. What is the coefficient of determination for the regression equation? Is the model you chose a good fit for the data over this interval? Explain why or why not.

4. Consider the data from the years 1989 through 1997.

    a. Describe the type of polynomial function that best models the data over this interval. Explain your reasoning.

    b. Determine a regression equation for this data over this interval.

    c. What is the coefficient of determination for the regression equation? Is the model you chose a good fit for the data over this interval? Explain why or why not.

5. Consider the data after the year 1997 and before the year 2006.

    a. Describe the type of polynomial function that best models the data over this interval. Explain your reasoning.

    b. Determine a regression equation for this data over this interval.

    c. What is the coefficient of determination for the regression equation? Is the model you chose a good fit for the data over this interval? Explain why or why not.

6. Consider the data from the years 2006 through 2009.

    a. Describe the type of polynomial function that best models the data over this interval. Explain your reasoning.

b. Determine a regression equation for this data over this interval.

c. What is the coefficient of determination for the regression equation? Is the model you chose a good fit for the data over this interval? Explain why or why not.

The year 1955 is represented by $x = 5$, not $x = 1955$. Remember this when you write each domain.

7. Write the equation of the function $f(x)$, where $f(x)$ includes each regression equation you used to model the absolute minimum wage data from the years 1955 through 2009. Write each equation on the line before the comma and write its corresponding domain on the line after the comma. Then, use a graphing calculator to sketch the graph of this function on the scatter plot at the beginning of the problem.

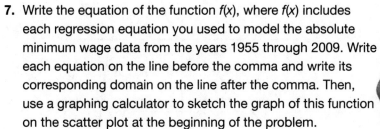

$$f(x) = \begin{cases} \underline{\hspace{6cm}}, & \underline{\hspace{2cm}} \\ \underline{\hspace{6cm}}, & \underline{\hspace{2cm}} \\ \underline{\hspace{6cm}}, & \underline{\hspace{2cm}} \\ \underline{\hspace{6cm}}, & \underline{\hspace{2cm}} \\ \underline{\hspace{6cm}}, & \underline{\hspace{2cm}} \end{cases}$$

8. Explain why the function you wrote in Question 7 is a better fit for the data than a single linear, quadratic, cubic, or quartic function.

You have just written the equation for a *piecewise function*. A **piecewise function** includes different functions that represent different parts of the domain.

A piecewise function and its graph are shown.

$$f(x) = \begin{cases} x, & x < 0 \\ x^2, & 0 \leq x < 3 \\ -(x-5)^3 + 1, & x \geq 3 \end{cases}$$

Notice the domain is the set of real numbers broken into three different parts.

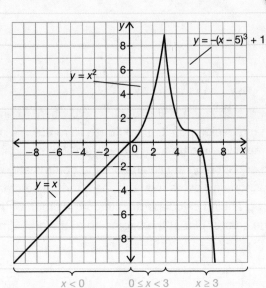

7

9. Sketch each piecewise function.

Pay attention to whether the endpoints are included or not included for each part of the piecewise function.

a. $g(x) = \begin{cases} \frac{1}{2}x + 1, & x < 4 \\ -(x - 4)^2 + 3, & x \geq 4 \end{cases}$

b. $t(x) = \begin{cases} x, & x < -2 \\ x^4 - 25x^2, & -2 \leq x \leq 2 \\ 2, & x > 2 \end{cases}$

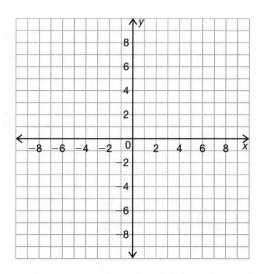

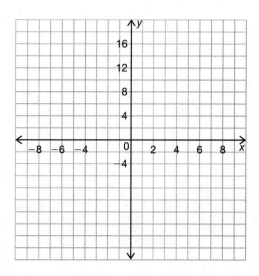

10. Billie, Kyle, and Avery were each asked to write the piecewise function to represent the graph shown.

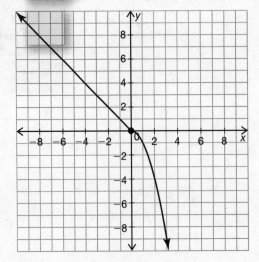

Kyle
$$f(x) = \begin{cases} -x, & x < 0 \\ -x^2, & x \geq 0 \end{cases}$$

Avery
$$f(x) = \begin{cases} -x, & x \leq 0 \\ -x^2, & x > 0 \end{cases}$$

Billie
$$f(x) = \begin{cases} -x, & x \leq 0 \\ -x^2, & x \geq 0 \end{cases}$$

Does analyzing a graph without a scenario change the way you write the function?

Who's correct? Explain your reasoning.

11. Write the equation for each piecewise function given its graph.

a. $h(x) =$

b. $b(x) =$

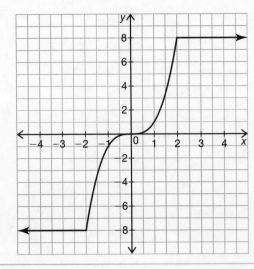

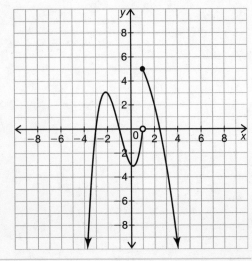

Salinity Now! Salinity Now!

Salinity is the measure of saltiness, or dissolved salt content in water. Salinity in an estuary changes due to location, tidal functions, seasonal weather changes, and volume of freshwater runoff. Ecologists routinely measure salinity in estuaries because of its impact on plants, animals, and people. Too much salinity can reduce vegetation in surrounding areas.

The table shows the salinity levels in an estuary in North Carolina over a period of 24 days. A scatter plot of this data is also shown.

Time (days)	1	2	3	4	5	6	7	8
Salinity (parts per thousand)	27.9	27.9	28.2	30.5	29.6	28.3	27.9	27.9

Time (days)	9	10	11	12	13	14	15	16
Salinity (parts per thousand)	28.6	30.1	29.9	30	29.5	29.5	29.5	29.4

Time (days)	17	18	19	20	21	22	23	24
Salinity (parts per thousand)	29.2	29.1	29.0	29.0	28.9	28.8	28.8	28.7

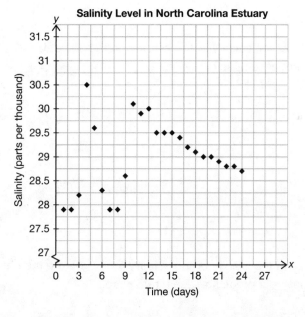

1. Consider the data for the first ten days. Determine the regression equation that is the best fit for the data over this interval. Explain your reasoning.

2. Consider the data after the tenth day. Determine the regression equation that is the best fit for the data over this interval. Explain your reasoning.

3. Use your answers to Questions 1 and 2 to write a piecewise function that models the salinity over the 24-day period. Then, graph the function on the scatter plot.

4. Predict the salinity of the estuary on the 30th day. Does your prediction seem reasonable?

 5. Predict the salinity of the estuary 5 days before the data in the table was recorded. Does your prediction seem reasonable?

The table shows the average price of a gallon of regular unleaded gas from the years 1980 through 2008.

Years Since 1980	0	1	2	3	4	5	6	7	8	9
Average Gas Price (dollars)	1.25	1.38	1.30	1.24	1.21	1.20	0.93	0.95	0.95	1.02

Years Since 1980	10	11	12	13	14	15	16	17	18	19
Average Gas Price (dollars)	1.16	1.14	1.13	1.11	1.11	1.15	1.23	1.23	1.06	1.17

Years Since 1980	20	21	22	23	24	25	26	27	28
Average Gas Price (dollars)	1.51	1.46	1.36	1.59	1.88	2.30	2.59	2.80	3.27

1. Create a scatter plot of the data on the grid shown.

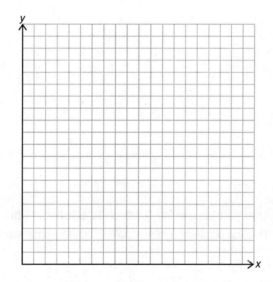

2. Describe the type of function(s) that best models this data. Explain your reasoning.

3. Consider using a piecewise function to model this data. Determine the intervals for the domain, and the type of polynomial function for each interval. Explain your reasoning.

4. Write a piecewise function to model the data. Then, graph the piecewise function on the grid in Question 1.

5. Use your piecewise function to predict the price of gas in the year 2020. Does your prediction seem reasonable? Explain your reasoning.

Life expectancy is a prediction of the number of years that a person will live. Life expectancies often vary significantly over time and across different groups such as country, gender, and race.

The table shows the average life expectancy of a person from the years 1910 through 1920.

Years Since 1910	0	1	2	3	4	5
Life Expectancy (years)	50.6	52.7	53.7	52.7	54.4	54.7

Years Since 1910	6	7	8	9	10
Life Expectancy (years)	52.0	51.2	39.4	54.8	54.1

1. Create a scatter plot of this data on the grid shown.

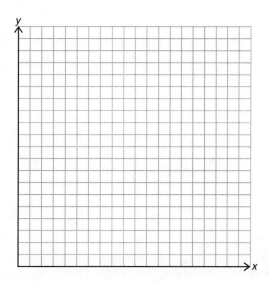

2. Write a piecewise function to model the data. Then, graph the piecewise function on the grid. Explain your reasoning.

 3. Write a brief report that explains the patterns shown by the data in terms of life expectancy from 1910 through 1920. Do some research and use facts to support your claims.

Talk the Talk

 Write a brief summary about what you've learned about using piecewise functions to model real-world data. Include advantages and disadvantages of using a piecewise function instead of a single function type to model data.

 Be prepared to share your solutions and methods.

Modeling Gig
Modeling Polynomial Data

LEARNING GOALS

In this lesson, you will:

- Model a problem situation with a polynomial function.
- Solve problems using a regression equation.

Americans watch a lot of movies. The first ever movie was made in the 1870s, but it wasn't until the early 20th century that movie theaters were invented. Americans lined up to pay a quarter to see black and white productions with no sound. As audio-visual technology advanced, so did the quality of movie productions. Changes in technology not only improved the quality of movies, they also led to changes in the entire industry.

The Video Home System (also known as VHS), developed in the 1970s, allowed consumers to rent or purchase movies and watch them on their TVs at home. With the invention of the remote control, people could even fast forward to their favorite parts, without even getting off the couch! Video stores were a huge business, leading way to newer technology that allowed customers to stream movies from their computers at home.

How do you think movies will change throughout the 21st Century? Do you think people will still go to "old-fashioned" movie theaters to watch movies?

The CALC_U-Now Company sells a variety of calculators. The table shows the relationship between the price of various models of graphing calculators and the monthly profit earned from the sale of the calculators.

 1. Analyze the data in the table of values.

Price of Calculators (dollars)	Monthly Profit (dollars)
65	15,950
70	17,600
75	19,060
80	19,300
85	19,290
90	19,240
95	18,000
100	17,150
105	15,300

    a. What patterns do you notice in the data?

    b. Describe the polynomial function that best models this data. Explain your reasoning.

2. Use a graphing calculator to determine the regression function that best models this data.

3. Write inequalities to represent the prices for which CALC-U-Now would lose money? Explain your reasoning.

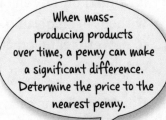

When mass-producing products over time, a penny can make a significant difference. Determine the price to the nearest penny.

 4. CALC-U-Now must make budget cuts! As a financial contractor, you must determine which calculator price will generate the most profit. Write a statement to support your decision including all relevant mathematics.

3,2,1.... Polynomial Modeling Action!

Inflation has influenced the price of a movie ticket over the years. The first movie theater opened in the year 1900, charging $.05 per ticket. The data provided shows how the average price of a movie ticket has increased over the years.

Years	Average Price of a Movie Ticket (dollars)
1900	0.05
1948	0.36
1958	0.68
1971	1.65
1983	3.15
1995	4.35
2003	6.03
2007	6.88
2009	7.50

Remember the function that best models the data has a coefficient of determination closest to 1.

1. Determine a regression function that best models this data.

2. Use your regression equation to predict when the average price of a movie ticket will reach $15.00. Explain your reasoning.

3. Use your regression equation to predict the cost of a movie ticket in the year 2100. Explain your reasoning.

7

4. Jessica and Lindsay disagree over how to model this situation with a polynomial function.

> **Jessica**
>
> A cubic function is the most appropriate model. The coefficient of determination is closest to 1.

> **Lindsay**
>
> A piece-wise function is most appropriate for this situation.

Who's correct? Explain your reasoning.

"Polynomial Models" for $500, Please!

 The Math Club sponsors an event each year to raise money for their trip to the Quiz Bowl. As the president of the Math Club, you propose having a movie night fundraiser. You survey the students to see how many students will attend. The number of students varies depending on the ticket price.

Ticket Price (dollars)	Students Who Will Attend
1.25	120
1.75	105
2.25	95
2.75	83
3.25	77
3.75	64
4.25	58
4.75	40
5.25	30

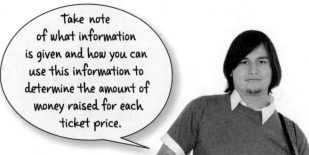

Take note of what information is given and how you can use this information to determine the amount of money raised for each ticket price.

Write a short letter to your principal about your findings. Include details about the exact ticket price that raises the most money as well as the approximate number of students who will attend.

 Be prepared to share your solutions and methods.

7

The Choice Is Yours
Comparing Polynomials in Different Representations

In this lesson, you will:

- Compare polynomials using different representations.
- Analyze key characteristics of polynomials.

Infinity refers to something that goes on without end. The set of natural numbers $\{1, 2, 3, \ldots\}$ and the set of integers $\{\ldots -2, -1, 0, 1, 2 \ldots\}$ are examples of infinite sets because they continue without end. Another example of an infinite set is the set of rational numbers between 0 and 1.

Seeing different infinite sets of numbers begs the question: do all infinite sets have the same quantity of numbers in them? The set of natural numbers are only positive, while the set of integers are positive and negative. Does this mean that the set of natural numbers has fewer numbers than the set of integers?

How do you compare the size of these sets of numbers? Is it possible for one infinite set to be greater than another infinite set?

Recall that you can represent a polynomial using a graph, table of values, equation, or description of its key characteristics. The ability to compare functions using different representations is an important mathematical habit. This skill allows you to model problems in different ways, solve problems using a variety of methods, and more easily identify patterns. At times you may need to compare functions when they are in different representations.

When comparing two functions in different forms, it may be helpful to ask yourself a series of questions. Examples include:

- *What information is given?*

- *What is the degree of each function?*

- *What do I know about all functions of this degree?*

- *What key characteristics do I need to know?*

- *How do the functions compare?*

Consider two polynomial functions $f(x)$ and $g(x)$. Which polynomial has a greater number of real zeros? Justify your choice.

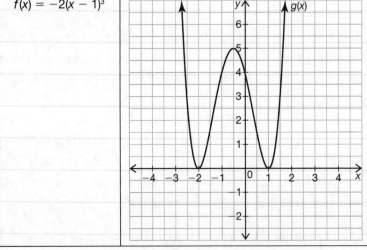

$f(x) = -2(x - 1)^3$

> Metacognition is an important mathematical habit that involves mentally asking yourself a series of questions to determine what you know about a problem and how you can reason your way to a solution.

- The Fundamental Theorem of Algebra states that the number of zeros must be equal to the degree of the function. Therefore, $f(x)$ has 3 zeros.

- The function $f(x)$ has a real zero at 1 (multiplicity 3), so all zeros are real.

- The graph of $g(x)$ shows each zero has multiplicity 2, for a total of 4 real zeros.

The function $g(x)$ has 4 real zeros while $f(x)$ has 3. Therefore the correct choice is $g(x)$.

1. Toby compared the table of values for $f(x)$ and the graph of $g(x)$ to determine which polynomial function has the greater number of real zeros.

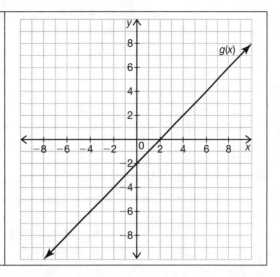

x	f(x)
−2	3
−1	−2
0	−5
1	−6
2	−5
3	−2
4	3

Toby

Function $g(x)$ has the greater number of real zeros. The graph has 1 zero at $x = 2$ while the table of values has no output value of 0, and therefore no zeros.

Is Toby correct? Explain your reasoning.

7

2. Analyze each pair of representations. Then, answer each question and justify your reasoning.

   a. Which function has a greater degree?

A polynomial function $h(x)$ has 1 absolute maximum and 1 relative maximum.	$j(x) = -40(x - 7)^2 + 30x^2 - 17x + 1$

   b. Which function has a greater degree?

x	m(x)	A polynomial function $n(x)$ has a real zero and an imaginary zero.
−2	9	
−1	3	
0	1	
1	3	
2	9	

   c. Which function has a degree divisible by 2?

x	p(x)	The function $q(x)$ has only imaginary solutions.
−2	2	
−1	4	
0	6	
1	8	
2	10	

7

d. Determine which function has the greater output as x approaches infinity.

An odd function $r(x)$ with $a < 0$.	$k(x) = x^6 + x^4 + 3x^2 + 5x - 10{,}000$

e. Determine which function has the greater output as x approaches negative infinity.

$t(x) = -3(x - 4)^8 + 130$	A quartic function $s(x)$ with y-intercept $(0, 5)$ and all imaginary roots.

3. Sam and Otis disagree when they compared the two functions shown to determine which one has an odd degree.

The function $f(x)$ has an absolute maximum value.	$g(x) = x^4(3 - x)(2x^2 + 3)(x^4 + 4)$

Sam

The function $f(x)$ has an odd degree because odd functions approach positive infinity as x either increases or decreases. This means $f(x)$ has a maximum value.

Otis

The function $g(x)$ has an odd degree. When I multiplied the factors, I got a term with a highest exponent of 11:
$x^4(-x)(2x^2)(x^4) = -2x^{11}$.
Therefore, $g(x)$ is odd.

Who is correct? Justify your reasoning.

Many problems in mathematics are unique, without specific step-by-step algorithms that lead to an answer. In Problem 1, *The Best of Both Representations*, you mentally asked yourself a series of metacognitive questions to compare functions in different representations. As you consider additional questions in this lesson, it may be helpful to compare the problems to ones that you have already completed.

Ask yourself:

* *How is this problem the same or different than the previous ones that I have already solved?*
* *What do I know about the function that is given? What can I conclude that is not directly stated?*

Consider the representations shown. Which function has a greater *y*-intercept? Justify your reasoning.

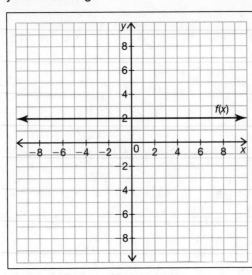

A function *g*(*x*) has an *a*-value less than zero and all roots have a multiplicity of 2.

Remember that the *a*-value is the coefficient of the leading term. For example, in the function $f(x) = 5x^2 + 3x + 4$, the *a*-value is 5.

Solution:

This problem is similar to previous problems in that you must consider functions with restrictions on the *a*-value and functions with multiple roots. The problem is also similar in that you must consider an output value for a given input. In this case, the input is 0.

In function *f*(*x*), the output value is 2 for any given input. Analyzing function *g*(*x*), the multiplicity 2 tells you that the function is even, and the negative *a*-value indicates that the function opens downward. The multiplicity of the roots also tells you that the function does not cross the *x*-axis. Instead, it reflects at a given point where the double root occurs.

Comparing the two functions, you know that function *g*(*x*) is always below the *x*-axis and function *f*(*x*) is above the *x*-axis. Therefore, *f*(*x*) has a greater *y*-intercept.

1. Isaac and Tina disagree over which function has a greater *y*-intercept.

		x	h(x)
$g(x) = 2(x - 2)(x + 2)(x - 3) - 4$		−2	−2
		−1	0
		0	4
		1	10
		2	18

Isaac

Function g(x) has a greater y-intercept. I calculated the y-intercept by substituting 0 for x. This value is greater than (0, 4) shown in the table for the function h(x).

Tina

Function h(x) has a greater y-intercept. The y-intercept of h(x) is (0, 4) and the y-intercept of g(x) is (0, −4).

Who is correct? Justify your reasoning.

2. Analyze each pair of representations. Then, answer each question and justify your reasoning.

   a. Which function has a greater average rate of change for the interval $(-4, 4)$?

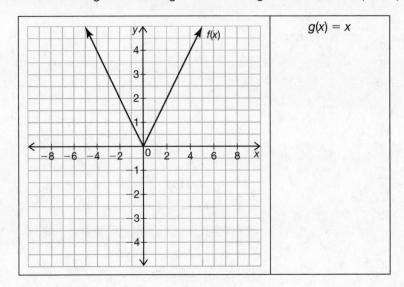

$g(x) = x$

   b. Which function has a greater average rate of change for the interval $(-1, 1)$?

x	j(x)
−2	4
−1	1
0	0
1	1
2	4

c. Which function has a greater relative minimum?

A cubic function $a(x)$ with $a > 0$ and 3 distinct real roots.

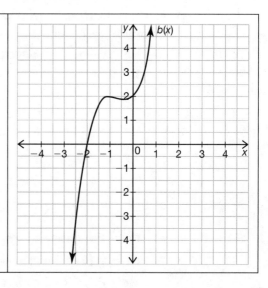

d. Which function's axis of symmetry has a greater x-value?

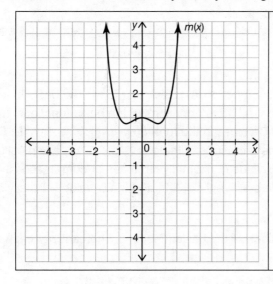

$$n(x) = x^2 - 3x + 1$$

3. Emilio studied the table of values and description of the key characteristics to determine which function has a greater minimum.

x	d(x)
−2	5
−1	2
0	1
1	2
2	5

A quartic function $m(x)$ has $a < 0$ and 2 pairs of real zeros (multiplicity 2).

Emilio

Function d(x) has a greater minimum. This function is a parabola opening up, with its vertex at (0, 1). Function m(x) opens down because a < 0. Since the real zeros have multiplicity 2, I know any real zeros occur when the function reflects off the x-axis. Therefore, the output values of m(x) never reach a point greater than y = 0.

Is Emilio correct? Justify your reasoning.

Recall that a basic function is a function in its simplest form. The basic function of a is $f(x) = x^n$ for any natural number n. Transformations of the basic functions are performed by changing the A-, B-, C-, and D-values in the form $g(x) = Af(B(x) − C) + D$. Remember, each value describes different transformations of the graph: the A-value vertically stretches or compresses the graph, the B-value horizontally stretches or compresses the graph, the C-value horizontally shifts the graph right or left, and the D-value vertically shifts the graph up or down.

4. Analyze the transformations of the basic functions. Then answer each question and justify your reasoning.

a. Which function has a greater output for a given input?

The basic quadratic function $f(x) = x^2$.	$g(x) = f(x − 2) + 1$

7

b. Which function has a lower minimum?

x	j(x)
−2	16
−1	1
0	0
1	1
2	16

$k(x) = 5f(x - 4) + 2$

c. Which function has the greater input for a given output value?

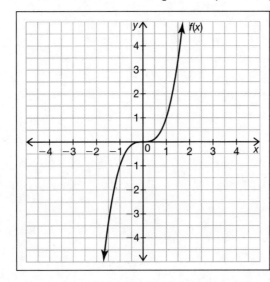

$g(x) = 3f(x - 5) + 1$

 Be prepared to share your solutions and methods.

7

7

- regression equation (7.2)
- coefficient of determination (7.2)
- piecewise function (7.3)

7.1 Determining When a Polynomial Function is Greater Than and When it is Less Than 0 Using Its Roots

To determine when a polynomial function is greater than or less than 0, first determine the zeros of the function or where the function equals 0. Then use the graph to determine whether the function is greater than or less than 0 for the intervals between the zeros.

Example

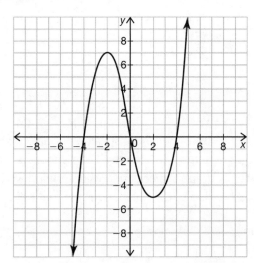

$f(x) < 0$ when $\begin{Bmatrix} x < -4 \\ 0 < x < 4 \end{Bmatrix}$

$f(x) > 0$ when $\begin{Bmatrix} -4 < x < 0 \\ x > 4 \end{Bmatrix}$

7.1 Determining the Solution to Polynomial Inequalities
Using a Graphing Calculator

You can use a graphing calculator to solve higher order polynomials that are not easily factorable.

Step 1:   Press **Y** = and input the expression.

Step 2:   Scroll to the left of the Y_1, when your cursor is blinking over the diagonal line, press **ENTER** 2 times, you will see the area above the diagonal shaded (this represents $y \geq$ expression). If you Press **ENTER** 1 more time, you will see the area below the diagonal line shaded (this represents $y \leq$ expression).

Step 3:   Make sure your viewing window is appropriate and press **GRAPH**.

Step 4:   To determine the particular values of x that makes the inequality true, press 2nd, **CALC, 2:ZERO**. Scroll to the appropriate bounds to determine the zeros.

Step 5:   Determine if x must be greater than or less than the roots depending on the inequality sign for your solution.

Example

$12 < x^2 - 2x + 3$

$x < -2.16$ or $x > 4.16$

7.1 Determining the Solution to Polynomial Inequalities
Algebraically and Graphically

When solving polynomial inequalities treat the inequality as an equation and solve. Factor or use the quadratic formula to determine the x-intercepts. Then choose a test point between each interval created by the roots or graph the equation to determine which values satisfy the inequality. The section(s) that provide a true solution for the test point is the solution to the inequality.

Example

$x^2 - x - 12 < 0$

$(x + 3)(x - 4) = 0$

$x = -3, 4$

$x^2 - x - 12 < 0$ when $-3 < x < 4$

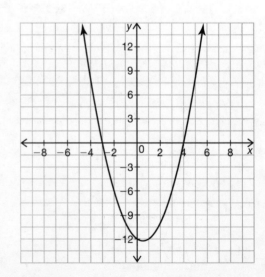

Determining the Appropriate Regression Equation to Model a Problem

Analyze data as a scatter plot to identify any patterns in the data. Based on how the data increases or decreases, determine the type of polynomial that best fits the data. Then, use a graphing calculator to determine the regression equation. A regression equation is a function that models the relationship between 2 variables in a scatter plot. Generally, there is 1 curve or degree of polynomial that will best fit the data. The coefficient of determination measures the strength of the relationship between the original data and the regression equation. The value ranges from 0 to 1 with a value of 1 indicating a perfect fit between the curve and the original data.

Example

The table shows the concentration of medication in a patient's blood as time passes.

Time (hours)	Concentration (mg/l)
0	0
0.5	78
1	100
1.5	84
2	50
2.5	15

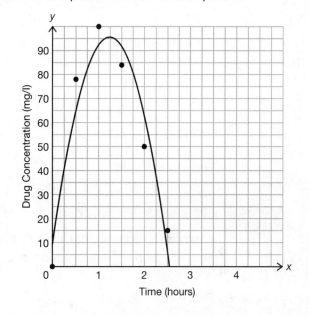

The data could be represented by a quadratic equation.

Regression equation:
$y = -56.357x^2 + 139.464x + 9.321$

Coefficient of determination: 0.924

The curve is a pretty good fit for the data.

Predicting Outcomes Using a Regression Equation

The regression equation is often used to make predictions about past and future events. Substitute various inputs into the regression equation to determine the likely outputs. Or, use intersecting lines to determine inputs.

Example

The medicine is considered at its most effective when the concentration in the blood is at least 60 mg/l. About for how long after administering is the medicine most effective? Use the regression equation: $g(x) = -56.357x^2 + 139.464x + 9.321$ where x is time in hours and $g(x)$ is the concentration of the medicine in the blood in mg/l.

The drug is most effective between 0.44 hour after administering and 2.03 hours after administering.

7.3 Graphing a Piecewise Function

A piecewise function includes different functions that represent different parts of the domain. Sometimes a single polynomial function is not the best model for a set of data. Data with breaks in the patterns can be better modeled by separating the data into pieces where each piece is modeled by a different polynomial function. Each equation can be graphed for its domain. Open points are associated with $<$ and $>$ and closed points are associated with $\leq$ and $\geq$.

Example

$$d(x) = \begin{cases} x^2 - 3x + 5, & x < 3 \\ 4x - 1, & x \geq 3 \end{cases}$$

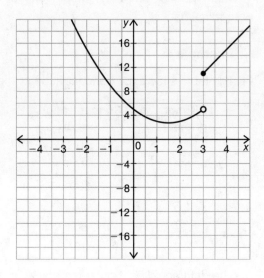

7.3 Writing a Piecewise Function Based on Its Graph

A regression equation can be determined for each interval on the graph of a piecewise function given with the appropriate domain.

Example

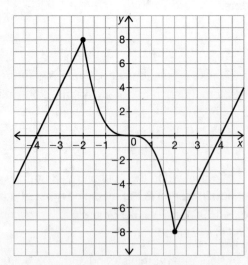

$$c(x) = \begin{cases} 4x + 16, & x \leq -2 \\ -x^3, & -2 < x < 2 \\ 4x - 16, & x \geq 2 \end{cases}$$

Modeling a Problem Situation with a Polynomial Function

Examine data in a table or scatter plot for patterns to determine what type of polynomial would best match the data. Use a graphing calculator to determine a regression equation to best model the data.

Example

Day	Attendance
1	40
2	70
3	50
4	60
5	75
6	45
7	0

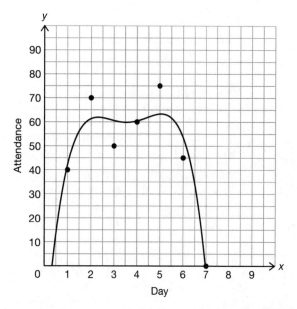

The data increases, decreases, increases, and decreases. A quartic function would best model the data.

Regression equation: $y = -0.758x^4 + 11.01x^3 - 57.083x^2 + 124.72x - 35.714$

Solving Problems Using Polynomial Regression Equations

Use the regression equation for the data to answer questions and make predictions about the data. The vertex, intersection of lines, or table of values can each be useful for solving problems about the data.

Example

Attendance at a local museum fluctuates throughout the week according to the regression equation $f(x) = -0.758x^4 + 11.01x^3 - 57.083x^2 + 124.72x - 35.714$, where x is the day and $f(x)$ is attendance. If the days 1–7 correspond to days of the week Monday through Sunday, how many people should the museum plan to expect on a typical Wednesday?

The museum can expect about 60–61 people on a typical Wednesday.

7

Polynomials can be represented using a graph, table of values, equation, or description of key characteristics. When comparing 2 functions in different forms, important information to look for includes the degree of each function, the shape of the graph, the number and type of zeros, transformations of a basic function, etc.

Example

Which polynomial function has an even degree?

$a(x)$	$b(x)$
A polynomial function with 2 absolute maximums and 1 relative minimum.	$b(x) = 4(3 - 2x) + 3(x + 6)$

The function $a(x)$ has an even degree. A function with 3 turns must have a degree greater than 3. And, having absolute maximums means the end behavior of the function is to approach negative infinity as x approaches both negative and positive infinity. This indicates an even degree function. The function $b(x)$ is a linear function—the x-values are added, not multiplied.

Sequences and Series

8

Covered in bees!
Bees build honeycombs to hold larvae, pollen, and of course honey. Honeycombs are constructed of hexagonal cells that tile a surface with no overlaps or gaps.

571

Sequence—Not Just Another Glittery Accessory

Arithmetic and Geometric Sequences

"Ostinato" is a musical term that indicates a repeating pattern of notes. A word that you might be familiar with that is related to "ostinato" is "obstinate," meaning "stubborn".

An ostinato is indeed a stubborn pattern. Musicians commonly use ostinati (the plural of ostinato) to underlay a particular feeling they want a certain song to portray. They may also use it to stabilize a variety of pitches to provide uniformity within a song.

A basso ostinato is a type of ostinato that is used to form a harmonic pattern and is repeated throughout a song. Some argue that the basso ostinato should be thought of more as a device than a form of music.

The term "riff" is the modern day ostinato for popular music. A riff is defined as a short series of notes that create a melody within a melody of a song. Unlike an ostinato, a riff does not need to be repeated throughout the whole song.

You may be familiar with Pachelbel's Canon in D, which features one of the most famous repeating patterns of all time.

Just as with ostinati, when dealing with sequences, you look to identify an underlying pattern. You try to identify what it is that is moving the pattern along, so that you may be able to determine what is coming next.

PROBLEM 1 **I Spy With My Little Eye, A Pattern!**

Patterns, both numerical and physical, can be defined as sequences. Recall, a sequence is a pattern involving an ordered arrangement of numbers, geometric figures, letters, or other objects called terms. An **arithmetic sequence** is a sequence of terms in which the difference between any two consecutive terms is a constant. A **geometric sequence** is a sequence of terms in which the ratio between any two consecutive terms is a constant. A sequence that is neither arithmetic or geometric has a pattern, but there is no common difference or ratio.

Sequences can have a fixed number of terms, or they can continue forever. If a sequence terminates it is called a **finite sequence**. If a sequence continues forever it is called an **infinite sequence**.

An ellipsis is 3 periods which means "and so on." Ellipses are used to represent infinite sequences.

1. Lisa and Ray give the next few terms in the sequence: 1, 1, 1, . . .

Lisa

2, 2, 2, 3, 3, 3

The sequence is writing each natural number three times.

Ray

1, 1, 1, 1, 1, 1, . . .

The sequence just repeats 1 forever.

Who is correct? Explain your reasoning.

It is important to recognize that when you are only given the first few terms in a sequence, you may not have enough information to determine the next term.

2. Analyze each sequence and then circle the appropriate type of sequence. If the sequence is arithmetic, identify the common difference. If the sequence is geometric, identify the common ratio. Finally, circle whether the sequence is finite or infinite.

a. number of tiles

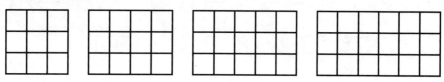

Arithmetic _____ Geometric _____ Neither
Sequence   Sequence

Infinite Sequence   Finite Sequence

b. number of toothpicks

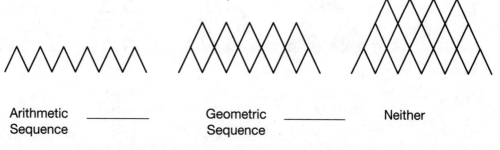

Arithmetic _____ Geometric _____ Neither
Sequence   Sequence

Infinite Sequence   Finite Sequence

c. number of rows

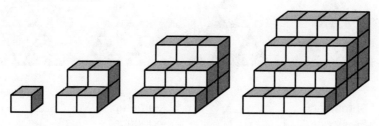

Arithmetic _____ Geometric _____ Neither
Sequence   Sequence

Infinite Sequence   Finite Sequence

d. number of cubes

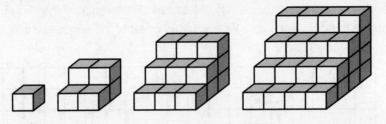

Arithmetic _____ Geometric _____ Neither
Sequence Sequence

Infinite Sequence Finite Sequence

e. number of black triangles

Arithmetic _____ Geometric _____ Neither
Sequence Sequence

Infinite Sequence Finite Sequence

f. number of white triangles

Arithmetic _____ Geometric _____ Neither
Sequence Sequence

Infinite Sequence Finite Sequence

g. Side length of smallest shaded square within the unit square

Arithmetic _____ Geometric _____ Neither
Sequence Sequence

Infinite Sequence Finite Sequence

h. Number of shaded squares

Arithmetic _____ Geometric _____ Neither
Sequence Sequence

Infinite Sequence Finite Sequence

3. Create your own sequence given the type indicated. Include the first three terms.

   a. Arithmetic Sequence

   b. Geometric Sequence

   c. Neither Arithmetic or Geometric Sequence

PROBLEM 2 **Formula: Not Just for Babies**

 Previously, you learned the explicit and recursive formulas for arithmetic and geometric sequences. An explicit formula for a sequence is a formula used for calculating each term of the sequence using the index, a term's position in the sequence. A recursive formula generates each new term of a sequence based on a preceding term of the sequence.

	Arithmetic Sequence	**Geometric Sequence**
Explicit Formula	$a_n = a_1 + d(n - 1)$ where a_1 is the first term, d is the common difference, and n is the nth term in the sequence.	$g_n = g_1 \cdot r^{n-1}$ where g_1 is the first term, and r is the common ratio.
Recursive Formula	$a_n = a_{n-1} + d$ where a_{n-1} is the term previous to a_n, and d is the common difference.	$g_n = g_{n-1} \cdot r$ where g_{n-1} is the term previous to g_n, and r is the common ratio.

 1. Consider the sequence in Problem 1, Question 2, part (a), *number of tiles*.

   a. Use the recursive formula to determine the 5th term.

   b. Use the explicit formula to determine the 5th term.

2. Consider the sequence in Problem 1, Question 1, part (e), *number of black triangles*.

   a. Use the recursive formula to determine the 5th term.

   b. Use the explicit formula to determine the 5th term.

 3. Which formula would you use if you wanted to determine the 95th term of either sequence? Explain your reasoning.

4. Identify each sequence as arithmetic, geometric, or neither. If possible, determine the 50th term of each sequence.

a. $-5, -1, 3, 7, 11, 15, 19, 23 \ldots$

Type of Sequence: _____

50th term: _____

b. $0, 1, 1, 2, 3, 5, 8, 13 \ldots$

Type of Sequence: _____

50th term: _____

c. $27, 9, 3, 1, \dfrac{1}{3}, \dfrac{1}{9}, \dfrac{1}{27}, \dfrac{1}{81}$

Type of Sequence: _____

50th term: _____

5. Use either the recursive or explicit formula to determine each answer.

a. The sum of the interior angles in a triangle is 180°, in a quadrilateral is 360°, and in a pentagon is 540°. How many degrees are in a decagon?

b. The employees at Franco's Pizza Shack turn the pizza ovens down to 200° overnight. When the workers open the shop in the morning, they turn the ovens up to 550°. The temperature of each oven increases by 40% every 30 minutes. Will the ovens reach the required 550° in 1.5 hours?

Talk the Talk

Complete each row in the table using the given information in that row.

	Sequences	Type of Sequence	Recursive Formula	Explicit Formula
A			$g_n = 3(g_{n-1})$ $g_1 = 4$	
B	320, 80, 20, 5, . . .			
C			$a_n = a_{n-1} + 10$ $a_1 = 20$	
D				$g_n = 10 \cdot 5^{n-1}$ $n = 1, 2, 3 \ldots$
E	3, 11, 19, 27 . . .			
F				$a_n = 5 + 20(n - 1)$ $n = 1, 2, 3 \ldots$

Be prepared to share your solutions and methods.

This Is Series(ous) Business

Finite Arithmetic Series

LEARNING GOALS

In this lesson, you will:

- Compute a finite series.
- Use sigma notation to represent a finite series.
- Use Gauss's method to compute finite arithmetic series.
- Write a function to represent a finite arithmetic series.
- Use finite arithmetic series to solve real-world problems.

KEY TERMS

- tessellation
- series
- finite series
- infinite series
- arithmetic series

Honey bees are fascinating little creatures. Did you know that honey bees are the only insects that produce food that humans eat? They also identify members of their colony by a unique smell.

Another amazing aspect of the honey bee is how they build their hive. Honey bees build hexagonal honey cells from a single cell. Layers of honey cells are then built around the edges, as shown.

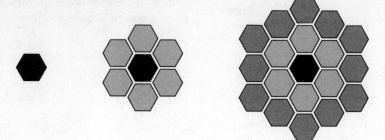

Could you sketch the next figure in the sequence? Could you predict how many total hexagons would be in the next term of the sequence? How does this pattern translate to an arithmetic sequence?

Josephine is helping her little brother Pauley with his latest art project. He is using toothpicks to create a *tessellation*. A **tessellation** is created when a geometric shape is repeated over a two-dimensional plane such that there are no overlaps and no gaps.

Pauley starts his tessellation project by gluing toothpicks to a large piece of poster board to make a single diamond shape. This is the first row.

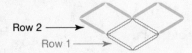

Then, he places additional toothpicks parallel to the first row to create the second row. The second row consists of two diamond shapes.

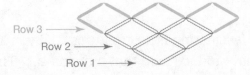

He continues to place toothpicks in this manner, so that each row has one more diamond shape than the previous row. The first three rows of Pauley's tessellation are shown.

 1. Sketch the next two rows of the tessellation on the previous diagram.

2. Complete the table to show the number of additional toothpicks used to create each row.

Row	Number of Additional Toothpicks Used to Create the Row
1	
2	
3	
4	
5	

3. Can this tessellation be represented by an arithmetic or geometric sequence? Explain how you know.

4. Write an explicit formula for this sequence. Let n represent the row number, and let a_n represent the number of additional toothpicks used to create that row.

5. Suppose that Pauley knows that he wants his tessellation to include 18 rows. How many additional toothpicks will he need for the 18th row? Explain how you determined your answer.

6. Describe how to calculate the total number of toothpicks that Pauley needs for a tessellation that includes 18 rows. (Do not actually perform the calculation.)

You know how to determine the *n*th term of a sequence. However, sometimes it is necessary to determine the *sum* of the terms in a sequence.

A **series** is the sum of terms in a given sequence. The sum of the first *n* terms of a sequence is denoted by S_n. For example, S_3 is the sum of the first three terms of a sequence.

There is a special notation for the summation of terms using a capital sigma, Σ:

upper bound of
summation

$$S_n = \sum_{i=1}^{n} a_i \leftarrow$$ an indexed variable representing each
successive term in the series

index of summation   lower bound of summation

This expression means sum the values of *a*, starting at a_1 and ending with a_n.

In other words, $S_n = \sum_{i=1}^{n} a_i = a_1 + a_2 + a_3 + \cdots + a_{n-1} + a_n$.

A series can be *finite* or *infinite*. A **finite series** is the sum of a finite number of terms. An **infinite series** is the sum of an infinite number of terms. For example, the sum of all of the even integers from 1 to 100 is a finite series, and the sum of all of the even whole numbers is an infinite series.

> Think about it . . . what is the sum of an infinite arithmetic series with a negative common difference? What is the sum of an infinite arithmetic series with a positive common difference?

7. Use sigma notation to rewrite each finite series, and then compute.

 a. 5 + 9 + 13 + 17 + 21

 $S_2 =$ _____

 $S_5 =$ _____

 b. 3 + 6 + 12 + 24 + 48 + 96 + 192

 $S_1 =$ _____

 $S_7 =$ _____

8. Use sigma notation to represent the total number of toothpicks Pauley needs to complete 5 rows of his tessellation. Then, use your table in Question 2 to calculate this amount.

PROBLEM 2   Gauss's Method to the Rescue!

Remember that an arithmetic sequence is a sequence of numbers in which the difference between any two consecutive terms is a constant. An **arithmetic series** is the sum of an arithmetic sequence.

You can compute a finite arithmetic series by adding each individual term, but this can take a lot of time. A famous mathematician named Carl Friedrich Gauss developed another way to compute a finite arithmetic series.

As the story goes, when Gauss was in elementary school, his teacher asked the class to calculate the sum of the first 100 positive integers. Apparently, Gauss determined the answer in a matter of seconds! How did Gauss determine his answer so quickly?

1. Complete the steps and answer the questions to see how Gauss was able to calculate the sum of the first 100 positive integers so quickly.

   a. The series S_{100} is shown. The same series in descending order is shown beneath it. Add the series by computing the sum of each pair of vertical, or partial sums.

$S_{100} =$	1	$+$	2	$+$	3	$+ \cdots +$	98	$+$	99	$+$	100
$+S_{100} =$	100	$+$	99	$+$	98	$+ \cdots +$	3	$+$	2	$+$	1
$2S_{100} =$	_____	$+$	_____	$+$	_____	$+ \cdots +$	_____	$+$	_____	$+$	_____

   b. What do you notice about each partial sum?

   c. How many partial sums are there in this series?

   d. Write the sum of the partial sums.

   $2S_{100} =$ _____

   e. To arrive at the total in part (d), you actually added each term of the series twice. How could you calculate the correct total from the sum of the partial sums, or S_{100}?

   f. What is S_{100}?

   $S_{100} =$ _____

Gauss's method can be generalized for any finite arithmetic series.

2. Consider a finite arithmetic series S_n written as a sum of its terms.

$$S_n = a_1 + a_2 + a_3 + \cdots + a_{n-2} + a_{n-1} + a_n$$

Complete the steps shown to determine Gauss's formula to compute any finite arithmetic series.

a. First, write S_n in terms of a_1, a_n, and the common difference d. Remember that for an arithmetic sequence, $a_n = a_1 + d(n - 1)$.

$$S_n = a_1 + (\underline{\hspace{1.5cm}}) + (a_1 + 2d) + \cdots + (a_n - 2d) + (\underline{\hspace{1.5cm}}) + \underline{\hspace{1cm}}$$

b. Then, write S_n in reverse order.

$$S_n = \underline{\hspace{1.5cm}} + (a_n - d) + (\underline{\hspace{1.5cm}}) + \cdots + (a_1 + 2d) + (\underline{\hspace{1.5cm}}) + a_1$$

c. Add the series, keeping the "+" and "=" signs vertically aligned.

$$S_n = \quad a_1 \quad + (\underline{\hspace{0.7cm}}) + (\underline{\hspace{0.7cm}}) + \cdots + (\underline{\hspace{0.7cm}}) + (\underline{\hspace{0.7cm}}) + \quad a_n$$

$$+S_n = \quad a_n \quad + (\underline{\hspace{0.7cm}}) + (\underline{\hspace{0.7cm}}) + \cdots + (\underline{\hspace{0.7cm}}) + (\underline{\hspace{0.7cm}}) + \quad a_1$$

$$2S_n = (\underline{\hspace{0.7cm}}) + (\underline{\hspace{0.7cm}}) + (\underline{\hspace{0.7cm}}) + \cdots + (\underline{\hspace{0.7cm}}) + (\underline{\hspace{0.7cm}}) + (\underline{\hspace{0.7cm}})$$

d. Identify each partial sum.

e. Fill in the blanks to show the sum of the partial sums.

$$2S_n = \underline{\hspace{1.5cm}}(a_1 + \underline{\hspace{1.5cm}})$$

f. Fill in the blanks to write the formula for S_n.

$$S_n = \frac{\underline{\hspace{0.7cm}}(a_1 + \underline{\hspace{1.2cm}})}{2}$$

g. Describe Gauss' rule to compute any finite arithmetic series by completing the sentence.

Add the _____ term and the _____ term of the series,

multiply the sum by the number of _____ of the series, and divide by

_____.

So, Gauss's formula to compute the first n terms of an arithmetic series is shown.

$$S_n = \frac{n(a_1 + a_n)}{2}$$

3. Use the *Toothpick Tessellation* problem situation to answer each question.

   a. Use Gauss's formula to calculate the total number of toothpicks Pauley needs to complete 5 rows of his tessellation. Show your work.

   b. Remember that Pauley wanted his tessellation to include a total of 18 rows. If he has a box of 350 toothpicks, does he have enough? Explain why or why not.

PROBLEM 3   **Human Calculator, or Inspiration from Gauss?**

In the previous problem, you learned a way to compute the first n-terms of any finite arithmetic series. Now, you will take a closer look at some special series of numbers.

1. Consider a sequence of odd whole numbers.

   a. Write an explicit formula to determine any term of the sequence.

If possible, use the distributive property and combine like terms when you write your answers. This way, you can be more efficient!

b. Use Gauss's formula to calculate the sum of the first 20 odd whole numbers. What information did you need to use Gauss's formula?

Emma claims that she can calculate the sum of the first 20 odd whole numbers using a different method. Emma's method does not require her to calculate the last term of the series.

2. Let's determine how Emma can perform this calculation.

    a. Substitute the known value of a_1 and the algebraic expression for a_n into Gauss's formula.

    b. Write your answer from part (a) using function notation. Describe the function.

    c. Use your function from part (b) to calculate the sum of the first 20 odd whole numbers. Verify that your result the same as your result in Question 1.

3. Calculate the sum of the first 100 odd whole numbers. Then, verify your result using Gauss's formula.

What about even numbers? You can use a similar process to compute the series of even whole numbers.

4. Follow the given steps to calculate the sum of the first 100 even whole numbers.

    a. Write an explicit formula to calculate any term of the sequence of even whole numbers.

    b. Substitute the known value of a_1 and the algebraic expression for a_n into Gauss's formula.

    c. Write your answer from part (b) using function notation.

    d. Use your function from part (c) to calculate the first 100 even whole numbers. Then, verify using Gauss's formula.

5. Compare the function for the series of even whole numbers with the function for the series of odd whole numbers. What makes them different? Explain why you think the difference exists.

"Chair"-ity Case

You are in charge of setting up for your high school band's annual Spring concert. The concert will be held outdoors on the school soccer field, and one of your duties is to arrange the seating for the show.

You have gathered the following information.

- The stage is 20 feet wide.

- The first row of chairs will be about the same width as the stage.

- Each successive row of chairs will have three more chairs than the previous row. This way, the chairs are offset so that each person does not have a chair directly in front of them for better viewing.

- Each chair is 1.5 feet wide and 1.5 feet deep.

- There needs to be 0.5 foot of spacing in between the chairs within a row so that the audience can sit comfortably.

- In order to have enough room for people to walk through the rows, there needs to be 4 feet of space in between each row, from the back of one chair to the back of the other chair.

Use the given information to answer each question.

1. What factors do you need to consider when determining how many rows of chairs there could be?

2. How many chairs are in the first row? Explain your reasoning.

3. Sketch a seating chart that includes the given information and dimensions.

Answer each question based on the additional given information. Show all your work.

4. Suppose that the first 5 rows of chairs make up the "gold circle" section.

    a. How many chairs are in the gold circle section?

    b. How many feet deep is the gold circle section?

5. Suppose that you need a total of 500 chairs for the concert.

    a. How many rows will you need with this number of chairs?

    b. How deep is the seating area with this number of chairs?

6. Suppose that no row can have more than 40 chairs.

    a. What is the maximum number of rows possible?

    b. What is the maximum number of people that can be seated?

 Be prepared to share your solutions and methods.

I Am Having a Series Craving (For Some Math)!

Geometric Series

In this lesson, you will:

- Generalize patterns to derive the formula for the sum of a finite geometric series.
- Compute a finite geometric series.

- geometric series

The art that is produced in a culture often reflects the peoples' social values, struggles, and important events over a given time period. While it is generally not considered one of the great art forms of our time, television drama is an art that regularly reflects current events and social issues.

Consider *Mission Impossible*, a spy series which brought millions of viewers the secret assignments of a group of government agents battling dictators around the globe. It's no accident that this series was hugely popular in the 1960's, a time of heightened Cold War anxieties. During the 1980s, a time when more women entered the work force, *Cagney and Lacey* featured a career-focused, single mother battling crime. During the 2000s, *West Wing* focused on political scandals, terrorism, and other foreign affairs issues that were in the news during that period.

What are some of the pressing current events right now? Are they reflected in any popular television series you watch?

A **geometric series** is the sum of the terms of a geometric sequence. Recall, that the sequence 1, 3, 9, 27, 81 is a geometric sequence because the ratio of any two consecutive terms is constant. Adding the terms creates the geometric series $1 + 3 + 9 + 27 + 81$.

> The constant ratio of this geometric sequence is 3 because
> $$\frac{3}{1} = \frac{9}{3} = \frac{27}{9} = \frac{81}{27} = 3$$
> Recall all geometric sequences have a constant ratio between successive terms.

Theresa raises her hand and claims that she has a "trick" for quickly calculating the sum of any geometric series. She asks members of the class to write any geometric series on the board. She boasts that she can quickly tell them how to determine the sum without adding all of the terms. Several examples are shown.

Paul:	Theresa:
"OK, so prove it! What is the sum of $1 + 3 + 9 + 27 + 81 + 243 + 729$?"	"Multiply 729(3) and subtract 1. Then divide by 2."
Stella:	**Theresa:**
"What is $5 + 20 + 80 + 320 + 1280 + 5120$?"	"I will have the answer if I multiply 5120(4), subtract 5, and then divide by 3."
Julian:	**Theresa:**
"Let me see . . . How about $10 + 50 + 250 + 1250$?"	"No problem. Multiply 1250(5), subtract 10, and then divide by 4."
Henry:	**Theresa:**
"Hmmm . . . I bet I can stump you with $10 + (-20) + 40 + (-80) + 160$."	"Pretty sneaky with the negatives, Henry, but the method still works. Multiply 160(-2) and subtract 10. This time divide by -3."

1. Verify that Theresa is correct for each series.

> How can you tell all of the series are geometric?

2. What is Theresa's "trick"? Describe in words how to calculate the sum of any geometric sequence.

3. Use Theresa's "trick" to calculate $1 + 2 + 4 + 8 + 16 + 32 + 64 + 128$. Show all work and explain your reasoning.

Remember, $g_n = g_1 r^{n-1}$.

Theresa's "trick" really isn't a trick. It is known as Euclid's Method. An example of this method, along with a justification for each step, is shown.

Compute $\displaystyle\sum_{i=1}^{5} 3^{i-1}$.

$S_5 = 1 + 3 + 9 + 27 + 81$
- The common ratio is 3.

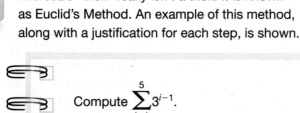

$3S_5 = \qquad 3 + 9 + 27 + 81 + 243$

$S_5 = 1 + 3 + 9 + 27 + 81$
- Write $3S_n$ above the original series. Multiply each term of the original series by the common ratio. Line up each product above the original series.

$3S_5 = \qquad\quad 3 + 9 + 27 + 81 + 243$

$- S_5 = -(1 + 3 + 9 + 27 + 81)$
- Subtract to determine $3S_n - S_n = 2S_n$.

$2S_5 = -1 + 243$

$\dfrac{2S_5}{2} = \dfrac{242}{2}$
- Divide by 2.

$S_5 = 121$

In all of the examples, Theresa knew that she could calculate each sum by first multiplying the last term by the common ratio and subtracting the first term. Then she could divide that quantity by one less than the common ratio.

In other words, $S_n = \dfrac{\text{(Last Term)(Common Ratio)} - \text{(First Term)}}{\text{(Common Ratio} - 1)}$.

4. Analyze the worked example.

a. In the worked example, why multiply both sides of the equation by 3? Does the algorithm still work if you multiply by a different number? Explain your reasoning.

b. Why do you always divide by one less than the common ratio?

The formula to compute any geometric series becomes $S_n = \dfrac{g_n(r) - g_1}{r - 1}$, where g_n is the last term, r is the common ratio, and g_1 is the first term.

5. Apply Euclid's Method to compute each.

a. $1 + 10 + 100 + \cdots + 1{,}000{,}000$

Do you need to know all of the terms? How can you determine just the terms that you need? Remember to work efficiently, looking for patterns and applying formulas that you already know.

b. $10 + 20 + 40 + 80 + 160 + 320$

c. $\displaystyle\sum_{k=1}^{8} 5^{k-1}$

d. A sequence with 9 terms, a common ratio of 2, and a first term of 3.

PROBLEM **2** **Return of Long Division: The Pattern Strikes Back**

Recall previously you used long division to determine each quotient:

Polynomial Long Division	$\longrightarrow$	**Rewritten Using the Reflexive and Commutative Properties of Equality**

Example 1

$\dfrac{r^3 - 1}{r - 1} = r^2 + r + 1$ $\longrightarrow$ $1 + r + r^2 = \dfrac{r^3 - 1}{r - 1}$

Example 2

$\dfrac{r^4 - 1}{r - 1} = r^3 + r^2 + r + 1$ $\longrightarrow$ $1 + r + r^2 + r^3 = \dfrac{r^4 - 1}{r - 1}$

Example 3

$\dfrac{r^5 - 1}{r - 1} = r^4 + r^3 + r^2 + r + 1$ $\longrightarrow$ $1 + r + r^2 + r^3 + r^4 = \dfrac{r^5 - 1}{r - 1}$

Each Example represents a geometric series, where r is the common ratio and $g_1 = 1$. Each geometric series can be written in summation notation.

Example 1: $n = 3$ $\quad \displaystyle\sum_{i=1}^{3} r^{i-1}$ or $\displaystyle\sum_{i=0}^{2} r^i$

Example 2: $n = 4$ $\quad \displaystyle\sum_{i=1}^{4} r^{i-1}$ or $\displaystyle\sum_{i=0}^{3} r^i$

1. For each Example, explain why the power of the common ratio in the summation notation is different, yet still represents the series.

2. Identify the number of terms in the series in Example 3, and then write the series in summation notation.

3. Use the pattern generated from repeated polynomial long division to write a formula to compute any geometric series $1 + r + r^2 + r^3 + \cdots + r^{n-1}$ where n is the number of terms in the series, r is the common ratio, and $g_1 = 1$.

$$\sum_{i=0}^{n} r^i = \underline{\hspace{3cm}}$$

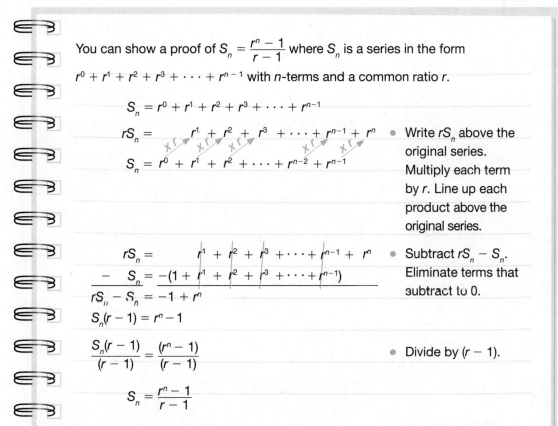

You can show a proof of $S_n = \dfrac{r^n - 1}{r - 1}$ where S_n is a series in the form

$r^0 + r^1 + r^2 + r^3 + \cdots + r^{n-1}$ with n-terms and a common ratio r.

$S_n = r^0 + r^1 + r^2 + r^3 + \cdots + r^{n-1}$

$rS_n = \qquad r^1 + r^2 + r^3 + \cdots + r^{n-1} + r^n$ • Write rS_n above the original series.

$S_n = r^0 + r^1 + r^2 + \cdots + r^{n-2} + r^{n-1}$ Multiply each term by r. Line up each product above the original series.

$rS_n = \qquad r^1 + r^2 + r^3 + \cdots + r^{n-1} + r^n$ • Subtract $rS_n - S_n$.

$-\ \underline{\ S_n = -(1 + r^1 + r^2 + r^3 + \cdots + r^{n-1})\ }$ Eliminate terms that subtract to 0.

$rS_n - S_n = -1 + r^n$

$S_n(r - 1) = r^n - 1$

$\dfrac{S_n(r - 1)}{(r - 1)} = \dfrac{(r^n - 1)}{(r - 1)}$ • Divide by $(r - 1)$.

$S_n = \dfrac{r^n - 1}{r - 1}$

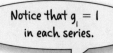

4. Identify the number of terms, the common ratio, and g_1 for each series. Then compute each.

a. $1 + 2^1 + 2^2 + 2^3 + 2^4$

Notice that $g_1 = 1$ in each series.

b. $1 + 5 + 25 + 125 + 625$

c. $1 + (-2) + 4 + (-8) + 16 + (-32)$

5. Angus and Perry each wrote the geometric series $7 + 14 + 28 + 56 + 112 + 224 + 448 + 896$ in summation notation and then computed the sum.

 Angus

I know that $g_n = g_1 r^{n-1}$. The number of terms is 8, the common ratio is 2, and the first term is 7, so I can write the series as $\sum_{i=1}^{8} 7 \cdot 2^{i-1}$.

I know the last term is 896, so I can use Euclid's Method to compute the sum.

$$\frac{896 \cdot 2 - 7}{2 - 1}$$

 Perry

I can rewrite the series as

$7(1 + 2 + 4 + 8 + 16 + 32 + 64 + 128)$.

I know the common ratio is 2, so I can rewrite the series using powers as

$7(2^0 + 2^1 + 2^2 + 2^3 + 2^4 + 2^5 + 2^6 + 2^7)$.

The number of terms is 8, so I can write the series in summation notation as

$$7 \sum_{i=1}^{8} 2^{i-1}.$$

Then, I can compute the series as $7\left(\dfrac{2^8 - 1}{2 - 1}\right)$.

Verify that both methods produce the same sum.

The formula to compute a geometric series that Perry used is $S_n = \dfrac{g_1(r^n - 1)}{r - 1}$.

Recall Euclid's Method to compute a geometric series is $S_n = \dfrac{g_n(r) - g_1}{r - 1}$.

You can use the fact that $g_n = g_1 r^{n-1}$ to verify that these two formulas are equivalent.

$$S_n = \frac{g_n(r) - g_1}{r - 1}$$ 　 • Given Euclid's Method.

$$= \frac{g_1 r^{n-1}(r) - g_1}{r - 1}$$ 　 • Substitute $g_n = g_1 r^{n-1}$.

$$= \frac{g_1 r^n - g_1}{r - 1}$$ 　 • Perform multiplication.

$$= \frac{g_1(r^n - 1)}{r - 1}$$ 　 • Factor out g_1.

6. When is it appropriate to use each formula?

7. Rewrite each series using summation notation.

    a. 4 + 12 + 36 + 108 + 324

    b. 64 + 32 + 16 + 8 + 4 + 2 + 1

8. Compute each geometric series.

    a. $\displaystyle\sum_{i=1}^{4} 6^{i-1}$
                    b. $10\displaystyle\sum_{i=0}^{4} 3^{i}$

    c. $6\displaystyle\sum_{i=0}^{4}\left(\frac{1}{3}\right)^{i}$

9. Analyze the table of values.

x	$f(x)$	$\dfrac{f(x + 1)}{f(x)}$
0	3	
1	4.5	
2	6.75	
3	10.125	
4	15.1875	
5		

a. Complete the table.

b. Describe any patterns that you notice.

c. Assume the geometric sequence continues, determine $f(0) + f(1) + \cdots + f(9)$. Show all work and explain your reasoning

d. Explain why the ratio of any two consecutive terms in a geometric sequence is always a constant.

PROBLEM 3 **Making Choices**

1. Jane analyzes the salary schedule for the same position at two different electrical engineering companies, Nothing's Shocking and High Voltage. The salary schedules for the first 5 years are provided with promises from each company that the rate of salary increase will be the same over time.

Time (years)	Nothing's Shocking Salary ($)	High Voltage Salary ($)
1	40,000	46,000
2	42,400	47,840
3	44,944	49,754
4	47,641	51,744
5	50,499	53,814

a. What is the salary in year 10 for each company? Show all work and explain your reasoning.

b. Assuming all other factors are equal, which company offers the better salary over a 10-year period? Show all work and explain your reasoning.

You're not determining who pays more on year 10, but who pays more over the entire 10-year period.

c. What would be the difference in total career salary if you choose one company over the other? Assume a 30-year career. Show all work and explain your reasoning.

2. A single elimination basketball tournament begins with 128 games in the first round. Each round eliminates half of the teams until an overall winner is decided. The tournament sponsor needs to purchase a new ball for every game that will be played throughout the tournament. How many basketballs must the sponsor purchase? Explain your reasoning.

 Be prepared to share your solutions and methods.

These Series Just Go On . . . And On . . . And On . . .

Infinite Geometric Series

LEARNING GOALS

In this lesson, you will:

- Write a formula for an infinite geometric series.
- Compute an infinite geometric series.
- Draw diagrams to model infinite geometric series.
- Determine whether series are convergent or divergent.
- Use a formula to compute a convergent infinite geometric series.

KEY TERMS

- convergent series
- divergent series

Infinity is a concept that philosophers and mathematicians have struggled with for centuries. Infinity is a very abstract idea. How can something be limitless? What does it mean for something to go on forever?

The following quote is from an Indian philosophical text dating back to the 4th or 3rd century B.C.

If you remove a part from infinity or add a part to infinity, still what remains is infinity.

How can this be so?

What does infinity mean to you?

PROBLEM 1 Hang On Bessie, We're Almost There

Previously, you calculated sums of finite series. What if a series was infinite? Let's see if there is a way to calculate the sum of an infinite series.

The first three terms of an infinite sequence are represented by the figures shown. In this sequence, each square represents a unit square, and the shaded part represents area.

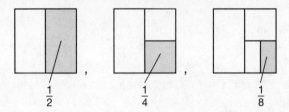

1. Sketch the next two figures to model this sequence, and write the numbers that correspond to each term.

2. Is this sequence arithmetic, geometric, or neither? Explain how you know. If possible, write an explicit formula for the sequence.

3. Consider the series, or sum, of the first two terms of this infinite sequence. The sum of the first two terms can be modeled with a diagram, as shown.

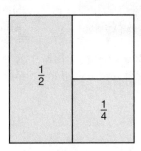

Continue shading the diagram to represent the sum of the first five terms of the series. What happens to the total area that is shaded every time you shade another piece of the unit square?

4. In the table shown, n represents the term number of the series, and S_n represents the sum of the first n terms of the series. Use the sequence from the unit square in Question 3 to answer each question.

n	1	2	3	4	5	10	25
S_n as a Fraction							
S_n as a Decimal							

a. Complete the table for $n = 1$ through $n = 5$ to show the sum of the series that corresponds to the previous diagram. Write each sum as a fraction and as a decimal.

b. Describe the pattern you see in the table.

c. Use the pattern to complete the table for the final two columns.

5. What value does the series approach as n gets greater?

In the figure that models this series, each additional part of the unit square is one half of the previous part. If you could continue to add these parts forever, the unit square would eventually be filled.

Likewise, in the table of values that models this series, the sums get closer and closer to 1 as n gets greater. Therefore, you can say that this infinite geometric series is equal to 1.

So, an infinite series can have a finite sum . . . it sounds crazy, but it's true!

6. Miley and Damian determined formulas they could use to compute the first n-terms of the series.

Miley

I noticed that when each sum is written as a fraction, the denominator is equal to 2^n and the numerator is one less than the denominator.

So, I can calculate the first n-terms of the series by using the formula shown.

$$S_n = \frac{2^n - 1}{2^n}$$

Damian

I know that $S_n = \dfrac{g_n \cdot r - g_1}{r - 1}$ can be used to compute the first n-terms of any geometric series. For this series, $g_n = \left(\frac{1}{2}\right)^n$, $g_1 = \frac{1}{2}$, and $r = \frac{1}{2}$.

Substituting these values gives:

$$S_n = \frac{\left(\frac{1}{2}\right)^n \left(\frac{1}{2}\right) - \frac{1}{2}}{\frac{1}{2} - 1}$$

Show that both representations for S_n are equivalent.

PROBLEM 2 **To Infinity, and Beyond!**

In the previous problem, you saw how an infinite geometric series can have a finite sum. Let's see if this is the case for *any* infinite geometric series.

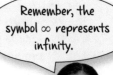

Remember, the symbol ∞ represents infinity.

1. Examine the given formula and accompanying diagram for each infinite geometric series. Identify both r and g_1 for each series. Then, determine if the sum is infinite or finite. If the sum is finite, estimate it.

   a. $\dfrac{1}{3} + \dfrac{1}{9} + \dfrac{1}{27} + \cdots = \displaystyle\sum_{i=1}^{\infty}\left(\dfrac{1}{3}\right)^i$

S_1 $\qquad$ S_2 $\qquad$ S_3

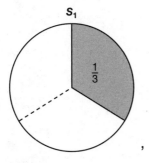

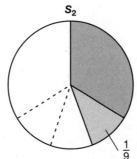

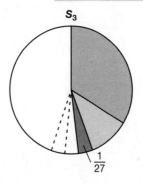

$r =$ _____

$g_1 =$ _____

$S =$ _____

b. $1 + 3 + 9 + 27 + \cdots = \sum_{i=1}^{\infty} \frac{1}{3}(3)^i$

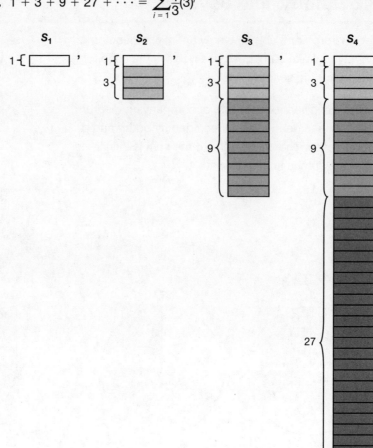

$r = $ _____

$g_1 = $ _____

$S = $ _____

c. $1 + \dfrac{3}{4} + \dfrac{9}{16} + \dfrac{27}{64} + \dfrac{81}{256} + \dfrac{243}{1024} + \dfrac{729}{4096} + \cdots = \displaystyle\sum_{i=1}^{\infty} \dfrac{4}{3}\left(\dfrac{3}{4}\right)^{i}$

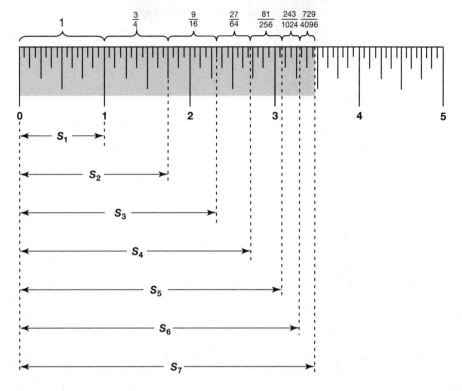

$r =$ _____

$g_1 =$ _____

$S =$ _____

d. $\dfrac{1}{4} + \dfrac{1}{16} + \dfrac{1}{64} + \cdots = \displaystyle\sum_{i=1}^{\infty} \left(\dfrac{1}{4}\right)^{i}$

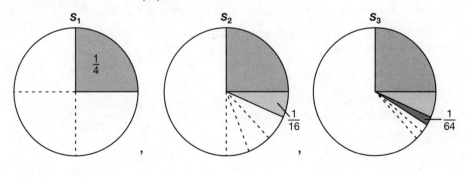

$r =$ _____

$g_1 =$ _____

$S =$ _____

e. $1 + \dfrac{3}{2} + \dfrac{9}{4} + \dfrac{27}{8} + \cdots = \displaystyle\sum_{i=1}^{\infty} \dfrac{2}{3}\left(\dfrac{3}{2}\right)^{i}$

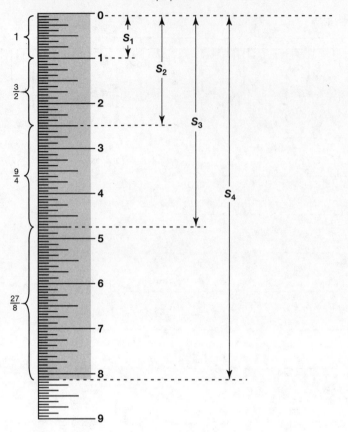

$r = $ _____

$g_1 = $ _____

$S = $ _____

2. Analyze the common ratio for each series in Question 1.

   a. What do you notice about the series with infinite sums?

   b. What do you notice about the series with finite sums?

A **convergent series** is an infinite series that has a finite sum. A **divergent series** is an infinite series that does not have a finite sum. If a series is divergent, the sum is infinity.

The formula to compute a convergent geometric series S is shown.

$$S = \frac{g_1}{1 - r}$$

Notice that S denotes the sum of an *infinite* series. This notation should not be confused with S_n, which represents the sum of the *n*th term of a series.

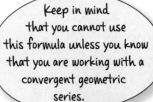

Keep in mind that you cannot use this formula unless you know that you are working with a convergent geometric series.

3. Consider each infinite geometric series from Question 1. Determine whether each series is convergent or divergent, and explain how you know. If a series is convergent, use the formula to compute the sum. If a series is divergent, write infinity.

a. $\dfrac{1}{3} + \dfrac{1}{9} + \dfrac{1}{27} + \cdots = \displaystyle\sum_{i=1}^{\infty}\left(\dfrac{1}{3}\right)^i$

Convergent or divergent? _____

Explanation:

$S =$ _____

b. $1 + 3 + 9 + 27 + \cdots = \displaystyle\sum_{i=1}^{\infty}\dfrac{1}{3}(3)^i$

Convergent or divergent? _____

Explanation:

$S =$ _____

c. $1 + \dfrac{3}{4} + \dfrac{9}{16} + \dfrac{27}{64} + \dfrac{81}{256} + \dfrac{243}{1024} + \dfrac{729}{4096} + \cdots = \displaystyle\sum_{i=1}^{\infty} \dfrac{4}{3}\left(\dfrac{3}{4}\right)^i$

Convergent or divergent? _____

Explanation:

$S = $ _____

d. $\dfrac{1}{4} + \dfrac{1}{16} + \dfrac{1}{64} + \cdots = \displaystyle\sum_{i=1}^{\infty} \left(\dfrac{1}{4}\right)^i$

Convergent or divergent? _____

Explanation:

$S = $ _____

e. $1 + \dfrac{3}{2} + \dfrac{9}{4} + \dfrac{27}{8} + \cdots = \displaystyle\sum_{i=1}^{\infty} \dfrac{2}{3}\left(\dfrac{3}{2}\right)^i$

Convergent or divergent? _____

Explanation:

$S = $ _____

4. Zoe computed the infinite geometric series.

$$\frac{5}{8} + \frac{25}{32} + \frac{125}{128} + \frac{625}{512} + \cdots = \sum_{i=1}^{\infty} \frac{1}{2}\left(\frac{5}{4}\right)^i$$

 Zoe

The formula to compute the series is $S = \dfrac{g_1}{1 - r}$.
In this series, $g_1 = \dfrac{5}{8}$ and $r = \dfrac{5}{4}$.

So, $S = \dfrac{\frac{5}{8}}{1 - \frac{5}{4}} = \dfrac{\frac{5}{8}}{-\frac{1}{4}} = \dfrac{5}{8}\left(-\dfrac{4}{1}\right) = -\dfrac{5}{2}$.

Explain why Zoe is incorrect, and then determine the correct sum.

5. Compute each infinite geometric series, if possible.

   a. $\dfrac{9}{10} + \dfrac{9}{100} + \dfrac{9}{1000} + \dfrac{9}{10,000} + \dfrac{9}{100,000} + \cdots$

   b. $0.9 + 0.09 + 0.009 + 0.0009 + \cdots$

   c. $0.9999999\ldots$

So far in this lesson, you have only seen infinite *geometric* series. What about infinite *arithmetic* series?

6. Consider the statements made by Ronald and Jeremiah about the infinite arithmetic series.

> **Ronald**
>
> Some infinite arithmetic series are convergent, and some are divergent; it all depends on the common difference.

> **Jeremiah**
>
> All infinite arithmetic series are divergent.

Who is correct? Explain your reasoning.

Talk the Talk

Write the formula to compute each type of series.

The First *n*-Terms of an Arithmetic Series:

$S_n =$

The First *n*-Terms of a Geometric Series:

$S_n =$

A Convergent Geometric Series:

$S =$

A Divergent Geometric Series:

$S =$

Be prepared to share your solutions and methods.

The Power of Interest (It's a Curious Thing)
Geometric Series Applications

LEARNING GOALS

In this lesson you will:

- Apply your understanding of series to problem situations.
- Write the formula for a geometric series representing a problem situation.

Imagine walking up to the counter of a major electronics store to purchase a new flat screen television for $999. When the salesperson rings up your purchase, she says: "After fees and interest charges, your total is $1950!" Would you still buy the television?

In another scenario, imagine walking into the tuition office at a local university. You are interested in taking 2 classes this fall while working part-time. The cost of the 6 credits is supposed to be $5000, but after discussing a particular payment option with the financial aid officer, you realize that the classes will cost more than $10,000 over the next 12 years. Would you still accept that payment option?

It may surprise you, but many people accept these terms for their purchases every day and don't even realize it. You may wonder how this could happen. The answer lies in the mathematics behind credit cards. When used wisely, credit cards can be convenient and flexible. They allow consumers to purchase expensive or necessary items and pay for them at a later date. On the other hand, if used unwisely, consumers waste a lot of money on interest charges.

How do credit cards work? How could you end up paying twice the amount for a television, or make monthly payments and still carry a balance on two college classes that you took over a decade ago?

PROBLEM **I Don't Want Credit For This**

Vince wants to purchase a laptop with high screen resolution for his gaming hobby. He charges the $1000 purchase to a credit card with 19% interest.

The credit card company requires a minimum monthly payment of the greater of:

- 2% of the balance on the card, or

- $15.00.

To determine how long it will take to pay off the credit card when paying the minimum balance, Vince calls the company. He learns that when making a monthly payment, 75% of the minimum payment goes toward interest and the remaining portion of the minimum monthly payment goes toward the principal.

1. Determine the percent of the payment that is paid toward interest and principal for each monthly payment.

   a. Monthly payment is 2% of balance.

Calculating finance charges is a very complex endeavor. The calculations in this lesson closely approximate what happens in real life.

   b. Monthly payment is 10% of balance.

   c. Monthly payment is 25% of balance.

Let's consider Vince's monthly payment.

In order to calculate the minimum monthly payment, you will need to calculate 2% of the balance.

$$\text{minimum payment} = (0.02)(\text{balance})$$
$$= 0.02(1000)$$
$$= 20$$

If the credit card balance is $1000.00, the minimum monthly payment would be $20.00.

The amount paid toward interest is 1.5% of the balance.

$$\text{amount paid toward interest} = 0.015(\text{balance})$$
$$= (0.015)(1000)$$
$$= 15$$

If the minimum monthly payment is $20.00, the amount paid toward interest would be $15.00.

The amount paid toward principal is 0.5% of the balance.

$$\text{amount paid toward principal} = (0.005)(\text{balance})$$
$$= (0.005)(1000)$$
$$= 5$$

If the minimum monthly payment is $20.00, the amount paid toward principal would be $5.00.

The remaining balance on the credit card will be the current balance minus the amount paid toward principal.

$$\text{remaining balance} = (\text{current balance}) - (\text{amount paid toward principal})$$
$$= 1000 - 5$$
$$= 995$$

So, if Vince makes a monthly payment of $20.00 on the $1000.00 balance, the balance after the monthly payment is $995.00.

2. Calculate the monthly payment details for the first 12 months of minimum payments. The first row of the table reflects the calculations from the worked example.

Number of Months (n)	Balance Before Monthly Payment ($)	Minimum Monthly Payment ($)	Amount Paid Toward Principal ($)	Amount Paid Toward Interest ($)	Balance After Monthly Payment ($)
1	1000.00	20.00	5.00	15.00	995.00
2					
3					
4					
5					
6					
7					
8					
9					
10					
11					
12					
n					

3. Consider the worked example and the answers to each part to complete the n-row of the table.

    a. Write the explicit formula for the geometric sequence represented in the "Balance Before Monthly Payment" column.

    b. Write the formula to calculate the minimum monthly payment.

To write the explicit formulas of each column in the n-row, consider the initial value and the rate of change.

c. Write the formula to calculate the amount paid toward interest.

d. Write the formula to calculate the amount paid toward principal.

e. Write the formula to calculate the balance after minimum payment.

Vince knows how much he is paying each month, but it would be helpful if he knew how much he had paid in both interest and principal over a certain amount of time instead of on any given month.

4. Calculate each.

a. the total monthly payment in the first 12 months

You developed two different formulas to compute a geometric series. Which one are you going to use in this situation?

b. the amount paid toward principal in the first 12 months

c. the amount paid toward interest in the first 12 months

5. Write a formula for the geometric series that represents:

    a. the total monthly payment.

    b. the total payment toward principal over time.

    c. the total payment toward interest over time.

6. Use the formulas you created in Question 5 to complete the table.

	Total Amount Paid Toward Principal	Total Amount Paid Toward Interest
2 years		
5 years		

7. Assume the credit card company does not require a monthly payment of $15.00. Determine how long will it take to pay off the credit card completely.

8. Does your answer to Question 7 seem reasonable? Explain your reasoning.

Use a graphing calculator to help solve these problems.

9. Determine the amount of time it will take to pay off the credit card balance, taking into account the minimum payment of $15.00.

   a. After how many months will the minimum monthly payment become $15.00?

   b. What will be the balance on Vince's credit card when the minimum monthly payment becomes $15.00?

   c. How much will Vince pay toward principal with every $15.00 payment?

   d. How much will Vince pay toward interest with every $15.00 payment?

   e. Suppose Vince continues to make $15.00 payments until the end of the loan. How many months will Vince have to make the $15.00 minimum payment to pay off the remaining balance?

   f. How many years will it take Vince to pay off the entire balance?

10. How much money will Vince end up spending on his $1000.00 laptop?

Keep in mind, Vince paid 2% of the balance for awhile, and then he made $15 monthly payments until the balance was paid in full.

11. How much money will Vince spend in interest to pay for his $1000.00 laptop?

PROBLEM 2   A Little Less Interest-ing

After realizing how long it would take to pay his entire credit card bill when only paying the minimum amount, Vince decides that he should pay more than the minimum amount every month. Vince determines that he can pay 10% of the balance every month.

Remember, amount paid toward interest is still 75% of the monthly payment. You might want to use a spreadsheet to perform these calculations.

1. Complete the table to represent this information for 12 months.

Number of Months (n)	Balance Before Monthly Payment ($)	10% Monthly Payment ($)	Amount Paid Toward Principal ($)	Amount Paid Toward Interest ($)	Balance After Monthly Payment ($)
1	1000.00	0.10(1000) = 100	25.00	75.00	975.00
2					
3					
4					
5					
6					
7					
8					
9					
10					
11					
12					
n					

2. Write the formula for the geometric series that represents:

    a. the total monthly payment.

Use the formulas from the table in Problem 1 to help you with the formulas for this table.

    b. the total payment toward principal over time.

    c. the total payment toward interest over time.

3. Use the formulas you created in Question 2 to complete the table.

	Total Money Spent in Principal	Total Money Spent in Interest
1.5 years		
2 years		

4. After how many months will the minimum monthly payment become $15.00?

Remember the minimum payment is the greater of 10% of the balance or $15.00.

5. What will the balance on his credit card, when the minimum payment becomes $15.00?

6. Vince decides that once he gets to the minimum payment, he will pay off the rest of the balance in one lump sum.

   a. How long will it take Vince to pay off the entire balance?

   b. How much money will Vince end up spending on his $1000.00 laptop?

   c. How much money will Vince spend in interest to pay for his $1000.00 laptop?

7. How much money will Vince save by paying 10% instead of the required 2% minimum payment?

PROBLEM 3 **Enough of These Interest Payments**

Vince is still concerned about paying so much money in interest on his credit card, and decides that he can afford to pay a flat amount of $100 each month.

1. Sean calculates how long it will take Vince to pay off his credit card this way.

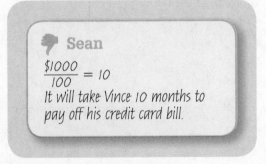

> **Sean**
>
> $$\frac{\$1000}{100} = 10$$
>
> It will take Vince 10 months to pay off his credit card bill.

What is wrong with Sean's work? Explain your reasoning.

2. How long do you think it will take Vince to pay off his credit card this way? Explain your reasoning.

3. Complete the table to represent this information for 12 months.

Number of Months (n)	Balance Before Monthly Payment ($)	$100 Monthly Payment ($)	Amount Paid Toward Principal ($)	Amount Paid Toward Interest ($)	Balance After Monthly Payment ($)
1	1000.00	100.00	25.00	75.00	975.00
2					
3					
4					
5					
6					
7					
8					
9					
10					
11					
12					
n					

4. What pattern do you notice in this table that is different from the tables in Problems 1 and 2?

5. How long will it take Vince to pay off the entire balance?

6. How much money will Vince end up spending on his $1000.00 laptop?

7. How much money will Vince spend in interest to pay for his $1000.00 laptop?

PROBLEM 4   **Interest Free? Whoopee!**

Now that Vince has become more educated about credit card finances and proven that he can be responsible for paying off his debt, he applies for a new credit card that offers the first 6 months interest free for any purchases. Like his other credit card, this new credit card requires a minimum monthly payment of the greater of:

- 2% of the balance on the card, or

- $15.00.

How will your calculations change for month 7?

Vince is approved for the card, and charges $1000 for a flat screen TV. He still decides to pay 10% of the balance after noticing how much money that saved him the last time.

1. Complete the table to show 12 months of payments.

Number of Months (n)	Balance Before Monthly Payment ($)	10% Monthly Payment ($)	Amount Paid Toward Principal ($)	Amount Paid Toward Interest ($)	Balance After Monthly Payment ($)
1	1000.00	0.10(1000) = 100	100.00	0.00	900.00
2					
3					
4					
5					
6					
Interest begins on the 7th month.					
7					
8					
9					
10					
11					
12					
n					

2. Describe the change in Vince's balance in the first 6 months compared to the last 6 months.

3. Analyze the 12 months of payments. What recommendations would you give Vince about paying off his credit card? Include the number of months he would be paying on the balance, the total amount that he would pay for the flat screen TV, and the amount of total interest he would pay.

Talk the Talk

Consider the four credit card payment scenarios Vince explored:

    a. Paying minimum payment

    b. Paying 10% of balance until minimum payment and then paying off in one lump sum

    c. Paying $100.00 a month

    d. Paying 10% interest free for 6 months and then continuing to pay 10%

1. Why might payment method (c) not be an option for some people?

2. Which method of payment do you consider the best option? Explain your reasoning.

3. When considering applying for a credit card, what details should you look for? How would you plan to pay off your bill?

Be prepared to share your solutions and methods.

A Series of Fortunate Events

Applications of Arithmetic and Geometric Series

In this lesson, you will:

- Apply your understanding of series to problem situations.
- Determine whether a situation is best modeled by a geometric or arithmetic series.

Have you ever heard the expression "money can't buy happiness"? Do you think it's true? People spend a lot of time and mental energy dreaming about having a lot of money or material possessions. It's interesting to think about whether winning the lottery or suddenly acquiring a lot of fancy things would actually make you a happier person. Researchers at universities across the globe have studied this question, and some of the results of the studies may surprise you.

- Lottery winners often become less satisfied with life's simple pleasures over time.
- Once earnings surpass the ability to purchase essential items (food, clothing, shelter, etc.), additional money generally doesn't lead to an increase in happiness.
- Wealthy people tend to relish positive life experiences much less than people who aren't wealthy.

That isn't to say that money isn't important. Making sound financial decisions can save you a lot of headaches and put you in a position where you aren't worrying about money. However, research says that having a lot of money won't necessarily make you a happier person.

What financial decisions have you made so far in your life? What important financial decisions are coming up?

PROBLEM 1 **A Time of Serious Financial Decisions**

Some of the most important financial decisions often occur during the years following the completion of high school or college. This is a time when young adults usually face their first serious choices about things such as a career, buying a car, assuming a mortgage for a house, or investing money in the bank.

1. Benjamin is anxious. After finishing his undergraduate degree he must take the GRE in order to get into graduate school, but the amount of information that he needs to cover is overwhelming. "I only have a month to prepare!" he exclaims. Sally tells him to calm down and start slowly. She recommends studying just 15 minutes the first day, but adding 3 minutes every day to his study time.

"But a friend told me that you have to study at least 20 hours to get ready for this thing! I think I need a different plan."

Will Sally's plan lead to enough study time? Show all work and explain your reasoning.

Did Sally describe an arithmetic or geometric series?

2. Carlos meets up with Jake after a visit to the bank. He has a confused look.
   Carlos said, "I wanted to determine the best way to invest my money, but everybody at
   the bank was busy. I found this graph showing how $50 increases over time from two of
   their investment options."

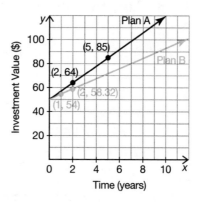

"So what's the problem?" Jake asks.

Carlos explains his dilemma: "I want to invest my money in a plan and keep it there for
20 years. This brochure was ripped and only shows the first few years. I need to know
which plan is a better long-term investment.

a. Are the investment plans arithmetic or geometric? Explain your reasoning.

b. Determine the better investment for Carlos. Show all work and explain
   your reasoning.

3. Rhonda is considering two different physical therapist positions.

- Range of Motion offers an initial salary of $50,000 per year with annual increases of $1,500 per year.

- Mobility, Inc. offers an initial salary of $42,000 with a guaranteed 4% increase in salary every year.

a. Is this situation arithmetic or geometric? Explain your reasoning.

b. Determine the years for which Range of Motion pays more than Mobility, Inc. Show all work and explain your reasoning.

c. Determine which company pays more salary over a 30-year career. Show all work and explain your reasoning.

1. A stomach virus spreads rapidly through a town. Initially only 12 people were infected, but the virus spreads quickly, increasing the number of people infected by 15% every day.

   a. How many new people are infected on the 10th day? Show all work and explain your reasoning.

   b. How many total people were infected on the 10th day? Show all work and explain your reasoning.

2. A total of 123,000 cases of a different cold virus were reported throughout the country in a particular year. The production and distribution of a vaccine is projected to decrease the number of reported cases by 26% every year.

   a. Approximately how many new cases will be reported in 15 years? Show all work and explain your reasoning.

   b. A company reports that vaccine production will cost approximately $9 per person. Estimate the total cost of production for the next 15 years.

   c. Will the virus be eliminated? If so, when? Show all work and explain your reasoning.

Be prepared to share your solutions and methods.

Chapter 8 Summary

KEY TERMS

- arithmetic sequence (8.1)
- geometric sequence (8.1)
- finite sequence (8.1)
- infinite sequence (8.1)
- tessellation (8.2)
- series (8.2)
- finite series (8.2)
- infinite series 8.2)
- arithmetic series (8.2)
- geometric series (8.3)
- convergent series (8.4)
- divergent series (8.4)

8.1 Identifying Whether a Sequence is Arithmetic, Geometric, or Neither

An arithmetic sequence is a sequence of numbers in which the difference between two consecutive terms is a constant. A geometric sequence is a sequence of numbers in which the ratio between two consecutive terms is a constant. A sequence that is neither arithmetic nor geometric has no common difference or ratio between two consecutive terms.

Example

The sequence 5, 11, 17, 23, 29 is arithmetic because the difference between consecutive terms is 6.

The sequence $\frac{1}{2}, \frac{1}{6}, \frac{1}{18}, \frac{1}{54}$ is geometric because the ratio between two consecutive terms is $\frac{1}{3}$.

The sequence $-2, 0, 4, 10$ is neither arithmetic nor geometric because there is no common difference or ratio between two consecutive terms.

Writing an Explicit Formula and/or Recursive Formula for Determining a Term of an Arithmetic or Geometric Sequence

An explicit formula for a sequence is a formula for calculating each term of the sequence using the index, which is a term's position in the sequence. A recursive formula expresses each new term of a sequence based on a preceding term of the sequence.

	Arithmetic Sequence	**Geometric Sequence**
Explicit Formula	$a_n = a_1 + d(n - 1)$ where a_1 is the first term, d is the common difference, and n is the nth term in the sequence.	$g_n = g_1 \cdot r^{n-1}$ where g_1 is the first term and r is the common ratio.
Recursive Formula	$a_n = a_{n-1} + d$ where a_{n-1} is the term previous to a_n and d is the common difference.	$g_n = g_{n-1} \cdot r$ where g_{n-1} is the term previous to g_n and r is the common ratio.

Example

The Explicit Formula for the arithmetic sequence 3, 7, 11, 15, 19 where $a_1 = 3$ and $d = 4$ is as shown.

$$a_n = a_1 + d(n - 1)$$

$$= 3 + 4(n - 1)$$

$$= 3 + 4n - 4$$

$$a_n = 4n - 1$$

The Recursive Formula for the geometric sequence $-2, -4, -8, -16$ where $g_1 = -2$ and $r = 2$ is as shown.

$$g_n = g_{n-1} \cdot r$$

$$g_n = g_{n-1} \cdot 2$$

Using an Explicit Formula and/or Recursive Formula for Determining a Term of an Arithmetic or Geometric Sequence

Deciding whether to use an explicit formula or recursive formula to determine a term in a sequence depends on what information is known. To determine the nth term in an arithmetic sequence use an explicit formula if the first term and common difference are known or use a recursive formula if the $(n - 1)$th term and common difference are know. To determine the nth term in an geometric sequence use an explicit formula if the first term and common ratio are known or use a recursive formula if the $(n - 1)$th term and common ratio are know.

Example

To determine the term a_7 of an arithmetic sequence given $a_6 = 15$ and $d = 3$ use a recursive formula.

$$a_n = a_{n-1} + d$$

$$a_7 = a_6 + 3$$

$$= 15 + 3$$

$$= 18$$

To determine the term g_7 of a geometric sequence given $g_1 = 2$ and $r = 4$ use an explicit formula.

$$g_n = g_1 \cdot r^{n-1}$$

$$g_7 = 2 \cdot 4^6$$

$$= 8192$$

Using Sigma Notation to Rewrite the Sum of a Series

Sigma notation is a convenient way to write the sum, S_n, of the series $a_1 + a_2 + a_3 + \cdots + a_n$.

The notation is as follows: $S_n = \displaystyle\sum_{i=1}^{n} a_i = a_1 + a_2 + a_3 + \cdots + a_{n-1} + a_n$

Example

Series: $2 + 7 + 12 + 17$

$$S_4 = \sum_{i=1}^{4} a_i$$

$$= 2 + 7 + 12 + 17$$

Using Gauss's Formula to Compute the First n Terms of an Arithmetic Series

To compute S_n, of the first n terms of an arithmetic series Gauss's Formula,

$S_n = \dfrac{n(a_1 + a_n)}{2}$, can be used providing the first term, a_1, and the last term, a_n, are known.

Example

Series: $-\dfrac{1}{2} + 0 + \dfrac{1}{2} + 1 + \dfrac{3}{2}$

$n = 5, a_1 = -\dfrac{1}{2}, a_5 = \dfrac{3}{2}$

$S_n = \dfrac{n(a_1 + a_n)}{2}$

$S_5 = \dfrac{5\left(-\dfrac{1}{2} + \dfrac{3}{2}\right)}{2}$

$= \dfrac{5}{2}$

Determining a Function that Computes the First n Terms of an Arithmetic Series

The explicit formula, $a_n = a_1 + d(n - 1)$, together with Gauss's Formula, $S_n = \dfrac{n(a_1 + a_n)}{2}$, can be used to determine a function that computes the first n terms of an arithmetic series.

Example

Series: $-1 + (-3) + (-5) + (-7) + (-9) + \cdots$

$a_1 = -1, d = -2$

$a_n = a_1 + d(n - 1)$

$\quad = -1 + (-2)(n - 1)$

$\quad = -1 - 2n + 2$

$a_n = 1 - 2_n$

$S_n = \dfrac{n(a_1 + a_n)}{2}$

$\quad = \dfrac{n[-1 + (1 - 2n)]}{2}$

$\quad = \dfrac{n[-2n]}{2}$

$\quad = \dfrac{-2n^2}{2}$

$S_n = -n^2$

Solving Real-World Problems Using Finite Arithmetic Series

Identify what the problem is asking. Then determine what information is provided so that the correct approach to the solution can be used. Choose the appropriate formula(s) need, make the correct substitution(s), and solve the problem. Check to see that the question asked has been answered.

Example

Barry planted sunflowers in his garden. In the first row he planted 4 plants, in the second row he planted 10 plants, and in the third row he planted 16 plants. If this pattern continued, how many plants did Barry place in the sixth row?

The problem asks how many sunflower plants are placed in the sixth row. The information provided is that $n = 6$, $a_1 = 4$, and $d = 6$.

$$a_n = a_1 + d(n - 1)$$

$$a_6 = 4 + 6(6 - 1)$$

$$= 34 \text{ sunflowers}$$

Barry placed 34 sunflower plants in the sixth row.

Using Euclid's Method to Determine the Sum of a Finite Geometric Series

Euclid's Method can be used to compute a finite geometric series provided the first term, g_1, the last term, g_n, and the common ratio, r, are known. In which case, the formula $S_n = \dfrac{g_n(r) - g_1}{r - 1}$ can be used.

Example

$$-5 + (-10) + (-20) + (-40)$$

$$g_1 = -5, n = 4, g_4 = -40, r = 2$$

$$S_n = \frac{g_n(r) - g_1}{r - 1}$$

$$S_4 = \frac{-40(2) - (-5)}{2 - 1}$$

$$= -75$$

8.3 Using the Formula $S_n = \dfrac{g_1(r^n - 1)}{r - 1}$ to Compute a Finite Geometric Series

The formula, $S_n = \dfrac{g_1(r^n - 1)}{r - 1}$, can be used to compute a finite geometric series provided the first term, g_1, the common ratio, r, and the number of terms, n, are known.

Example

$2 + 6 + 18 + 54 + 162$

$g_1 = 2, r = 3, n = 5$

$S_n = \dfrac{g_1(r^n - 1)}{r - 1}$

$S_5 = \dfrac{2(3^5 - 1)}{3 - 1}$

$ = 242$

8.4 Determining Whether an Infinite Geometric Series Converges or Diverges

A convergent series is an infinite series that has a finite sum. A divergent series is an infinite series that does not have a finite sum. If a series is divergent, it is said that the sum is infinity. An infinite geometric series converges providing the common ratio, r, is greater than zero and less than 1.

Example

$\dfrac{2}{3} + \dfrac{2}{9} + \dfrac{2}{27} + \dfrac{2}{81} + \cdots$

The common ratio for the infinite geometric series is $\dfrac{1}{3}$ which is greater than zero and less than 1. The series converges.

8.4 Computing an Infinite Convergent Geometric Series

The formula to compute S of a convergent geometric series with a first term g_1 and common ratio r is $S = \dfrac{g_1}{1 - r}$ provided $0 < r < 1$.

Example

$5 + \dfrac{5}{2} + \dfrac{5}{4} + \dfrac{5}{8} + \cdots$

Observe that $g_1 = 5$ and $r = \dfrac{1}{2}$. Since r is greater than zero and less than 1, the infinite geometric series converges.

$$S = \frac{g_1}{1 - r}$$

$$S = \frac{5}{1 - \dfrac{1}{2}}$$

$$= 10$$

8.5 Solving Real-World Problems Involving Geometric Sequences or Series

Identify what the problem is asking. Then determine what information is provided so that the correct approach to the solution can be used. Choose the appropriate formula(s) need, make the correct substitution(s), and solve the problem. Check to see that the question asked has been answered.

Example

Every Saturday Chloe places money in her piggy bank. On the first Saturday she placed $0.02 in the piggy bank, on the second Saturday she placed $0.06 in the piggy bank, and on the third Saturday she place $0.18 in the piggy bank. If Chloe continues to place money in her piggy bank using the same pattern, how much money will she place in her piggy bank on the seventh Saturday?

The problem is asking how much money Chloe places in her piggy bank on the seventh Saturday. The information indicates that Chloe is using a geometric pattern where the first term, g_1, is $0.02 and the common ratio, r, is 3. The formula needed to answer the question is $g_n = g_1 \cdot r^{n-1}$ where $n = 7$.

$$g_n = g_1 \cdot r^{n-1}$$

$$g_7 = 0.02 \cdot 3^6$$

$$= \$14.58$$

The amount of money Chloe places in her piggy bank on the seventh Saturday is $14.58.

8.6 Determining Whether a Situation Is Best Modeled by a Arithmetic or Geometric Series

When solving a problem involving a series it is important to determine whether the given situation is arithmetic or geometric. If consecutive terms of the series have a common difference then the series is arithmetic. If consecutive terms of the series have a common ratio then the series is geometric.

Example

Gia applied for a job that initially pays her $13 per hour but she is guaranteed a yearly raise of $1.50 per hour.

The progression in her yearly salary is arithmetic with a common difference of $1.50.

8.6 Solving Real-World Problems Involving Arithmetic or Geometric Sequences or Series

Identify what the problem is asking. Then determine what information is provided so that the correct approach to the solution can be found. Choose the appropriate formula(s) need, make the correct substitution(s), and solve the problem. Check to see that the question asked has been answered.

Example

Belinda likes to write poetry. The table shows how many poems she wrote over the course of 5 weeks. Determine how many poems Belinda wrote.

Week	Number of Poems Written
1	4
2	8
3	16
4	32
5	64

The problem asks for the number of poems written by Belinda. The number of poems written forms a geometric series. Using Euclid's Method, $S_n = \dfrac{g_n(r) - g_1}{r - 1}$, where $n = 5$, $g_5 = 64$, $r = 2$, and $g_1 = 4$ the number of poems written by Belinda can be determined.

$$S_5 = \frac{g_5(r) - g_1}{r - 1}$$

$$= \frac{64(2) - 4}{2 - 1}$$

$$= 124 \text{ poems}$$

Belinda wrote 124 poems during the 5 week period.

Glossary

A

absolute maximum

A function has an absolute maximum if there is a point that has a y-coordinate that is greater than the y-coordinates of every other point on the graph.

Example

The ordered pair (4, 2) is the absolute maximum of the graph of the function $f(x) = -\frac{1}{2}x^2 + 4x - 6$.

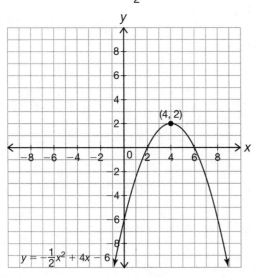

absolute minimum

A function has an absolute minimum if there is a point that has a y-coordinate that is less than the y-coordinates of every other point on the graph.

Example

The ordered pair (1, −4) is the absolute minimum of the graph of the function $y = \frac{2}{3}x^2 - \frac{4}{3}x - \frac{10}{3}$.

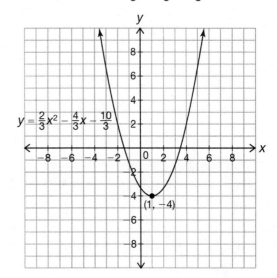

Glossary

amplitude

The amplitude of a periodic function is one-half of the distance between the maximum and minimum values of the function.

Example

The function $y = \sin(x)$ has a maximum of 1 and a minimum of -1. The distance between the maximum and minimum is 2. So, the amplitude of $y = \sin(x)$ is 1.

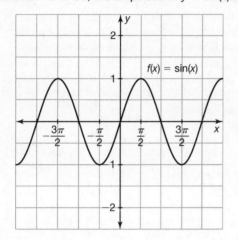

argument of a function

The argument of a function is the variable, term, or expression on which the function operates.

Example

In the function $f(x + 5) = 32$, the argument is $x + 5$.

arithmetic sequence

An arithmetic sequence is a sequence of numbers in which the difference between any two consecutive terms is a constant.

Example

The sequence 1, 3, 5, 7 is an arithmetic sequence with a common difference of 2.

arithmetic series

An arithmetic series is the sum of the terms of an arithmetic sequence.

Example

The arithmetic series corresponding to the arithmetic sequence 1, 3, 5, 7 is $1 + 3 + 5 + 7$, or 16.

average rate of change

The average rate of change of a function is the ratio of the independent variable to the dependent variable over a specific interval. The formula for average rate of change is $\dfrac{f(b) - f(a)}{b - a}$ for an interval (a, b). The expression $a - b$ represents the change in the input of the function f. The expression $f(b) - f(a)$ represents the change in the function f as the input changes from a to b.

Example

Consider the function $f(x) = x^2$.

The average rate of change of the interval $(1, 3)$ is $\dfrac{3^2 - 1^2}{3 - 1} = \dfrac{9 - 1}{3 - 1} = \dfrac{8}{2} = 4$.

B

biased sample

A biased sample is a sample that does not accurately represent all of a population.

Example

A survey is conducted asking students their favorite class. Only students in the math club are surveyed. The sample of students is a biased sample.

binomial

A binomial is a polynomial with exactly two terms.

Example

The polynomial $3x + 5$ is a binomial.

Binomial Theorem

The Binomial Theorem is used to calculate any term of any binomial expansion. It is written in the form:

$$(x + y)^k = \sum_{r=0}^{k} \binom{k}{r} x^{k-r} y^r$$
$$= \binom{k}{0} x^k y^0 + \binom{k}{1} x^{k-1} y^1 + \binom{k}{2} x^{k-2} y^2 + \cdots$$
$$+ \binom{k}{k-2} x^2 y^{k-2} + \binom{k}{k-1} x^1 y^{k-1}$$
$$+ \binom{k}{k} x^0 y^k$$

where k is the degree of the binomial exponent. Note that a given term is the $(r + 1)$th term.

Example

Use the Binomial Theorem to find the third term of $(x + y)^{20}$.

$$(x + y)^{20} = \binom{20}{2} x^{20-2} y^2 = \frac{20!}{18!2!} x^{18} y^2$$
$$= \frac{20 \cdot 19}{2 \cdot 1} x^{18} y^2 = 190 x^{18} y^2$$

carrying capacity

The carrying capacity of a species is the maximum population size of the species that the environment can sustain. In logistic functions $f(x) = \dfrac{C}{1 + Ae^{-Bx}}$, C is the carrying capacity.

Example

The number of fish in a small pond is modeled by the logistic growth function $f(x) = \dfrac{150}{1 + 7e^{-0.06x}}$. The carrying capacity of the pond is 150 fish.

Change of Base Formula

The Change of Base Formula allows you to calculate an exact value for a logarithm by rewriting it in terms of a different base. It is especially helpful when using a calculator.

The Change of Base Formula states: $\log_b (c) = \dfrac{\log_a (c)}{\log_a (b)}$, where $a, b, c > 0$ and $a, b \neq 1$.

Example

$$\log_4 (50) = \dfrac{\log 50}{\log 4}$$
$$\approx 2.821928095$$

characteristic of interest

A characteristic of interest is the specific question that you are trying to answer or specific information that a study is trying to gather.

Example

In a sample survey to determine teenagers' online habits, a characteristic of interest is the amount of time that a teenager spends online per day.

closed under an operation

A set is closed under an operation if the operation is performed on any of the numbers in the set and the result is a number that is also in the same set.

Example

The set of whole numbers is closed under addition. The sum of any two whole numbers is always another whole number.

clusters

Clusters are area of the graph where data are grouped close together.

Example

A city manager randomly selects one block in the city and surveys all of the residents of that block. Each block is considered a cluster.

cluster sample

A cluster sample is a sample obtained by creating clusters, with each cluster containing the characteristics of the population, and randomly selecting a cluster.

Example

If students in a high school are divided into clusters of 20 students based on their student I.D. number and then one cluster is randomly selected, this is a cluster sample.

coefficient of determination

The coefficient of determination (R^2) measures the "strength" of the relationship between the original data and its regression equation. The value of the coefficient of determination ranges from 0 to 1 with a value of 1 indicating a perfect fit between the regression equation and the original data.

common logarithm

A common logarithm is a logarithm with a base of 10. Common logarithms are usually written without a base.

Example

$\log (10x)$ or $\log x$ are examples of a common logarithm.

complex conjugates

Complex conjugates are pairs of numbers of the form $a + bi$ and $a - bi$. The product of a pair of complex conjugates is always a real number.

Example

The expressions $(1 + i)$ and $(1 - i)$ are complex conjugates. The product of $(1 + i)$ and $(1 - i)$ is a real number: $(1 + i)(1 - i) = 1 - i^2 = 1 - (-1) = 2$.

Glossary

composition of functions

Composition of functions is the process of substituting one function for the variable in another function.

Example

If $f(x) = 3x - 5$ and $g(x) = x^2$, then the composition of the functions $f(g(x))$ can be written as $f(g(x)) = 3(x^2) - 5 = 3x^2 - 5$.

The composition of functions $g(f(x))$ can be written as $g(f(x)) = (3x + 5)^2$.

concavity of a parabola

The concavity of a parabola describes the orientation of the curvature of the parabola.

Example

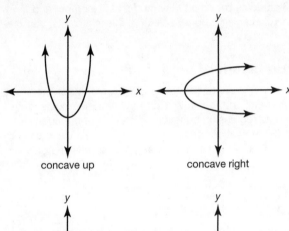

concave up   concave right

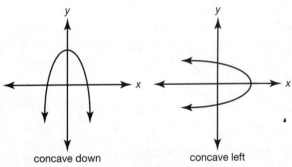

concave down   concave left

confidence interval

A confidence interval is an estimated range of values, based on the results of a sample survey, that will likely include the population proportion. Typically, a confidence interval of 95%, or 2 standard deviations from the mean, is used. The formula for calculating the confidence interval for proportions is $\sqrt{\dfrac{\hat{p}(1 - \hat{p})}{n}}$, where $\hat{p}$ is the sample population and n is the sample size. The formula $\dfrac{S}{\sqrt{n}}$, where S is the standard deviation of the sample and n is the sample size, is used for continuous data.

Example

A survey of 2000 teenagers reports that 42% have a part-time job.

$$\sqrt{\frac{0.42(1 - 0.42)}{2000}}$$

$$\sqrt{\frac{0.42(0.58)}{2000}}$$

≈ 0.011

The interval from 40.9% to 43.1% represents a 95% confidence interval for the population proportion.

confounding

Confounding is the process of overlooking factors and situations that distort the final results when seeking to gather information or data.

Example

Suppose that a study is conducted to determine if there is a link between a certain type of insulin that some diabetic patients use and cancer. Confounding can occur due to the fact that there are other potential causes of cancer that could be involved in the sample.

continuous data

Continuous data are data that have an infinite number of possible values.

Example

The heights of students is an example of continuous data.

convenience sample

A convenience sample is a sample whose data are based on what is convenient for the person choosing the sample.

Example

If you choose the students sitting closest to you in math class as your sample, you have a convenience sample.

convergent series

A convergent series is an infinite series that has a finite sum. The sum of a convergent series S can be calculated as $\dfrac{g_1}{1-r}$ where g_1 is the first term of the series and r is the common ratio.

Example

The infinite geometric series $1 + \dfrac{1}{2} + \dfrac{1}{4} + \dfrac{1}{8} + \cdots$ can be calculated as $S = \dfrac{1}{1 - \dfrac{1}{2}} = \dfrac{1}{\dfrac{1}{2}} = 2$.

cosine function

A cosine function is a periodic function. It takes angle measures (θ values) as inputs and then outputs real number values based on coordinates of points on the unit circle.

Example

The function $h(\theta) = 4\cos(\theta + \pi)$ is a cosine function.

cube root function

The cube root function is the inverse of the power function $f(x) = x^3$.

Example

The cube root function is $g(x) = \sqrt[3]{x}$.

cubic function

A cubic function is a function that can be written in the standard form $f(x) = ax^3 + bx^2 + cx + d$ where $a \neq 0$.

Example

The function $f(x) = x^3 - 5x^2 + 3x + 1$ is a cubic function.

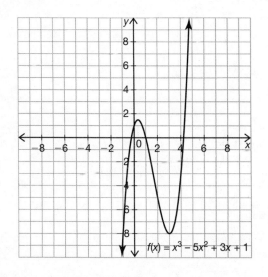

$f(x) = x^3 - 5x^2 + 3x + 1$

damping function

A damping function is a function that is multiplied to a periodic function to decrease its amplitude over time. It can be from a multitude of function families, including linear, quadratic, or exponential.

Example

In the function $f(x) = 2^x \cdot \sin(x) + 1$, the exponential function 2^x is the damping function.

degree of a polynomial

The degree of a polynomial is the greatest variable exponent in the expression.

Example

The polynomial $2x^3 + 5x^2 - 6x + 1$ has a degree of 3 because the greatest exponent is 3.

discrete data

Discrete data are data that have a finite number of possible values.

Example

If you roll a number cube 10 times and record the results, the results are discrete data.

discriminant

The radicand expression in the Quadratic Formula, $b^2 - 4ac$, is called the discriminant because it "discriminates" the number and type of roots of a quadratic equation.

Example

For the function $f(x) = 2x^2 - 5x + 1$, the discriminant is $(-5)^2 - 4(2)(1)$, or 17.

divergent series

A divergent series is an infinite series that does not have a finite sum.

Example

The infinite geometric series $1 + 2 + 4 + 8 + 16 + \cdots$ is a divergent series.

Glossary

double root

A double root of an equation is a root that appears twice.

Example

The equation $x^2 + 2x + 1 = 0$ has a double root at $x = -1$.

$$x^2 + 2x + 1 = 0$$
$$(x + 1)(x + 1) = 0$$
$$x + 1 = 0 \quad \text{or } x + 1 = 0$$
$$x = -1 \quad \text{or} \quad x = -1$$

E

Empirical Rule for Normal Distributions

The Empirical Rule for Normal Distributions states that:

- Approximately 68% of the area under the normal curve is within one standard deviation of the mean.
- Approximately 95% of the area under the normal curve is within two standard deviations of the mean.
- Approximately 99.7% of the area under the normal curve is within three standard deviations of the mean.

Example

For a data set that is normally distributed with a mean of 10 and a standard deviation of 1, the following are true:

- Approximately 68% of the data values are between 9 and 11.
- Approximately 95% of the data values are between 8 and 12.
- Approximately 99.7% of the data values are between 7 and 13.

end behavior

The end behavior of the graph of a function is the behavior of the graph as x approaches infinity and as x approaches negative infinity.

Example

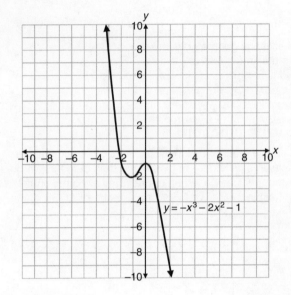

$$y = -x^3 - 2x^2 - 1$$

The end behavior of the graph shown can be described as follows:

As x approaches infinity, y approaches negative infinity.

As x approaches negative infinity, y approaches infinity.

Euclid's Formula

Euclid's Formula is a formula used to generate Pythagorean triples given any two positive integers. Given positive integers r and s, where $r > s$, Euclid's Formula is $(r^2 + s^2)^2 = (r^2 - s^2)^2 + (2rs)^2$.

Example

Let $r = 3$ and $s = 1$.

$$(3^2 + 1^2)^2 = (3^2 - 1^2)^2 + (2 \cdot 3 \cdot 1)^2$$
$$10^2 = 8^2 + 6^2$$

So, one Pythagorean triple is 6, 8, 10.

even function

An even function f is a function for which $f(-x) = f(x)$ for all values of x in the domain.

Example

The function $f(x) = x^2$ is an even function because $(-x)^2 = x^2$.

experiment

An experiment gathers data on the effect of one or more treatments, or experimental conditions, on the characteristic of interest.

Example

The following is an example of an experiment.

A sample of 200 asthma patients participated in the clinical trial for a new asthma drug. One hundred of the patients received a placebo treatment along with an inhaler, while the remaining 100 patients received the new drug along with an inhaler. Monthly blood and breathing tests were performed on all 200 patients to determine if the new drug was effective.

experimental unit

An experimental unit is a member of a sample in an experiment.

Example

Suppose that an experiment is conducted to test the effects of a new drug on a sample of patients. Each patient is an experimental unit in the experiment.

extraneous solution

Extraneous solutions are solutions that result from the process of solving an equation; but are not valid solutions to the equation.

Example

$$\log_2 (x) + \log_2 (x + 7) = 3$$
$$\log_2 (x^2 + 7x) = 3$$
$$x^2 + 7x = 2^3$$
$$x^2 + 7x = 8$$
$$x^2 + 7x - 8 = 0$$
$$(x + 8)(x - 1) = 0$$
$$x + 8 = 0 \quad \text{or} \quad x - 1 = 0$$
$$x = -8 \qquad\qquad x = 1$$

The solution $x = -8$ is an extraneous solution because the argument of a logarithm must be greater than zero.

extrema

Extrema are the set of all relative maxima and minima for a graph.

Example

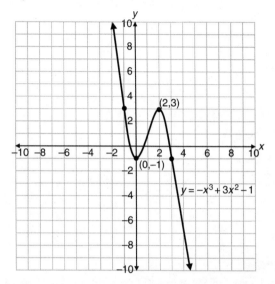

The graph shown has 2 extrema, a relative maximum at (2, 3) and a relative minimum at (0, −1).

F

Factor Theorem

The Factor Theorem states that a polynomial is divisible by $(x - r)$ if the value of the polynomial at r is zero.

Example

The polynomial $x^3 - 2x^2 + 2x - 1$ is divisible by $x - 1$ because $(1)^3 - 2(1)^2 + 2(1) - 1 = 0$.

factored form of a quadratic function

A quadratic function written in factored form is in the form $f(x) = a(x - r_1)(x - r_2)$, where $a \neq 0$.

Example

The function $h(x) = x^2 - 8x + 12$ written in factored form is $h(x) = (x - 6)(x - 2)$.

finite sequence

If a sequence terminates, it is called a finite sequence.

Example

The sequence 22, 26, 30 is a finite sequence.

finite series

A finite series is the sum of a finite number of terms.

Example

The sum of all of the even integers from 1 to 100 is a finite series.

fractal

A fractal is a complex geometric shape that is constructed by a mathematical pattern. Fractals are infinite and self-similar.

Example

Stage 0   Stage 1   Stage 2   Stage 3

frequency

The frequency of a periodic function is the reciprocal of the period and specifies the number of repetitions of the graph of a periodic function per unit. It is calculated by the formula $\frac{|B|}{2\pi}$.

Example

The function $f(x) = 3 \cos (2x)$ has a B-value of 2, so the frequency is $\frac{|2|}{2\pi}$ or $\frac{1}{\pi}$ units.

function

A function is a relation such that for each element of the domain there exists exactly one element in the range.

Example

The equation $y = 2x$ is a function. Every x-value has exactly one corresponding y-value.

function notation

Function notation is a way of representing functions algebraically. The function $f(x)$ is read as "f of x" and indicates that x is the input and $f(x)$ is the output.

Example

The function $f(x) = 0.75x$ is written using function notation.

Fundamental Theorem of Algebra

The Fundamental Theorem of Algebra states that any polynomial equation of degree n must have exactly n complex roots or solutions; also, every polynomial function of degree n must have exactly n complex zeros. However, any root or zero may be a multiple root or zero.

Example

The polynomial equation $x^5 + x^2 - 6 = 0$ has 5 complex roots because the polynomial $x^5 + x^2 - 6$ has a degree of 5.

G

geometric sequence

A geometric sequence is a sequence of terms in which the ratio between any two consecutive terms is a constant.

Example

The sequence 2, 4, 8, 16 is a geometric sequence with a common ratio of 2.

geometric series

A geometric series is the sum of the terms of a geometric sequence.

Example

The geometric series corresponding to the geometric sequence 2, 4, 8, 16 is 2 + 4 + 8 + 16, or 30.

H

half-life

The half-life of a sample is the time it takes for half of the atoms in the sample to decay.

Example

The radioactive isotope strontium-90 has a half life of about 30 years. A 1000-gram sample of strontium-90 will decay to 500 grams in 30 years.

Glossary

horizontal compression

Horizontal compression is the squeezing of a graph toward the y-axis.

Example

The graph of $g(x) = (2x)^2$ is a horizontal compression compared to the graph of $f(x) = x^2$.

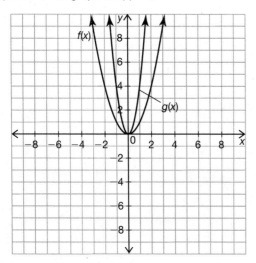

horizontal dilation

A horizontal dilation is a type of transformation that stretches or compresses the entire graph.

Example

The graphs of $g(x) = (2x)^2$ and $h(x) = \left(\frac{1}{2}x\right)^2$ are horizontal dilations of the graph of $f(x) = x^2$.

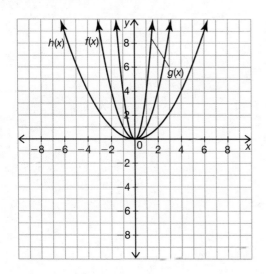

Horizontal Line Test

The Horizontal Line Test is a test to determine if a function is one to one. To use the test, imagine drawing every possible horizontal line on the coordinate plane. If no horizontal line intersects the graph of a function at more than one point, then the function is one to one.

Example

The function $y = x$ passes the Horizontal Line Test because no horizontal line can be drawn that intersects the graph at more than one point. So, the function is one to one.

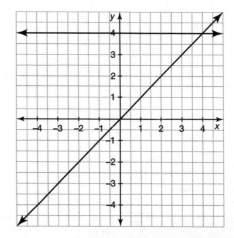

The function $y = x^2$ does not pass the Horizontal Line Test because a horizontal line can be drawn that intersects the graph at more than one point. So, the function is not one to one.

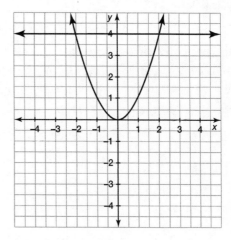

horizontal stretching

Horizontal stretching is the stretching of a graph away from the *y*-axis.

Example

The graph of $g(x) = \left(\frac{1}{2}x\right)^2$ is a horizontal stretching compared to the graph of $f(x) = x^2$.

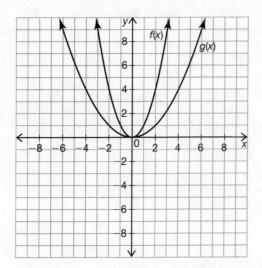

I

identity function

The identity function, also known as the composition identity, is defined as $f(x) = x$.

imaginary part of a complex number

In a complex number of the form $a + bi$, the term bi is called the imaginary part of a complex number.

Example

The imaginary part of the complex number $3 + 2i$ is $2i$.

imaginary roots

Imaginary roots are imaginary solutions to equations.

Example

The quadratic equation $x^2 - 2x + 2$ has two imaginary roots: $1 + i$ and $1 - i$.

infinite sequence

If a sequence continues forever, it is called an infinite sequence.

Example

The sequence 22, 26, 30, 34 . . . is an infinite sequence.

infinite series

An infinite series is the sum of an infinite number of terms.

Example

The sum of all of the even whole numbers is an infinite series.

initial ray of an angle

The initial ray of an angle in standard position is the ray with its endpoint at the origin and extending along the positive *x*-axis.

Example

The initial ray of the angle is labeled in the diagram.

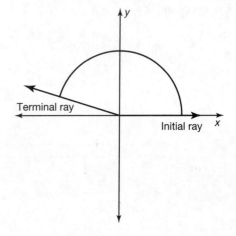

inverse cosine (cos⁻¹)

The cos⁻¹ function is the inverse of the cosine function. The inverse cosine function is written as arccos or cos⁻¹.

Example

$\cos(60°) = \frac{1}{2}$ so $\cos^{-1}\left(\frac{1}{2}\right) = 60°$

inverse of a function

The inverse of a one-to-one function is a function that results from exchanging the independent and dependent variables. A function $f(x)$ with coordinates $(x, f(x))$ will have an inverse with coordinates $(f(x), x)$.

Example

The inverse of the function $y = 2x$ can be found by exchanging the variables x and y.

The inverse of $y = 2x$ is $x = 2y$.

inverse sine (sin⁻¹)

The sin⁻¹ function is the inverse of the sine function. The inverse sine function is written as arcsin or sin⁻¹.

Example

$\sin(30°) = \frac{1}{2}$ so $\sin^{-1}\left(\frac{1}{2}\right) = 30°$

inverse tangent (tan⁻¹)

The tan⁻¹ function is the inverse of the tangent function. The inverse tangent function is written as arctan or tan⁻¹.

Example

$\tan(45°) = 1$ so $\tan^{-1}(1) = 45°$

invertible function

An invertible function is a function whose inverse exists. It is one-to-one and passes the Horizontal Line Test, so its inverse will also be a function.

Example

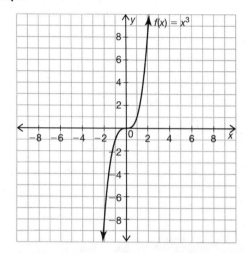

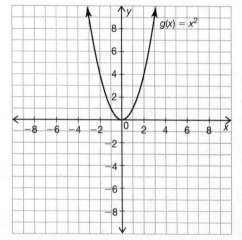

The graph of $f(x) = x^3$ is an invertible function because it is one-to-one and passes the Horizontal Line Test. Therefore its inverse will also be a function.

The graph of $g(x) = x^2$ is not an invertible function because it does not pass the Horizontal Line Test.

iterative process

An iterative process is one in which the output from one iteration is used as the input for the next iteration.

Example

A recursive sequence uses an iterative process to generate its terms.

$a_n = 3a_{n-1} + 1$

$a_1 = 2$

Begin with the first term, which is 2, and substitute it into the sequence to get the next term.

$a_2 = 3a_1 + 1$

$\quad = 3(2) + 1$

$\quad = 7$

Then substitute a_2 into the sequence to produce a_3, and so on.

L

line of reflection

A line of reflection is the line that a graph is reflected about.

Example

The line of reflection for the graph of the function $f(x) = x^2$ is the y-axis, or the line $x = 0$.

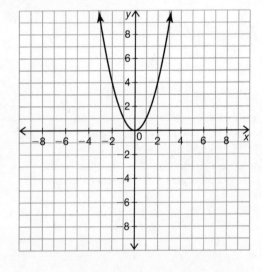

logarithm

The logarithm of a positive number is the exponent to which the base must be raised to result in that number.

Example

Because $10^2 = 100$, the logarithm of 100 to the base 10 is 2.

$\log 100 = 2$

Because $2^3 = 8$, the logarithm of 8 to the base 2 is 3.

$\log_2 (8) = 3$

logarithm with same base and argument

The logarithm of a number, with the base equal to the same number, is always equal to 1.

$$\log_b(b) = 1$$

Example

$\log_4(4) = 1$

logarithmic equation

A logarithmic equation is an equation that contains a logarithm.

Example

The equation $\log_2 (x) = 4$ is a logarithmic equation.

logarithmic function

A logarithmic function is a function involving a logarithm.

Example

The function $f(x) = 3 \log x$ is a logarithmic function.

logistic functions

Logistic functions are functions that can be written in the form $f(x) = \dfrac{C}{1 + Ae^{-Bx}}$. It is used to model population growth. The graph of a logistic growth function is shaped like an S-curve. The function appears to grow exponentially during the initial growth stage, but as it approaches the carrying capacity C, the growth slows and then stops when it reaches equilibrium.

Example

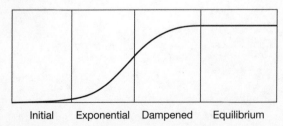

Initial   Exponential   Dampened   Equilibrium

Glossary

mean

The mean of a data set is the sum of all of the values of the data set divided by the number of values in the data set. With normal curves, the mean of a population is represented with the symbol μ, and the mean of a sample is represented with the symbol $\bar{x}$.

Example

The mean of the numbers 7, 9, 13, 4, and 7 is $\frac{7 + 9 + 13 + 4 + 7}{5}$, or 8.

The mean of a set of normally distributed data is aligned with the peak of the normal curve.

midline

The midline of a periodic function is a reference line whose equation is the average of the minimum and maximum values of the function.

Example

In the graph of $g(x) = -2 \cos(x) + 3$ the midline occurs at $y = 3$ because the maximum value is 5 and the minimum value is 1.

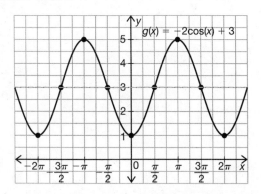

monomial

A monomial is a polynomial with exactly one term.

Example

The expressions $5x$, 7, $-2xy$, and $13x^3$ are monomials.

multiplicity

Multiplicity is how many times a particular number is a zero for a given function.

Example

The equation $x^2 + 2x + 1 = 0$ has a double root at $x = -1$. The root -1 has a multiplicity of 2.

$$x^2 + 2x + 1 = 0$$
$$(x + 1)(x + 1) = 0$$
$$x + 1 = 0 \quad \text{or } x + 1 = 0$$
$$x = -1 \quad \text{or} \quad x = -1$$

natural base, e

The natural base e is an irrational number equal to approximately 2.71828.

Example

$e^2 \approx 2.7183^2 \approx 7.3892$

natural logarithm

A natural logarithm is a logarithm with a base of e. Natural logarithms are usually written as ln.

Example

$\log_e (x)$ or ln x is a natural logarithm.

normal curve

A normal curve is a curve that is bell-shaped and symmetric about the mean.

Example

A normal curve is shown.

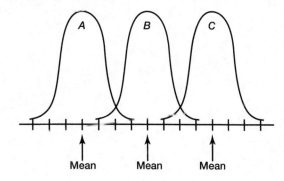

Glossary

normal distribution

A normal distribution, or normal probability distribution, describes a continuous data set that can be modeled using a normal curve.

Example

Adult IQ scores, gas mileage of certain cars, and SAT scores are all continuous data that follow a normal distribution.

observational study

An observational study gathers data about a characteristic of the population without trying to influence the data.

Example

The following is an example of an observational study.

New research funded by a pediatric agency found that nearly 70% of in-house day care centers show as much as 2.5 hours of television to the children in the center per day. The study examined 132 day care programs in 2 Midwestern states.

odd function

An odd function f is a function for which $f(-x) = -f(x)$ for all values of x in the domain.

Example

The function $f(x) = x^3$ is an odd function because $(-x)^3 = -x^3$.

parameter

When data are gathered from a population, the characteristic used to describe the population is called a parameter.

Example

If you wanted to find out the average height of the students at your school, and you measured every student at the school, the characteristic "average height" would be a parameter.

percentile

A percentile divides a data set into 100 equal parts.

period

A period of a periodic function is the length of the smallest interval over which the function repeats.

Example

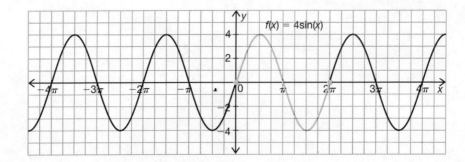

periodic function

A periodic function is a function whose graph consists of repeated instances of a portion of the graph.

Example

The function $f(x) = \sin(x)$ is a periodic function. The portion of the graph between $x = 0$ and $x = 2\pi$ repeats.

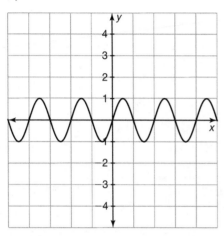

phase shift

A phase shift of a periodic function is a horizontal translation.

Example

The function $y = \sin(x - \pi)$ has a phase shift of π units from the basic function $y = \sin(x)$.

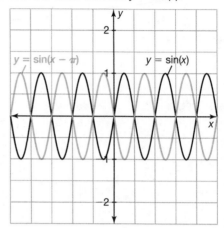

periodicity identity

A periodicity identity is a trigonometric identity based on the period of the trigonometric functions.

Example

The six periodicity identities are:
$\sin(x + 2\pi) = \sin(x)$; $\cos(x + 2\pi) = \cos(x)$
$\sec(x + 2\pi) = \sec(x)$; $\csc(x + 2\pi) = \csc(x)$
$\tan(x + \pi) = \tan(x)$; $\cot(x + \pi) = \cot(x)$

piecewise function

A piecewise function includes different functions that represent different parts of the domain.

Example

The function $f(x)$ is a piecewise function.

$$f(x) = \begin{cases} x + 5, & x \le -2 \\ -2x + 1, & -2 < x \le 2 \\ 2x - 9, & x > 2 \end{cases}$$

polynomial

A polynomial is a mathematical expression involving the sum of powers in one or more variables multiplied by coefficients.

Example

The expression $3x^3 + 5x^2 - 6x + 1$ is a polynomial.

polynomial function

A polynomial function is a function that can be written in the form

$p(x) = a_n x^n + a_{n-1} x^{n-1} + \cdots + a_2 x^2 + a_1 x + a_0$, where the coefficients $a_n, a_{n-1}, \ldots a_2, a_1, a_0$ are complex numbers and the exponents are nonnegative integers.

Example

The function $f(x) = 5x^3 + 3x^2 + x + 1$ is a polynomial function.

polynomial long division

Polynomial long division is an algorithm for dividing one polynomial by another of equal or lesser degree.

Example

$$
\begin{array}{r}
4x^2 - 6x + 3 \\
2x + 3 \,\overline{)\, 8x^3 + 0x^2 - 12x - 7} \\
-(8x^3 + 12x^2) \\
\hline
-12x^2 - 12x \\
-(-12x^2 - 18x) \\
\hline
6x - 7 \\
-(6x + 9) \\
\hline
\text{Remainder } -16
\end{array}
$$

population

The population is the entire set of items from which data can be selected. When you decide what you want to study, the population is the set of all elements in which you are interested. The elements of that population can be people or objects.

Example

If you wanted to find out the average height of the students at your school, the number of students at the school would be the population.

population proportion

A population proportion is the percentage of an entire population that yields a favorable outcome in an experiment.

Example

In an election, the population proportion represents the percentage of people in the entire town who vote to re-elect the mayor.

power function

A power function is a function of the form $P(x) = ax^n$ where n is a non-negative integer.

Example

The functions $f(x) = x$, $f(x) = x^2$, and $f(x) = x^3$ are power functions.

Power Rule of Logarithms

The Power Rule of Logarithms states that the logarithm of a power is equal to the product of the exponent and the logarithm of the base of the power.

$$\log_b (x)^n = n \cdot \log_b (x)$$

Example

$\ln (x)^2 = 2 \ln x$

principal square root of a negative number

For any positive real number n, the principal square root of a negative number, $-n$, is defined by $\sqrt{-n} = i\sqrt{n}$.

Example

The principal square root of -5 is $\sqrt{-5} = i\sqrt{5}$.

Product Rule of Logarithms

The Product Rule of Logarithms states that the logarithm of a product is equal to the sum of the logarithms of the factors.

$$\log_b (xy) = \log_b (x) + \log_b (y)$$

Example

$\log (5x) = \log (5) + \log (x)$

pure imaginary number

A pure imaginary number is a number of the form bi, where b is not equal to 0.

Example

The imaginary numbers $-4i$ and $15i$ are pure imaginary numbers.

Pythagorean identity

A Pythagorean identity is a trigonometric identity based on the Pythagorean Theorem.

Example

The three Pythagorean identities are:
$\sin^2(x) + \cos^2(x) = 1$
$1 + \tan^2(x) = \sec^2(x)$
$1 + \cot^2(x) = \csc^2(x)$

Q

quartic function

A quartic function is a polynomial function with a degree of four.

Example

The function $f(x) = 3x^4 - 2x + 5$ is a quartic function.

quintic function

A quintic function is a polynomial function with a degree of five.

Example

The function $f(x) = 5x^5 + 3x^4 + x^3$ is a quintic function

Quotient Rule of Logarithms

The Quotient Rule of Logarithms states that the logarithm of a quotient is equal to the difference of the logarithms of the dividend and the divisor.

$$\log_b \left(\frac{x}{y}\right) = \log_b (x) - \log_b (y)$$

Example

$\log\left(\frac{x}{2}\right) = \log x - \log 2$

R

radians

A radian is a unit of measurement for an angle in standard position. It is equal to the length of its intercepted arc in the unit circle.

Example

The angle shown has a radian measure of π radians.

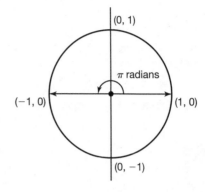

radical function

A radical function is a function that contains one or more radical expressions.

Example

The function $f(x) = \sqrt{3x + 5}$ is a radical function.

random sample

A random sample is a sample that is selected from the population in such a way that every member of the population has the same chance of being selected.

Example

Choosing 100 fans at random to participate in a survey from crowd of 5000 people is an example of random sample.

rational equation

A rational equation is an equation that contains one or more rational expressions.

Example

The equation $\frac{1}{x - 1} + \frac{1}{x + 1} = 4$ is a rational equation.

rational function

A rational function is any function that can be written as the ratio of two polynomial functions. A rational function can be written in the form $f(x) = \dfrac{P(x)}{Q(x)}$ where $P(x)$ and $Q(x)$ are polynomial functions, and $Q(x) \neq 0$.

Example

The function $f(x) = \dfrac{1}{x - 1} + \dfrac{1}{x + 1}$ is a rational function.

Rational Root Theorem

The Rational Root Theorem states that a rational root of a polynomial $a_n x^n + a_{n-1} x^{n-1} + \cdots + a_2 x^2 + a_1 x + a_0 x^0$ must be of the form $\dfrac{p}{q}$, where p is a factor of the constant term and q is a factor of the leading coefficient.

Example

For the polynomial $2x^2 - x + 4$, $p = 4$, and $q = 2$. So, the possible rational roots of the polynomial are ± 4, ± 2, ± 1, $\pm \dfrac{1}{2}$.

real part of a complex number

In a complex number of the form $a + bi$, the term a is called the real part of a complex number.

Example

The real part of the complex number $3 + 2i$ is 3.

reference points

Reference points are a set of key points that help identify the basic form of any function.

Example

The reference points of the basic quadratic function are $(0, 0)$, $(1, 1)$, and $(2, 4)$.

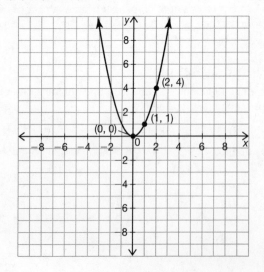

reflection

A reflection of a graph is a mirror image of the graph about a line of reflection.

Example

The triangle on the right is a reflection of the triangle on the left.

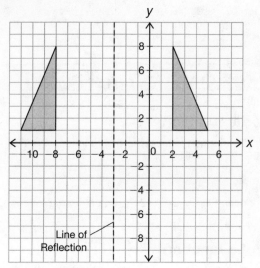

regression equation

A regression equation is a function that models the relationship between two variables in a scatter plot.

Example

The regression equation
$y = -0.41x^3 + 3.50x^2 - 4.47x + 8.44$ models the relationship between time and the number of vehicles.

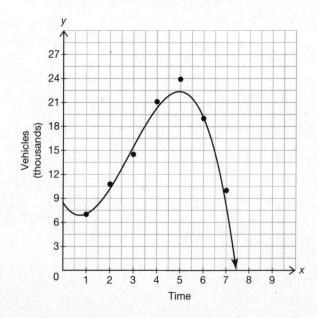

Glossary

relation

A relation is the mapping between a set of input values called the domain and a set of output values called the range.

Example

The set of points {(0, 1), (1, 8), (2, 5), (3, 7)} is a relation.

relative maximum

A relative maximum is the highest point in a particular section of a graph.

Example

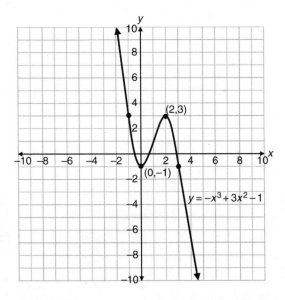

The graph shown has a relative maximum at (2, 3).

relative minimum

A relative minimum is the lowest point in a particular section of a graph.

Example

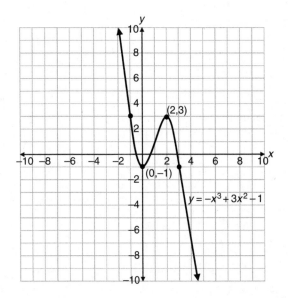

The graph shown has a relative minimum at (0, −1).

Remainder Theorem

The Remainder Theorem states that the remainder when dividing a polynomial by $(x - r)$ is the value of the polynomial at r.

Example

The value of the polynomial $x^2 + 5x + 2$ at 1 is $(1)^2 + 5(1) + 2 = 8$. So, the remainder when $x^2 + 5x + 2$ is divided by $x - 1$ is 8.

$$
\begin{array}{r}
x + 6 \\
x - 1 \overline{)\, x^2 + 5x + 2} \\
\underline{x^2 - x} \\
6x + 2 \\
\underline{6x - 6} \\
8
\end{array}
$$

Glossary

removable discontinuity

A removable discontinuity is a single point at which the graph of a function is not defined.

Example

The graph of the function $f(x) = \frac{x^2}{x}$ has a removable discontinuity at $x = 0$.

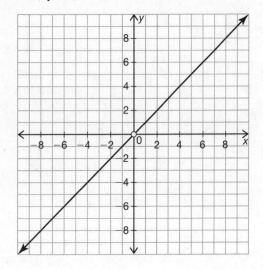

rigid motion

A rigid motion is a transformation that preserves size and shape.

Example

Reflections, rotations, and translations are examples of rigid motion.

S

sample

Where data are collected from a selection of the population, the data are called a sample.

Example

If you wanted to find out the average height of the students in your school, you could choose just a certain number of students and measure their heights. The heights of the students in this group would be the sample.

sample proportion

A sample proportion is the percentage of a sample that yields a favorable outcome in an experiment. This is often used to make predictions about a population.

Example

In an election, a sample of townspeople is surveyed. The sample proportion represents the percentage of the survey results that indicate that they will vote to re-elect the mayor.

sample survey

A sample survey poses one or more questions of interest to obtain sample data from a population.

Example

The following is an example of a sample survey.

A recent survey of nearly 1200 young people from across the U.S. shows that 40% of 16- to 20- year-olds who have a driver's license admit to texting on a regular basis while they are driving.

sampling distribution

A sampling distribution consists of every possible sample of equal size from a given population. A sampling distribution provides an estimate for population parameters. The mean or proportion of a sampling distribution is estimated by the mean or proportion of a sample. For categorical data, the standard deviation of a sampling distribution is estimated by calculating $\sqrt{\frac{\hat{p}(1 - \hat{p})}{n}}$ where $\hat{p}$ (p-hat) is the sample proportion and n is the sample size. For continuous data, the standard deviation of a sampling distribution is estimated by calculating $\frac{S}{\sqrt{n}}$ where S is the standard deviation of the original sample and n is the sample size.

Example

A sleep survey of 50 teens resulted in a sample mean of 7.7 hours and sample standard deviation of 0.8 hours.

The estimated mean of the sampling distribution is 7.7 hours. The estimated standard deviation of the sampling distribution is approximately 0.11 hours.

$$\frac{S}{\sqrt{n}} = \frac{0.8}{\sqrt{50}} \approx 0.11$$

self-similar

A self-similar object is exactly or approximately similar to a part of itself.

Example

A Koch snowflake is considered to be self-similar.

series

A series is the sum of the terms of a sequence. The sum of the first n terms of a sequence is denoted by S_n.

Example

The series corresponding to the sequence 1, 1, 2, 3, 5 is $1 + 1 + 2 + 3 + 5$, or 12.

set of complex numbers

The set of complex numbers is the set of all numbers written in the form $a + bi$, where a and b are real numbers. The set of complex numbers consists of the set of imaginary numbers and the set of real numbers.

Example

The numbers $1 + 2i$, 7, and $-3i$ are complex numbers.

set of imaginary numbers

The set of imaginary numbers is the set of all numbers written in the form $a + bi$, where a and b are real numbers and b is not equal to 0.

Example

The numbers $2 - 3i$ and $5i$ are imaginary numbers. The number 6 is not an imaginary number.

simple random sample

A simple random sample is a sample in which every member of the population has the same chance of being selected.

Example

Using a random number generator to select a sample is an example of simple random sampling.

sine function

A sine function is a periodic function. It takes angle measures (θ values) as inputs and then outputs real number values based on coordinates of points on the unit circle.

Example

The function $h(\theta) = -\sin(2\theta) + 1$ is a sine function.

square root function

The square root function is the inverse of the power function $f(x) = x^2$ when the domain is restricted to $x \geq 0$.

Example

The square root function is $g(x) = \sqrt{x}$.

standard deviation

Standard deviation is a measure of the variation of the values in a data set from the mean of the data. A lower standard deviation represents data that are more tightly clustered near the mean. A higher standard deviation represents data that are more spread out from the mean. Use the formula below to calculate standard deviation.

$$\text{standard deviation} = \sqrt{\frac{\sum_{i=1}^{n}(x_1 - \bar{x})^2}{n}}$$

where $\bar{x}$ is the mean and n is the number of data values in the data set $\{x_1, x_2, \ldots, x_n\}$.

Example

In the data set of test scores
60, 70, 80, 90, 100,
the mean $\bar{x}$ is 80 and the number of data elements n is 5. So, the standard deviation of the test scores is
standard deviation =

$$\sqrt{\frac{\begin{array}{c}(60 - 80)^2 + (70 - 80)^2 + (80 - 80)^2 + \\ (90 - 80)^2 + (100 - 80)^2\end{array}}{5}}$$

$$= \sqrt{\frac{1000}{5}}$$

$$= \sqrt{200}$$

$$\approx 14.14.$$

standard form (general form) of a quadratic function

A quadratic function written in the form $f(x) = ax^2 + bx + c$, where $a \neq 0$, is in standard form, or general form.

Example

The function $f(x) = -5x^2 - 10x + 1$ is written in standard form.

standard normal distribution

The standard normal distribution is a normal probability distribution with the following properties:

- The mean is equal to 0.
- The standard deviation is 1.
- The curve is bell-shaped and symmetric about the mean.

Example

A standard normal distribution curve is shown.

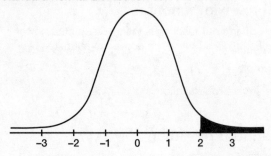

standard position of an angle

The standard position of an angle occurs when the vertex of the angle is at the origin and one ray of the angle is on the *x*-axis.

Example

The angle shown is in standard position.

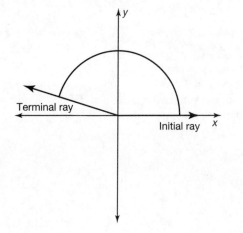

statistic

When data are gathered from a sample, the characteristic used to describe the sample is called a statistic.

Example

If you wanted to find out the average height of the students in your school, and you chose just a certain number of students randomly and measured their heights, the characteristic "average height" would be called a statistic.

statistically significant

A survey that has a result that is statistically significant indicates that the result did not likely occur by chance, but is likely linked to a specific cause. Typically, a result that is more than 2 standard deviations away from the mean is considered statistically significant.

Example

A survey of 2000 teenagers reports that 42% have a part-time job. The interval from 40.9% to 43.1% represents a 95% confidence interval for the population proportion. A survey that yields a report of 50% of teenager with a part-time job would be considered statistically significant.

stratified random sample

A stratified random sample is a sample obtained by dividing the population into different groups, or strata, according to a characteristic, and randomly selecting data from each group.

Example

If students in a high school are divided by class, and random samples are then taken from each class, the result is a stratified random sample.

subjective sample

A subjective sample is a sample that is chosen based on some criteria, rather than at random.

Example

From a set of students, "choosing five students you know" is a subjective sample. In contrast, "choosing five students at random" is a random sample.

Glossary

symmetric about a line

If a graph is symmetric about a line, the line divides the graph into two identical parts.

Example

The graph of $f(x) = x^2$ is symmetric about the line $x = 0$.

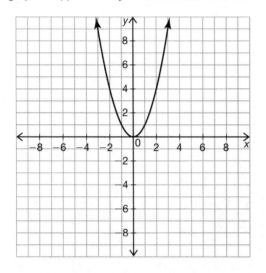

symmetric about a point

A function is symmetric about a point if each point on the graph has a point the same distance from the central point, but in the opposite direction.

Example

The graph of $f(x) = x^3$ is symmetric about the point $(0, 0)$.

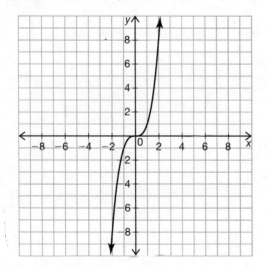

synthetic division

Synthetic division is a method for dividing a polynomial by a linear factor of the form $(x - r)$.

Example

The quotient of $2x^2 - 3x - 9$ and $x - 3$ can be calculated using synthetic division.

$$
\begin{array}{c|ccc}
3 & 2 & -3 & -9 \\
  &   & 6 & 9 \\
\hline
  & 2 & 3 & 0
\end{array}
$$

The quotient of $2x^2 - 3x - 9$ and $x - 3$ is $2x + 3$.

systematic sample

A systematic sample is a sample obtained by selecting every nth data in the population.

Example

If you choose every 12th student that walks into school, your sample is a systematic sample.

T

tangent function

A tangent function is a periodic function. It takes angle measures (θ values) as inputs and then outputs real number values based on coordinates of points on the unit circle.

Example

The function $f(\theta) = \tan\left(\dfrac{\theta}{2}\right)$ is a tangent function.

terminal ray of an angle

The terminal ray of an angle in standard position is the ray with its endpoint at the origin that is not the initial ray.

Example

The terminal ray of the angle is labeled in the diagram.

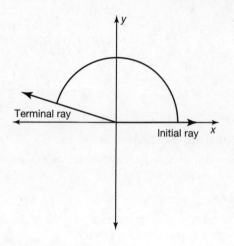

theta (θ)

Theta is a symbol typically used to represent the measure of an angle in standard position.

Example

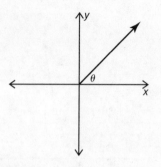

transformation

A transformation is the mapping, or movement, of all the points of a figure in a plane according to a common operation. Translations, reflections, rotations, and dilations are examples of transformations.

Example

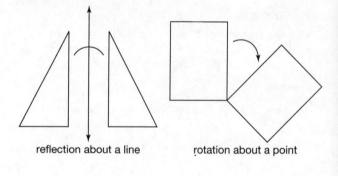

reflection about a line   rotation about a point

tessellation

A tessellation is created when a geometric shape is repeated over a two-dimensional plane such that there are no overlaps among the shapes and no gaps.

Example

A tessellation of diamonds is shown.

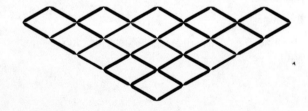

the imaginary number *i*

The number *i* is a number such that $i^2 = -1$.

Glossary

translation

A translation is a type of transformation that shifts an entire figure or graph the same distance and direction.

Example

The graph of $g(x) = (x - 2)^2$ is a translation of the graph of $f(x) = x^2$ right 2 units.

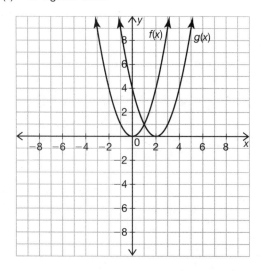

treatment

A treatment is a condition in an experiment.

Example

Suppose that an experiment is conducted to test the effects of a new drug on a sample of patients. The distribution of the drug to the patients is the treatment in the experiment.

trigonometric equation

A trigonometric equation is an equation that includes one or more trigonometric functions.

Example

The equation $\cos(x) = \frac{\sqrt{2}}{2}$ is a trigonometric equation.

trigonometric function

A trigonometric function is a periodic function that takes angle measures (θ values) as inputs and then outputs real number values based on coordinates of points on the unit circle.

Example

The function $g(x) = \sin(x)$ is a trigonometric function. The graph of the sine function $g(\theta) = \sin(\theta)$ is obtained by evaluating the θ values of the unit circle and graphing the coordinates.

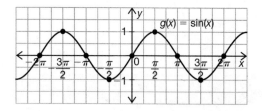

θ	$g(\theta) = \sin(\theta)$	$(\theta, g(\theta))$
0	$\sin(0) = 0$	$(0, 0)$
$\dfrac{\pi}{2}$	$\sin\left(\dfrac{\pi}{2}\right) = 1$	$\left(\dfrac{\pi}{2}, 1\right)$
π	$\sin(\pi) = 0$	$(\pi, 0)$
$\dfrac{3\pi}{2}$	$\sin\left(\dfrac{3\pi}{2}\right) = -1$	$\left(\dfrac{3\pi}{2}, -1\right)$
2π	$\sin(2\pi) = 0$	$(2\pi, 0)$

trinomial

A trinomial is a polynomial with exactly three terms.

Example

The polynomial $5x^2 - 6x + 9$ is a trinomial.

U

unit circle

A unit circle is a circle whose radius is one unit of distance.

Example

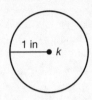

Circle K is a unit circle.

V

vertex form of a quadratic function

A quadratic function written in vertex form is in the form $f(x) = a(x - h)^2 + k$, where $a \neq 0$.

Example

The quadratic equation $y = 2(x - 5)^2 + 10$ is written in vertex form. The vertex of the graph is the point (5, 10).

vertical asymptote

A vertical asymptote is a vertical line that a function gets closer and closer to, but never intersects. The asymptote does not represent points on the graph of the function. It represents the output value that the graph approaches.

Example

The graph has two asymptotes: a vertical asymptote $x = 2$ and a horizontal asymptote $y = -1$.

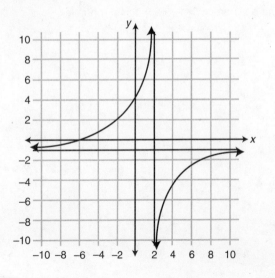

vertical compression

Vertical compression is the squeezing of a graph toward the x-axis.

Example

The graph of $g(x) = \frac{1}{2}x^2$ is a vertical compression compared to the graph of $f(x) = x^2$.

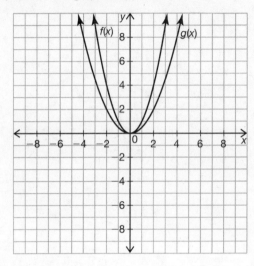

vertical dilation

A vertical dilation is a type of transformation that stretches or compresses an entire figure or graph. In a vertical dilation, notice that the y-coordinate of every point on the graph of a function is multiplied by a common factor, A.

Example

The graphs of $g(x) = 2x^2$ and $h(x) = \frac{1}{2}x^2$ are vertical dilations of the graph of $f(x) = x^2$.

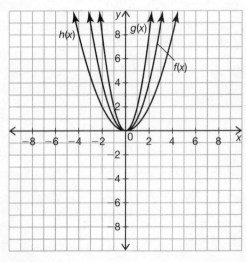

vertical stretching

Vertical stretching is the stretching of a graph away from the x-axis.

Example

The graph of $g(x) = 2x^2$ is a vertical stretching compared to the graph of $f(x) = x^2$.

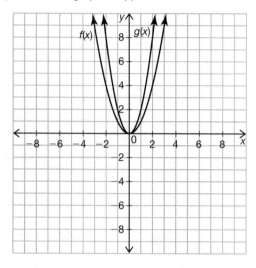

volunteer sample

A volunteer sample is a sample whose data consists of those who volunteer to be part of the sample.

Example

If you ask students in your school to complete and submit an optional survey so that you can collect data, your sample is a volunteer sample.

z-score

A z-score is a number that describes how many standard deviations from the mean a particular value is. The following formula can be used to calculate a z-score for a particular value, where z represents the z-score, x represents the particular data value, μ represents the mean, and σ represents the standard deviation.

$$z = \frac{x - \mu}{\sigma}$$

Example

Suppose that a set of data follows a normal distribution with a mean of 22 and a standard deviation of 2.4.

The z-score for a data value of 25 is $z = \dfrac{25 - 22}{2.4} = 1.25$.

Zero Product Property

The Zero Product Property states that if the product of two or more factors is equal to zero, then at least one factor must be equal to zero. This is also called the Converse of Multiplication Property of Zero.

Example

According to the Zero Product Property, if $(x - 2)(x + 3) = 0$ then $x - 2 = 0$ or $x + 3 = 0$.

Zero Property of Logarithms

The Zero Property of Logarithms states that the logarithm of 1, with any base, is always equal to 0.

$$\log_b (1) = 0$$

Example

$\log_3 (1) = 0$

Glossary

Glossary

Index

and irrational number *e*, 867–870
range, 863, 875–878
of functions
   analyzing graphs in terms of
      problem situations, 1031
   building functions from graphs,
      172–174, 176–179, 181–183
   contextual meaning of, 1031
   difference of two functions,
      172–174
   interpreting, 1029–1036
   modeling operations on functions
      with, 166–169
   predicting and verifying behavior of
      functions with, 171, 176–179
   product of two functions, 178–183
   sum of two functions, 170–171,
      176–178
input value from, 563
of invertible functions, 777–778
of logarithmic functions, 883–888
   asymptotes, 883, 884, 888, 897,
      899
   end behavior, 883, 884, 888
   intercepts, 883, 888
   intervals of increase/decrease, 884,
      888
modeling functions with, 150–151,
   153–154
modeling periodic functions with,
   1070–1077
of odd *vs.* even functions, 343–344
of periodic functions, 1168–1172
of polynomial functions
   identifying functions from graphs,
      368, 376–378
   sketching, based on key
      characteristics, 380–382
   solving equations and inequalities
      with, 428
of polynomials
   comparing functions based on, 554
   determining zeros from, 478
of power functions, 334–337
properties of polynomials in, 404
of quadratic functions
   effects of translations on, 219–221
   matching quadratic equations and,
      198–202
   writing functions from, 219–221,
      240, 252–253
of rational functions, 650–655
   determining function from, 664
   key characteristics, 652, 654–655
   power functions *vs.*, 656–659
   reciprocal of basic linear function,
      650–653
   with removable discontinuities,
      670–679
relative minimum from, 561
solving polynomial inequalities with,
   516–519, 521–522
solving rational equations with, 733
and structure of functions, 450
of tangent function, 1114–1118
of trigonometric functions,
   1159–1165

constructing trigonometric function,
   1160–1162
interpreting graphs, 1163–1165
writing equations for piecewise
   functions from, 540
x-value of axis of symmetry on, 561
y-intercept on, 558
Greatest common factor (GCF),
   460–462, 469
Grouping, factoring by, 463–464, 469
Growth
   exponential growth functions,
      851–853, 859–863
   logistic growth experiment,
      1033–1036
   modeling population growth, 975–978

H

Half-life
   defined, 853
   from exponential decay functions,
      853–856
Hexagonal numbers, 493
Higher-degree functions, inverses of,
   776–778
Higher order polynomials
   factoring, 459–469
      chunking method, 462–463, 469
      with difference of squares, 467,
         469
      factoring by grouping, 463–464, 469
      with greatest common factor,
         460–462, 469
      perfect square trinomials, 468, 469
      with quadratic form, 464, 469
      with sums and differences of
         cubes, 465–467, 469
   solving, with roots, 476–478
"Holes," in graphs of rational functions,
   679–681
   See also Removable discontinuities
Horizontal asymptotes
   defined, 653
   determining, for reciprocal of
      quadratic function, 653
   effect of *c*-value on, 662, 663
   of rational functions, 655, 674
   in structure of rational functions, 666
   and transformations of exponential
      functions, 875–878
Horizontal compression
   of cubic functions, 352, 356
   of exponential functions, 874–880
   function form and equation
      information for, 1015
   of quadratic functions, 243–250, 349
   of quartic functions, 357
Horizontal dilations
   of cubic functions, 352, 356
   of exponential functions, 874–880
   of logarithmic functions, 906–908
   of quadratic functions, 241–254, 350
      defined, 243
      effect of *B*-value on graph,
         242–247
      graphing functions with, 247–251,
         254

writing functions from graphs of,
   252–253
of quartic functions, 357
of rational functions, 675
Horizontal line, determining maximum
   value with, 320
Horizontal Line Test, for invertible
   functions, 778–779, 886
Horizontal stretching
   of cubic functions, 352, 356
   function form and equation
      information for, 1015
   of quadratic functions, 243–250, 349
   of quartic functions, 357
Horizontal translation(s)
   of cubic function, 354, 356
   of exponential functions,
      874–880
   function form and equation
      information for, 1015
   of logarithmic functions, 898,
      902–905
   of quadratic functions, 349, 350
   of rational functions, 675, 676
H-value, effect of, on basic quadratic
   function, 219, 220

I

i. *See* Imaginary numbers
Identities
   additive, 168, 175, 1000
   multiplicative, 499, 683, 1000
   periodicity
      for cosine, 1098
      for sine, 1098
      solving trigonometric equations
         with, 1136
   polynomial, 479–491
      generating Pythagorean triples
         with, 482–485
      patterns in numbers generated by,
         486–489
      proving algebraic statements with,
         490–491
      rewriting numeric expressions with,
         480–481
   Pythagorean
      defined, 1144
      in determining values of
         trigonometric functions,
         1145–1147
      proving, 1144
Identity function, 1001
Imaginary numbers (*i*)
   defined, 274
   polynomials with, 281–284
   powers of, 274–277
   pure, 278
   set of, 278
Imaginary part of a complex number,
   278
Imaginary roots, 290
   building cubic functions based on,
      389, 390
   building quartic functions based on,
      400
   of quartic functions, 398

Imaginary zeros
building cubic functions based on, 388, 391
in cubic functions, 390–391
in quadratic functions, 291
of quartic functions, 399
and table of values of polynomial functions, 400
Inequalities, polynomial
algebraic solutions, 516–519, 521–522
and determining roots of polynomial functions, 514–515
graphical solutions, 516–519, 521–522
representation of, in problem situations, 520–522
Inferences, 49–107
confidence intervals, 71–84
for categorical data, 72–79
for continuous data, 80–81
defined, 77
margin of error for population means, 80–81
margin of error for population proportions, 72, 75–79
and samples *vs.* sampling distributions, 75–76
designing studies, 101–102
estimating population means
with confidence intervals, 80–81
sampling methods for, 65
experiments, 53, 102
observational studies, 52, 102
sample surveys, 49–52, 102
sampling methods, 57–69
and biased data, 59
for estimating population mean, 65
randomization in, 60–64
types of, 58–64
statistical significance, 85–100
defined, 87
of differences in population means, 90–91, 94–97
of differences in population proportions, 86–89, 92–93, 96
Infinite arithmetic series, 618
Infinite geometric series, 607–618
calculating sum of terms for, 608–611
convergent *vs.* divergent, 617–618
determining convergence and divergence of, 615–616
determining formulas for, 610
diagrams for modeling, 611–614
Infinite sequences
defined, 574
identifying, 575–577
Infinite series
defined, 584
notation for, 615
Infinite sets, 553
Initial growth stage (logistic functions), 1032, 1035
Initial ray, 1074
Integers
closure property for, 406, 408
infinite set of, 553
polynomials *vs.*, 437

in set of complex numbers, 279
sum of reciprocal and, 697
Intercept(s)
on exponential graphs, 863
on graphs of logarithmic functions, 883, 888
of square root function, 487
Interest
calculating portion of credit card payment for, 620, 621, 623, 624, 627, 629
compound, 864–867
Interest-free periods, credit cards with, 630–631
Intersection points
of cubic function, 321
for graphs of power functions, 337, 338
solving polynomial inequalities with, 517
Intervals
Empirical Rule for Normal Distributions for percent of data in, 18–21
identifying, in problem situation, 428
modeling polynomials with regression equations for, 527
for piecewise functions, 544, 546
selecting, for piecewise functions, 535
Intervals of increase or decrease
on exponential graphs, 863, 873, 874
on graphs of logarithmic functions, 884, 888
Inverse cosine ($\cos^{-1}$), 1138
Inverse functions
function notation for, 883
for problem situations, 1053–1055
solving trigonometric equations using, 1138–1140
of transformations, 902–908
Inverse relations, Vertical Line Test for, 773, 774, 776, 779
Inverse sine ($\sin^{-1}$), 1138
Inverses of functions
defined, 777
evaluating, with composition of functions, 789–790, 1000–1003
exponential functions, 882–888
power functions, 771–782
asymptotes, 788
evaluating, with composition of functions, 789–790
graphing, 772–777
graphs of invertible functions, 777–778
Horizontal Line Test for invertible functions, 778–779
inverses of even- *vs.* odd-degree power functions, 778
inverses of higher-degree functions, 776–778
Vertical Line Test for inverse relations, 773, 774, 776, 779
Inverse tangent ($\tan^{-1}$), 1138
Invertible functions
exponential functions as, 886

graphs of, 777–778
Horizontal Line Test for, 778–779, 886
Irrational number(s)
closure property for, 406
e, 867–870
in set of complex numbers, 279
Iterative process
defined, 1038
for Koch Snowflake, 1044–1045
for Menger Sponge, 1041–1042
for Sierpinski Triangle, 1038–1040

K

Karmakar, Bhaskar, 868
Key characteristics
choosing functions for problem situations based on, 1053–1055, 1058
of cubic functions, 319–320, 325, 379
determining minimum from, 562
determining relative minimum from, 561
of periodic functions, 1073
of polynomial functions, 369–384
and degree of functions, 373–376, 378
generalizations about, 372–376
identifying, from a table of values, 436
identifying, from graphs, 376–378
in problem situations, 370–372, 426–427, 429
sketching graphs based on, 380–382
of quartic functions, 379, 398–403
of rational functions, 654–655
effect of *c*-value on, 662–663
and form of rational equation, 674
power functions *vs.*, 658–659
reciprocal of basic linear function, 652
in representations of polynomials, 560–563
of square root function, 787
of tangent function, 1119
and transformations of exponential functions, 875–878
See also specific characteristics
Key points, of graphs for functions, 170
Koch, Helge von, 1043
K-value, effect of, on basic quadratic function, 219, 220

L

LCD. *See* Lowest common denominator
Least possible value, for sum of integer and reciprocal, 697
Like terms, combining, 123, 440, 825–826
Linear expressions, identifying, 122
Linear factors, dividing polynomials by, 443–450, 452–453
Linear function(s)
addition and subtraction of, 171–176
addition of quadratic and, 176–177
common differences of, 326
cubic *vs.*, 326, 332
extrema of, 378

Index

T

Index

of polynomial functions
  building cubic functions based on, 388
  matching graphs and functions based on, 382
  in problem situation, 371
  sketching graphs of functions based on, 380, 381
of quadratic functions, 332
of quartic functions, 398
of square root function, 487
writing quadratic function for given, 262–264
and Zero Product Property, 180

Y

y-axis
  as axis of symmetry, 339, 341, 342
  and reciprocal of basic linear function, 652
  reflections across, 353, 356, 357, 872–874, 1015
y-intercept(s), 126
  building quartic functions based on, 401
  comparing representations of functions based on, 558–559
  drawing parabolas for given, 259, 261
  and form of quadratic function, 203, 205–207

identifying, in problem situation, 426
of polynomial functions
  building cubic functions based on, 388, 391
  in problem situation, 372
  sketching graphs of functions based on, 380
of rational functions, 674
of square root function, 487
of tangent function, 1119

Z

Zeno's paradox, 729
Zero power, 805
Zero Product Property, 181, 395, 518
Zero Property of Logarithms, 934, 938
Zero Property of Powers, 934, 938
Zero(s)
  of cubic functions, 331
    building functions based on, 386–387, 390, 391, 393–396
    imaginary zeros, 390–391
    and multiplication by a constant, 391
    number of, 326, 332, 379, 397
  and degree of polynomials, 379, 398–402
  in denominator of rational expressions, 715

determining number of real, from graphs of polynomial functions, 554–555
division by, 655
factoring polynomials based on, 434
of higher-order polynomials, 478
imaginary
  building cubic functions based on, 388, 391
  in cubic functions, 390–391
  in quadratic functions, 291
  of quartic functions, 399
  tables of values of polynomials and, 400
of linear functions, 397
of polynomials, from tables of values, 434
of quadratic functions
  determining, 288–289, 294–295
  number of, 332, 379, 397
of quartic functions, 397, 399
solving polynomial inequalities with, 517
z-scores
  defined, 26
  negative, 26
  for percentiles, 31
  for percent of data in normal distributions, 24–27, 29–30, 32–33

Index